Created and Directed by Hans Höfer

INSIGHT GUIDES

VIETNAM

Edited by Helen West
Photography by Tim Page and others
Editorial Director: Geoffrey Eu

APA PUBLICATIONS

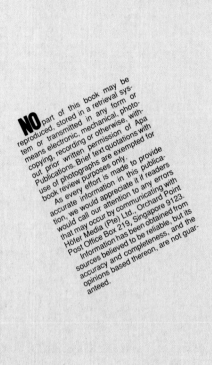
VIETNAM

First Edition

ABOUT THIS BOOK

The making of this book began more than a decade ago, when publisher **Hans Höfer** first mooted the idea of a Vietnam guidebook to a Vietnamese friend. In the intervening years, Vietnam has emerged as one of the newest and most attractive frontiers for travelers. *Insight Guide: Vietnam* appears at a time when the country is in a state of transition, and rapid changes are taking place even as this book reaches the bookstores.

Vietnam's appeal is based not only on the emotions the name itself evokes, but also on the mystery of the unknown, the many gaps in our knowledge of the country. While Vietnam has always been an inexaustible source of captivating literature, little is known about its ancient past, the traditional hospitality of its people and the wonders of its varied landscape. Apa Publications set out to produce a reference book — hopefully a landmark in the *Insight Guide* series — that would do justice to the country. To that end, we enlisted the aid of several knowledgeable writers and expert photographers to form the core of the *Vietnam* team.

The Right Staff

New Zealander **Helen West** had been studying Vietnamese history for years before she took on the post of project editor for *Insight Guide: Vietnam*. When the project began to take shape in 1989 and 1990, West traveled extensively in Vietnam, in search of its cultural heritage. She wrote several pieces for this book and together with Apa Editorial Director **Geoffrey Eu**, helped *Vietnam* over the usual editorial hurdles.

Tran Van Dinh, Vietnamese born and bred in Hue, the ancient capital of Vietnam, is perhaps among the few scholars who have inherited the best of both Eastern and Western cultures. He was the ideal choice to convey to non-Vietnamese readers the complex spiritual universe of the Vietnamese. Author of several novels and many articles on his homeland, Tran Van Dinh — who now lives in the US and lectures at Temple University in Pennsylvania — has a profound knowledge of the Vietnamese culture. His love of tradition provides an authentic Vietnamese flavor to this guide.

Professor **Nguyen Tan Dac**, ethnologist and Deputy Director of the Institute of Southeast Asian Studies in Hanoi, is intimately acquainted with almost every corner of his native land. After the Vietnam War, he undertook extensive research work on the hill tribe minorities of the northern and central regions. His first-hand expertise of the country's ethnographic roots has been a valuable contribution to the travel section of this book.

For freelance writer **Diana Reid**, her trip to Vietnam in 1990 was the realization of a life-long dream. She traveled the length of the country on the trans-Viet Reunification Express, and her impressions of that journey constitute a special feature of this guide.

A significant number of our readers are Americans, and in recognition of the fact that Vietnam holds a special place in recent American history, we have included a feature on "Namstalgia", a term coined by writer/photographer **Tim Page**, and which refers to perhaps the most lingering form of the Vietnam syndrome. Page is a celebrated wartime photographer whose pictures of the Vietnam conflict were seen in newspapers and

West

Dinh

Dac

Page

magazines across the globe. He regularly returns to Vietnam and other parts of Indochina and continues to work on book and film projects on the region. he is one of the few western photographers who has traveled throughout Vietnam, and the results of his many journeys can be appreciated in this volume.

American photographer **Joseph Lynch** is a relative newcomer to the region, having made Singapore his home base in 1991. Prior to his move, he made several photographic tours of the region, and his many compelling images in this book, including the cover picture, attest to the success of those trips. An intrepid traveler, Joe has traversedthe length and breadth of Vietnam in search of authentic scenes. His presentation of the Vietnamese, their festivals and lifestyles, is a revelation rarely seen.

Frequent Apa contributors **Kim Naylor** and **Catherine Karnow** put their considerable photographic talents to good use on *Vietnam*, as do Apa stalwarts **Jean-Leo Dugast**, **Bill Wassman**, **Alain Evrard** and **Zdenek Thoma**. Newcomers **Wim Van Cappellen** and **Brenda Turnnidge** also join the Insight Guide team for the first time.

As usual, maps were drawn by **Berndtson & Berndtson** of Munich.

Thanks are due to **Vietnam Tourism**, who provided several photographs and helped in making ground arrangements for Apa staff. Our appreciation also goes to **M. Rajaretnam**, Director of the Information and Resource Center in Singapore, who generously put its research material on Vietnam at our disposal.
    – APA Publications

Lynch   Karnow

History And Culture

Places

Maps

MANY RIVERS TO CROSS

As Vietnam opens its doors to welcome the world at large, many people have no idea of the stunning visual beauty and traditional culture that lie beyond the threshold. To many, the name Vietnam brings to mind only haunting images of a war-torn land in some remote corner of Southeast Asia, an image which continues to be exploited on the big screen and in print, and which remains deeply etched in the minds of all who found themselves a part of that war and its aftermath. Beyond such images lies the real Vietnam, a unique and fascinating land of great physical and rich cultural diversity whose history spans over 4,000 years.

Picture a land of idyllic tree-lined beaches, tranquil bays dotted with the sails of junks and sampans, offshore coral islands, mountains, valleys, primal forests, plains crossed by countless rivers and emerald rice fields enriched with the varied scenes of everyday life. The traditional rural life, embodied in the villagers tilling the land with rudimentary tools under their conical hats in the patchwork paddy fields, and children riding their water buffaloes home from the fields at the end of the day, contrasts dramatically with the sights, sounds and pace of the cities whose busy streets overflow with humanity borne along on a rising tide of bicycles and motor scooters. Such are the images of present-day Vietnam.

The country's long history is an ever present companion; the land is imbued with it – sites of ancient battles, ancient civilizations and kingdoms which flourished in this enigmatic land long before the French colonialists, Communism and the tragic war of the more recent past.

The changing tides of fortune that have swept over this country and its people have left their mark, greatly emphasizing the contrast between past and present.

Much of Vietnam's ancient past is shrouded in myths and legends of dragons and kings, heroes and heroines, gods and deities, brought to life in the present in the many colorful time-honored traditional festivals and rituals commemorating revered ancestors, who are worshipped alongside Buddhist, Taoist and Hindu deities in the thousands of temples and pagodas throughout the country.

In a traditionally agricultural country, so new to the concept of tourism that you have to expect the unexpected, you won't be disappointed.

This book traces the complex history and culture of Vietnam and its people, introducing some of the many different faces and places of this fascinating country. Exploring Vietnam through these pages may help lend an understanding to the background and events leading up to the tragic war and its aftermath and provide some insight into the diverse cultures and customs of its people.

Preceding pages: Emperor Khai Dinh's mausoleum, Hue; sunrise on the Mekong River; rice factory near Saigon; guardroom duty in Thai Nguyen; early to work, Bac Thai Province. Left, pearly whites on display in Haiphong.

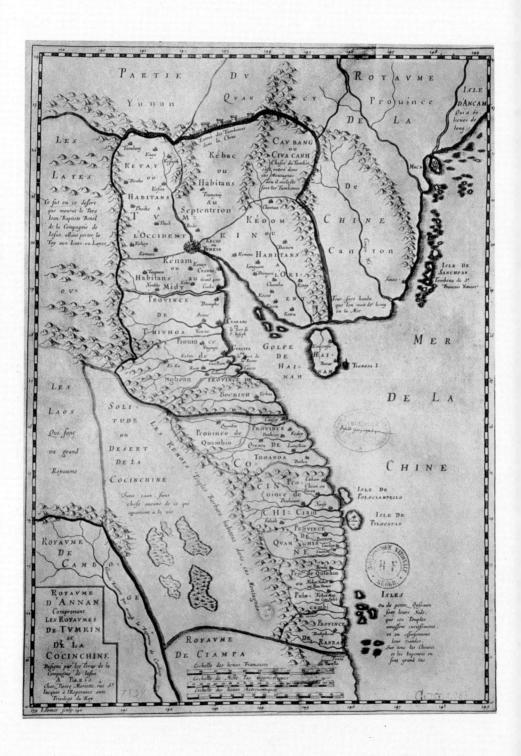

HOW VIETNAM WAS NAMED

To many people the name Vietnam conjures up images of war in some remote corner of Southeast Asia, yet few know the significance of the name, even though the war with its interminable sequels, has brought the country and its people to the forefront of the world scene for more than half a century.

The first national name of Van Lang was given to Vietnam by the Hung or Lac ethnic group, inventors of the wet rice cultivation technique and bronze drums still used today by the Muong minority. The Lac were followed by the Au or Tay Au who arrived from the Chinese province of Kwang Si. The two peoples integrated and formed the new kingdom of Au Lac. Following them came the Viet or Yue, an ethnic group who emigrated from the coastal provinces of ancient China towards the 5th century B.C. Together with the other ethnic groups of the Bach Viet (100 Viet Principalities) they began their long southward march towards the Indochinese peninsula which continued for more than 15 centuries.

The name Vietnam came about when Emperor Gia Long wanted to rename the country Nam Viet. Seeking the Chinese emperor's approval of the new national name, Gia Long sent his Ambassador, Le Quang Dinh, to China in 1802. Le Quang Dinh addressed the Emperor as follows: The new King of the Nguyen has succeeded in realizing under his rule, what the former reigns of the Tran and Le could not – the reunification of the old land of An Nam and the new land of Viet Thuong. Consequently, we would like to ask your permission to change the ancient name of An Nam to Nam Viet.

After consulting his court, the Chinese Emperor decided that the name Nam Viet would bring to mind Trieu Da's ancient kingdom of Nam Viet Dong which had included the two Chinese provinces of Guang Dong and Kwang Si, and therefore the proposed name of Nam Viet could lead to mis-

understandings or even conceal territorial ambitions. The problem was solved by simply reversing the order of the two words to Viet Nam.

Viet Nam means the Viets of the South (Nam) or the south populated by the Viet – the main ethnic group in Vietnam.

Etymologists and anthropologists have defined the origins of the Viet people by separating the components of the calligraphy for Viet, or Yue, as it is known in

Mandarin. On the left side of this ideogram is a character pronounced *tau* in Vietnamese, meaning to run. On the right is the complementary component pronounced Viet, with the meaning and profile of an axe. This component carries with it the particle *qua*, which signifies a lance or javelin.

This small ideographic analysis depicts the Viet as a race known since antiquity as a migratory, hunting people, perpetually moving and spreading beyond their frontiers of origin, carrying bow and arrow, axe and javelin.

The word Viet is the Vietnamese pronunciation of a Chinese character meaning be-

Preceding pages: young King Duy Tan and his entourage. Left, 1653 map of Tonkin. Above, Chinese motif, 17th-century building.

yond or far. It also has the sense of "to cross", "to go through", "to set onself right". The character Nam, meaning South, probably served to differentiate between the Viets in the North who remained in China and those who had left and headed South.

The name Viet referred to the territories located in the south of China during the 11th century B.C. These were so named by the Zhou dynasty (1050-249 B.C.).

Marco Polo skirted the coast of Vietnam in 1292. The name Caugigu which corresponds to Giao Chi Quan, (Vietnam's name under the Han Dynasty, 111 B.C.-203 A.D.) appears in his writings *The Wonders of the World*. This name was transformed to Kutchi by the Malays then Kotchi by the Japanese. The Portuguese in turn named it Cauchi Chine, (the Cauchi obedient to the Chinese), to distinguish it from Cauchi or Kutchi in India, also known as Cochin. These names when written or pronounced in the occidental manner evoked a far more ancient name, Cattigara, which first appeared on one of 14 maps drawn by Ptolemy, the famous Greek mathematician and geographer. These maps were used by the Roman conquerors and Arab navigators, then by Ptolemy himself on his voyage to the Indies and Southeast Asia. The terminating point of these voyages was the maritime port located in Southern Indochina at Oc Eo in the pre-Cambodian

In the course of its long history Vietnam has been known by many different national names:

Van Lang under the 18 Hung or Lac-Vuong kings (500 B.C. to 257 B.C.)
Au Lac under the Thuc Dynasty (257 B.C. to 207 B.C.)
Nam Viet under the Trieu Dynasty (207 B.C. to 111 B.C.)
Giao Chi under the early Chinese Han Dynasty (111 B.C. to 203 A.D.)
Giao Chau under the later Chinese Han Dynasty (203 to 544)
Van Xuan under the early Ly Dynasty (544 to 603)
An Nam under the Chinese Tang Dynasty (603 to 939)
Dai Viet under the Ngo Dynasty (939 to 967)
Dai Co Viet under the Dinh Dynasty and its successors (968-1054)

Dai Viet under the later Ly and Tran dynasties (1054-1400)
Dai Ngu under the Ho Dynasty (1400-1407)
An Nam under the Tran and Chinese Ming dynasties (1407-1428)
Dai Viet under the Le and Nguyen dynasties (1428-1802)
Viet Nam under Emperor Gia Long in 1802.
Dai Nam under Emperor Minh-Mang in 1832 and his successors.
Viet Nam renamed in April 1945 by the National government headed by Tran Trong Kim.

Under the French colonial administration, North Vietnam became known as Tonkin, the Centre as Annam and the South as Cochinchina.

Kingdom of Funan, (Phu Nam in Vietnamese) which occupied large areas of present-day South Vietnam and Cambodia from the 1st to the 6th centuries A.D. This kingdom twice came under Indian influence – during the 1st century B.C. and at the end of the 5th and early 6th centuries A.D. This advanced agricultural civilization cultivated rice, beans, cotton, raised pigs, sheep and elephants, and worshipped Brahma, Vishnu and Siva. Archaeological discoveries suggest that the kingdom had to struggle constantly against the flooding of the low-lying Mekong delta area. Many remains of this ancient culture probably lie buried under alluvium deposited over the centuries. An ironwood statue

artefacts at the site of Oc Eo. Among the findings were a great number of gold Roman coins; Greek, Indian and Chinese objects, including a gold medal bearing the effigy of Anthony the Pious dating from 152; Hellenic coins and seals; Indian rings; Burmese jade; Chinese pearls and jewellery; and Chinese bronzes of the later Han period. The Funan kingdom in exchange exported gold, silver, bronze, copper, lapis lazuli, mother-of-pearl, silk, cotton, sandalwood, rhinoceros horn, ivory and colorful parrots. The Oc Eo civilization was renowned for its crystal glass and beautifully crafted jewellery, and it remains a mystery why this highly developed kingdom collapsed and was swallowed up

of Buddha, today in Saigon's National Museum, discovered here in 1937, attests to the high level of Funan's artistic development. Excavations carried out in the Oc Eo area in My Lam village, Kien Hoa district by the French produced a quantity of artefacts of an impressive quality. Oc Eo appeared as the early capital of Funan and an import center of trade, with sea-links as far reaching as Rome, Persia, India, Burma and China. Evidence of this trade came to light when archaeologists unearthed a great number of

by the pre-Khmer Chan La Empire during the 7th century A.D.

Since the earliest antiquity, the Indochinese peninsula has played a major role in international trade relations and migrations, forming the link between India and China, which explains the name Indochina, first coined by the Danish geographer, Konrad Malte-Burn (1775-1826) in his Universal Geographic. Vietnam's central and strategic geographical position in Southeast Asia is of great importance. It has been used in turn by the world's great powers, much to the detriment of the independence and freedom of the Vietnamese people.

Left, detail of a Dong Son drum. **Above**, an example of a Dong Son bronze.

GEOGRAPHY

Designed like an immense elongated S, Vietnam stretches the length of the Indochinese peninsula bordering the China Sea in the East. Its 2,317 mile (3,730 km) frontier shares a 714 mile (1,150 km) border with China in the North, a border of 1,250 miles (1,650 km) with Laos, and 577 miles (930 km) with Cambodia in the West. With a total surface area of 126,500 square miles (327,500 square km), Vietnam's territory also encompasses a vast sea area including a large continental shelf and a string of thousands of archipelagoes stretching from the Tonkin Gulf to the Gulf of Thailand. These include the disputed Spratley (Truong Sa) and Paracel (Hoang Sa) archipelagoes which China also lays claim to. Its 1,600 mile (2,500 km) coastline is dotted with beautiful beaches and unspoilt resorts.

As the crow flies, Vietnam stretches 1,030 miles (1,650 km) from Mong Cai in the North to Ha Tien in the South, exceeding not more than 373 miles (600 km) across at its widest point in the North and 31 miles (50 km) at its narrowest in the Center.

Situated between 8° 33' and 23° 20' latitude North and 102° and 109° 27' longitude East of Greenwich, Vietnam is a land endowed with great physical beauty and diversity. The fertile imaginations of some geographers have likened the country with its three regions, Bac Bo (North), Trung Bo (Center) and Nam Bo (South) to a set of scales, the North and South constituting two balancing baskets of rice supplied by the rich alluvial deltas of the Red River Delta in the north and the Mekong in the south.

Chains of mountains and profoundly carved valleys separate North Vietnam from China. The most important valley is that of the Red River and the highest summit, the Fan Si Pan rises to 9,550 feet (3,160 meters) in the region of Hoang Lien Son.

The plains of Cao Bang, Lang Son, Vinh Yen and the valleys watered by the Lo, Chay, Cau, Luc, Nam and Cung rivers, occupy the

Preceding pages: picturesque paddies in North Vietnam. Left, sunset in Halong Bay. Above, lightning strikes over the Perfume River, Hue.

Northern part of the region and extend over the immense Red River Delta, home to nine-tenths of North Vietnam's population. The Red River flows from its source in the Yunnan region of China across the north of Vietnam southeastwards to its coastal mouth.

Central Vietnam form a long convex curve within which are small plains, jammed between the China Sea and the high plateaus of the Truong Son mountain range, characterized by dunes and lagoons in the east towards the coast and terraces of ancient alluvial

deposits towards the mountains. The limestone peaks of Pu Sam Sao stretch along the border with Laos in the northwest.

The Central Highlands are rich in volcanic basalt soil and constitute one of Vietnam's most important forestry, tea and coffee growing regions.

The Mekong River, known in Sino-Vietnamese as Cuu Long Giang, the River of Nine Dragons, is one of the longest rivers in Asia. 2,597 miles (4,180 km) long, it flows from its source in the mountains of Tibet, across China, through Burma's northern frontiers to Laos and northern Thailand and across Cambodia, before flowing across

South Vietnam and finally into the South China Sea.

Over the centuries the Mekong's alluvial deposits built up on a shallow, undersea shelf, forming an immense low-lying alluvial plain 29,000 miles square (75,000 square km), the vast South Vietnamese delta. These alluvial deposits do not accumulate on the natural delta but at the mouth of the Mekong and around the Camau Peninsula, where they contribute to enlarging the territory of South Vietnam by around 247 feet (75 meters) annually.

Mountains and forests make up more than three-quarters of Vietnam's total area. The country's tremendous topographical diver-

Siberia and China, which often bring temperatures as low as 32°F (0°C) in the mountainous regions North and East of Hanoi and fine drizzle starting in February. The average temperature of 71.6°F (22°C), varies slightly from one season to another, but like anywhere, is prone to sudden changes. Summer, from May to October, is characterized by higher temperatures, heavy rain and often typhoons. Both the North and Center experience their hottest months during June, July and August.

In Central Vietnam, the climate varies from North to South. The climate in the Northern provinces is almost identical to that of the Red River delta, whereas the Southern

sity is surpassed by the diverse species of flora and fauna found in its mountains and tropical forests, plains and plateaus.

Climate: Vietnam's location between the Tropic of Cancer and the Equator in the Southeast Asian monsoon zone gives rise to a complex and humid climate which varies from region to region. North Vietnam's climate is influenced by the winds of Central Asia which give rise to a climate similar to that of China. Generally two distinct seasons prevail. From November to April the North experiences a relatively cold and humid winter. This is precipitated by the invading polar air currents sweeping down across

provinces have more in common climatically with the Mekong delta area. In Hue, the cold season lasts from November to March with almost continual drizzle falling, often for periods of up to a week.

South Vietnam's climate is characterized by a relatively constant temperature, sudden changes during the monsoon and a punctual rainy season. The three seasons are a rainy season from May to October, a relatively dry season from November to February and a dry season from February to April before the rains. The South experiences its hottest months in March, April and May, when temperatures may reach 95°F (35°C). Average annual temperatures in the main cities are Saigon: 29°C (82.4°F), Hue: 25°C (77°F) and Hanoi: 21°C (70°F).

The rains, affected by the monsoon winds arriving across the ocean and the geographical position and relief of the various regions, are usually abundant. Between May and December the warm and humid Summer monsoon brings higher temperatures, a humidity of between 80 percent to 100 percent and heavy rain to both the North and South. During this season, violent typhoons often sweep across the South seas, ravaging the coastline from Qui Nhon to Camau, and causing a great deal of damage in their wake. The country's high plateau regions are usu-

accelerated this deforestation trend. Despite efforts to reverse this alarming trend, the government's reforestation program which replants some 620 square miles (1,600 square km) annually is not enough to cover the annual forest losses of 770 square miles (2,000 square km).

The much diminished but still immense tropical forests cover two-fifths of the country and contain over 700 identified plant species, constituting a rich source of oils, resins, precious woods and industrial timber and medicinal plants. Precious hardwoods are being felled in massive quantities for export, in order to supply the country with desperately needed hard currency. However,

ally much cooler than the coastal areas and experience a marked nightly drop in temperature all year round.

Flora and Fauna: In prehistoric times, much of Vietnam was covered in dense forest. Man's exploitation of the environment over the millennia has greatly reduced these vast forested regions, which have virtually been halved since 1945.

War, chemical defoliation, and an ever increasing population growth, have greatly

Left, keeping above the waterline in Ha Son Binh Province. Above, beauty of the Red River Delta in North Vietnam.

this wholesale depletion of forest reserves could cost the country far more in the long run as the subsequent flooding and erosion take their toll on the environment of this traditionally agricultural country.

Vietnam's wildlife is in general identical to that of Bengal and the Malaysian peninsula. It includes species extinct in other parts of Asia among its 273 species of mammals, 180 species of reptiles, 273 species of birds and hundreds of species of fish and invertebrates. Among these are elephant, wild buffalo, rhinoceros, antelope, tapir, monkey, wild boar, tortoise, crocodiles, hornbill and pheasant.

Vietnam's ancient history reads like a book of legend with many pages torn or missing, due to a lack of early historical records, many of which were destroyed as its history was in the making. Like any ancient nation, Vietnam's earliest history has been generously embellished with legend and fairy tales, rather daunting to the Western understanding. However, by combining Chinese and Vietnamese historical records, Vietnamese folklore and recent archaeological discoveries, some of the missing pages have come to light.

In ancient times, Eastern cosmogony viewed the world through the concept of The Five Elements: metal, wood, water, fire and earth, or Nghu Han, which represents Five Regions: the Center, the South, the North, the East and the West. The Center was represented by the earth and the color yellow, the South by fire and the color red, the North by water and the color black, the East by wood and the color green, the West by metal and the color white. The first threads of Vietnam's history are inextricably intertwined with the history of China.

At the source of the legend:
The Han and the Viet

From time immemorial, a kingdom reigned in the heart of the Asian continent. Known as the Middle Kingdom or Chung Hoa, its power center was located in the Five Mounts (Ngu Linh) Territory. It was peopled by many races, the two major being those of the Han and the Viet. Unlike the homogeneous Han, the Viets incorporated hundreds of tribes and were known as the Pac Yeuh (One hundred Yeuh) or Bach Viet, whose chief ruled the Five Mounts Territory. The Viets settled south of the Yellow River and developed an agricultural culture, whereas the Han in the northwest became expert in hunting and battle skills.

The Five Mounts Territory of the Middle

Kingdom was ruled by three consecutive chiefs: Toai Nhan – who discovered fire; Phuc Hi – who discovered the I Ching and domesticated wild animals; and Shen Nong – who cultivated wild plants for domestic use and taught his people to grow rice. By the end of Shen Nong's era the Han had invaded the Five Mounts territory and occupied the highest mount, Thai Son.

Their chief proclaimed himself Hwangdi, the Yellow Emperor of the Center, in accordance with the Five Elements concept. Hwangdi inherited the heritage of the Tam Hoang, Three Yellows era, which his invasion of The Five Mounts Territory ended. He referred to the Viets settled in the South as the southern barbarians, *Nam Man*. The Viets fled to the south where their chief proclaimed himself Viem De, the Red Emperor of the South, and named their territory Xich Qui, the territory of the Red Devils. This marked the first Viet exodus from Chung Hoa, the Middle Kingdom. The Viets regarded themselves as descendents of the first three chiefs of China's Three Yellows era. The last of the three, Shen Nong, is the direct Viet link.

According to Vietnamese historical folklore, De Minh, a third generation descendent of Shen Nong, fled to the southern territory of the Five Mounts and married Princess Vu Tien. Their son, Loc Tuc, became king of the south and called himself Kinh Duong Vuong, King of the Kinh and Duong Territory. He married one of the daughters of Dong Dinh Quang, a king from the lake of Dong Dinh territory. Their son, Sung Lam, succeeded his father to become Lac Long Quan, meaning the Lac Dragon.

The Quasi-Legendary Epoch and
Hoa Binh Civilization

Vietnam's National Annals tell of the marriage between King Lac Long Quan, the Dragon Lord of the Mighty Seas, and the beautiful Princess Au Co, descendant of the Immortals of the High Mountains, the daughter of King De Lai. Their union gave birth to one hundred sons and the Kingdom of Bach Viet, whose principalities extended from the lower Yang Tse Kiang to the north of Indochina. The Kingdom prospered, but the Lord of the Dragon and the Princess of the Mountains, convinced that the difference in their origins would always deny them earthly happiness, decided to separate. Half the children returned with their mother to the mountains, the others followed their father and established themselves beside the eastern sea.

The symbolism of Lac Long Quan's descendancy from the Dragon Lord and Au Co from the Immortals, holds significance for the Vietnamese as the Dragon symbolizes *yang* and Immortal is the symbol for *ying*. Thus the Vietnamese believe they are the descendents of Tien Rong, the Immortal

then called the "Calendar of the Sacred Turtle".

The southern Viet kingdom of Xich Qui was divided into one hundred principalities, each one governed by one of the 100 sons. In 2879 B.C. the eldest son was crowned King of Lac Viet. He named himself King Hung Vuong and Lac Viet was renamed Van Lang. His Kingdom of Van Lang was the most powerful and comprised most of present-day North Vietnam and the north of Central Vietnam.

The kingdom of Van Lang prospered during the first millennium B.C. under the rule of eighteen successive Hung kings who formed the dynasty of Hung Vuong. His

and the Dragon, and these symbols constitute their earliest totems.

Civilized norms governed early relations between the Han Court and the Viet kingdom. The Chinese historian Kim Ly Tuong recorded that in the Fifth Year of Dao Duong, Emperor of the Yao dynasty (2361 B.C.), the Viet Thuong kingdom sent a diplomatic delegation to the Han court and offered a "sacred turtle" (Linh Qui) as a friendship present. The turtle was thought to be a thousand years old and its shell was covered with precious inscriptions in hieroglyphics. It was learnt later that Emperor Yao transcribed all these inscriptions into a *vade-mecum*, which he

capital was founded in present day Vinh Phu Province which was then divided into fifteen provinces. At this time a certain King Thuc Phan governed the neighboring kingdom of Au Viet, another Viet tribe, to the north of Van Lang. His desire to bring about a marriage between his daughter and Hung Vuong's son was not shared by Hung Vuong who scornfully rejected the proposal. The hereditary hatred this rebuff bred between the two Viet dynasties led to conflict and eventually, in 258 B.C., during the rule of the rather weak 18th king, the destruction of Van Lang.

Under the title of King An Duong Vuong,

Thuc Pham established the new kingdom of Au Lac and installed his capital at Phuc An where a spiral citadel was built. The remains of the citadel can still be seen to this day in the village of Co Loa to the west of Hanoi in North Vietnam.

Fifty years later, the kingdom fell into the hands of the northern hordes of an ambitious general, Trieu Da from the South of the Middle Kingdom. After vanquishing the other Chinese generals, Trieu Da founded the independent kingdom of Nam Viet, which included much of present-day Southern China. He proclaimed himself king in 208 B.C. and founded the Trieu dynasty which lasted until the 3rd century B.C. His capital was located near present day Guangzhou.

Under the Trieu dynasty Nam Viet progressively entered the Chinese sphere of influence. In exchange for periodic tributes to the Court of the Han Emperor, Nam Viet received protection against foreign invasion. This period was marked by continual intrigues, including a plot aimed at seizing Nam Viet led by a Chinese Emperor, which was exposed and denounced. Less than a century later, in the year 3 B.C., the Han Emperor Wudi sent his mighty armies to conquer Nam Viet. Despite the defending army's fierce resistance Nam Viet finally fell into the hands of the Han invaders.

It is generally believed that with the decline of the Hung Vuong Dynasty and the ensuing decades, came the fusion of legend with known history in which much of Vietnam's ancient history has been recorded.

The Period of Chinese Domination

The first Chinese occupation lasted from 3 B.C. until A.D. 42. After Trieu Dau's defeat the country became a Chinese protectorate under the new name of Giao Chi. Highly qualified administrators were appointed as governors to rule the country, but their endeavors to introduce Chinese literature, arts and agricultural techniques met with fierce resistance from the Vietnamese. Greatly frustrated by decades of Chinese influence and culture, the Vietnamese not only guarded

Folk art woodblock prints: Left, the big cat (China) receives tributes from servile mice (Vietnamese royal court). Above, traditional theme of simple pleasures.

their national identity but fought fiercely to preserve it.

Finally, in 39 A.D., the oppressive rule and injustices of a cruel governor, To Dinh, provoked the victorious armed revolt against the Chinese authorities led by two sisters, Trung Trac and Trung Nhi. Their reign, however, was short-lived. Three years later, the better generals and arms of the Chinese Han armies saw to their downfall and the country was once more subjected to Chinese control. The fall of the Trung sisters marked the second period of Chinese occupation which lasted until 543. During this time Nam Viet was administered as a Chinese province and a campaign was launched against the King-

dom of Champa in the south.

This period of Chinese occupation ended abruptly when a scholar named Ly Bon led an armed revolt and succeeded in chasing out the Chinese authorities.

Ly Bon took control of the territory and founded the Ly Dynasty which lasted until the Chinese once again regained their supremacy in 545. The particularly troubled era that followed was marked by frequent outbreaks of violent battles between the Chinese and the Vietnamese. It ended with the third period of Chinese occupation which lasted from 603 until 938. During this time the Chinese made concerted efforts to establish their culture and civilization in Nam Viet, which they renamed Annam. However, numerous insurrections broke out despite the solid administrative structure imposed by the Chinese government of the Tang Dynasty.

The Great National Dynasties:

The Ngo Dynasty (939-967): Disorder accompanied the decline of the Chinese Tang Dynasty, giving the Vietnamese the chance they had long waited for. In a protracted war which ended with the celebrated battle of Bach Dang, General Ngo Quyen vanquished the Chinese invaders and founded the first

The Dinh Dynasty (968-980): The most powerful of the twelve feudal lords, Dinh Bo Linh, rapidly ruled out the others. He reunified the country under the name of Dai Co Viet and took the imperial title of "Dinh Tien Hoang De" (The First August Emperor Dinh). Well aware of the new Chinese Song dynasty's military might, Dinh Bo Linh negotiated a non-aggression treaty in exchange for tributes payable to the Chinese every three years. This set the foundation of future relations with China which were to last for centuries.

On the domestic front, Dinh Tien Hoang established a royal court and a hierarchy of civil and military servants. He instated a

National Dynasty in 939. Ngo Quyen then decided to transfer the capital to Co Loa, the capital of the Au Lac Kingdom, thus affirming the continuity of the traditions of the Lac Viet people.

Ngo Quyen spent the six years of his reign fighting the continual revolts of the feudal lords. At his death in 967, the kingdom fell into chaos and became known as the land of "Thap Nhi Su Quan", the twelve feudal principalities constantly fighting each other. For more than twenty years, the country remained fragmented and the external threat from the Song dynasty loomed large on the Northern horizon.

rigorous justice system and introduced the death penalty to serve as a deterrent to all who threatened the new order in the kingdom. He organized a regular army divided into ten Dao or military corps. Security and order were progressively re-established, inaugurating a new era of "Thai Binh" (peace).

However, Tien Hoang's reign was not to last long. He was assassinated in 979 by a palace guard, who, according to the Annals, saw "a star falling into his mouth" – a celestial omen heralding promotion. The heir to the throne was only six years old and could no way stand firm against the mounting intrigues of the court.

The Early Le Dynasty (980-1009): With the Queen Mother's blessing, Le Hoan dethroned Dinh Bo Linh's heir and proclaimed himself King Le Dai Hanh. He retained the capital in Hoa Lu and succeeded in warding off several Chinese invasions by the Song Court, but continued paying them tributes every three years in exchange for friendly relations.

With peace assured on the northern border, he decided to pacify the South. In 982, Le Dai Hanh launched a military expedition against the Champa kingdom, entered Indrapura (present-day Quang Nam) and burnt the Champa citadel. The conquest of this northern part of the Champa Kingdom brought about a marked Cham influence on Viet-

ensuing period, the famous monk, Khuong Viet managed to establish the Buddhist religion as a stabilizing pillar of the Kingdom. The Tien Le dynasty eventually collapsed after the death of one of Le Dai Hanh's heirs in 1009.

The Ly Dynasty (1009-1225): The Ly, who reigned over the country for more than two centuries, were the first of the great national dynasties. Ly Cong Uan was a disciple of a famous monk, Van Hanh, who helped him to power in the Hoa Lu Court. Assuming the name Ly Thai To, the new sovereign inaugurated his dynasty with a change of capital. The Annals mentioned that King Ly Thai To saw the apparition of an ascending dragon on

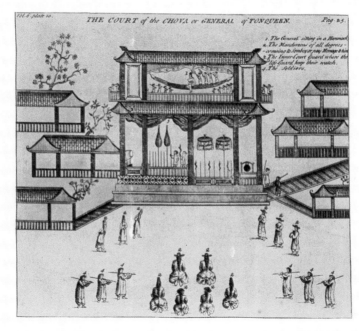

namese culture, particularly in the fields of music and dance.

Le Dai Hanh's reign marked the first attempt to consolidate the Viet nation. He devoted a great deal of energy to developing the road network in order to better administer the country's different regions. However, the local forces were still reluctant to toe the line to the central authority and mounted a succession of revolts. In 1005, after 24 years of difficult rule, Le Dai Hanh died. In the

the site of the future capital and decided to name it Thang Long(Ascending Dragon). In 1054, one of his successors, King Ly Thanh Ton, rechristened the country Dai Viet.

During the Ly dynasty, Buddhism flourished as the national religion. Buddhist masters, who acted as "Quoc Su", supreme advisors, assisted the Ly kings in their rule. Several Ly Kings – Thai Tong, Anh Tong and Cao Tong – led the Buddhist sects of Thao Duong and founded some 150 monasteries in the region of Thang Long.

Under the impulse of Confucian administrators, the Ly dynasty consolidated the monarchy by setting up a centralized government

Left, 17th-century view of Tonkin. **Above,** the royal court at Tonkin.

and establishing a tax system, a judiciary system and a professional army. Important public works, including the building of dikes and canals, were undertaken in order to develop agriculture and settle the population.

The monarchist centralization endowed the King with three roles: absolute monarch and religious chief of the Empire; mediator between the people and Heaven; and father of the nation. Meanwhile, the mandarinat became an institution composed of six departments: staff, finances, rites, justice, armed forces and public works.

In 1070 a National College was founded to educate future mandarins. Knowledge of the Confucian classics plus the mastery of liter-

ary composition and poetry were the main requirements of the rigorous three year course which culminated in a very competitive diploma examination.

The Tran Dynasty (1225-1400): An ambitious commoner, Tran Canh, married the Ly dynasty's last Queen, Chieu Hoang. He shrewdly plotted and manoeuvred his way to power and finally founded the Tran Dynasty. During this period, Buddhism, which had become predominant under the Ly Dynasty, continued to play an important role, but was subsequently weakened by its co-existence with Confucianism, Taoism and various other popular beliefs and customs. The century-

old competitive examination system introduced during the first period of Chinese occupation underwent draconian revisions. An administration incorporating both the reigning King and the heir to the title of the previous reign was officially adopted to ensure its continuity and prevent any dispute between the two families.

The Tran Dynasty is renowned for its brilliant military victories, especially that carried off by the King's brother, Tran Hung Dao, against Kublai Khan's much larger Mongol armies on the Bach Dang River. Another historic event in the course of that reign was the King's sister's – Princess Huyen Tran's – marriage to the King of Champa in 1307. The marriage extended the national territory southwards with the peaceful annexation of the Hue region and at the same time inaugurated the politics of diplomatic marriage.

The Ho Dynasty (1400-1428): The King's marriage to the aunt of a minister, Le Qui Ly, was to prove a fatal move for the Tran Dynasty. Taking full advantage of his aunt's union, Le Qui Ly shrewdly manoeuvred his way to power. He finally assumed control of the kingdom and founded a dynasty under his ancestral name of Ho.

During his reign the army was reorganized and reinforced. Taxes were revised and ports opened to trading ships which were obliged to pay taxes. Under a new fiscal system, coins were taken out of circulation and replaced with bank notes. Restrictions were imposed on land ownership. In the administrative domain, Ho introduced the extension of royal appointments to his loyal servants. The competitive examination system for administrators was modified to demand more practical knowledge of peasant life, mathematics, history, the Confucian classics and literature. Legal reforms were undertaken and a medical service established.

Well aware that Ho had usurped the throne, the Chinese Ming Emperor sent 5,000 soldiers into the country under the pretext of helping the movement faithful to the Tran Dynasty.

The Ming intervention provoked the fall of the Ho Dynasty in 1407. During the short period of Chinese occupation that followed, the Vietnamese suffered the most inhuman exploitation.

The Chinese resolutely strove to destroy

the Vietnamese national identity. Vietnamese literature, artistic and historical works were either burnt or taken to China and were replaced by the Chinese classics in all the schools. The Chinese dress and hair style were imposed on the Vietnamese women; local religious rites and costumes were replaced or banished; private fortunes were confiscated and taken to China.

The Late Le Dynasty (1428-1776): The oppressed people found a new leader in the person of Le Loi, a man renowned for his courage and generosity. Under the title, Prince of Pacification, he organized a resistance movement from his village and waged a guerrilla war against the enemy. By employ-

To. He renamed the country **Dai Viet** and immediately began the task of its reconstruction after the devastation caused by the war. He reduced his army from 250,000 to 10,000 men and adopted a rotation system which enabled four-fifths of his soldiers to return to the countryside to work to help boost food production. The legal system was reorganized and the penal system revised. A new College of National Sons (Quoc Tu Giam) was founded to educate future administrators, with admission based entirely on merit and not on the prior prerequisite of social or family status.

Le Thai To died in 1443, leaving the throne to his son, Le Thai Tong. Le Thai Tong's

ing a strategy of surprise attacks targeting his adversary's weakest points, Le Loi managed to further weaken the enemy and at the same time avoid combat with the superior Chinese forces. His enforcement of strict military discipline ensured that no pillaging was carried out by his troops in the regions under his control and this made him a very popular hero.

Le Loi founded the Le Dynasty in 1428 and became king under the name of Le Thai

Those who aspired to ascend to court officialdom had to pass strict literary exams. <u>Above</u>, river scene at Hoi An.

sudden death not long after was followed by a decade of confusion marked by intrigues and plots within the Royal Court. This troubled period ceased only when Le Thanh Tong affirmed his power.

Under his thirty six year reign the country prospered as never before. He revised the fiscal system, encouraged agriculture and placed great emphasis on customs and moral principles. A writer himself, he founded the Tao Dan Academy and wrote the first volume of national history.

Le Thanh Tong was by no means only a recorder of history. His reorganized army won an easy victory over the Champa army in 1471. His farmer-soldiers excelled not only on the battlefields, but also in the fields where they established militarized agricultural communities wherever they went. In this way the national territory was gradually expanded southwards, until finally the Champa Kingdom was completely absorbed and assimilated.

The Trinh and Nguyen Lords' Secession Wars: The increasing decadence of the Le dynasty in the late 16th century saw to the country's division into two rival principalities as some corrupt and useless kings succeeded Le Thanh Tong. Mac Dang Dung, a shrewd and scheming adviser at the Royal Court, seized control of the country, and founded the Mac Dy-

fying the north and re-establishing the Le authority in Hanoi, Lord Trinh returned only to find Nguyen Hoang well entrenched in the southern court reigning as lord and master of all.

In 1672, after repeated tentative attempts failed to remove Nguyen Hoang, Lord Trinh finally consented to the partition of the country at the Linh River which marked the 18th parallel. It was not, however, until after about fifty years of civil war, that the Trinh and Nguyen Lords eventually agreed to a period of co-existence. This respite lasted for more than a century, during which time the Le Emperors played no more than a ceremonial role.

nasty. During this time descendants of the Le Dynasty rallied around Nguyen Kim and Trinh Kiem, looking for a way to overthrow Mac Dang Dung. After a series of fierce battles they succeeded in occupying the country's southern capital and in 1543 founded the Southern Court near Thanh Hoa. The war continued indecisively until the death of the Mac Dynasty's last king, Mac Mau Hop, in 1592.

In an effort to restore law and order to the territory controlled by the Macs, Lord Trinh left the Southern Court under the temporary control of Nguyen Kim's nephew Nguyen Hoang, and set out for the north. After paci-

The Tay-Son Uprising (1776-1792): Frequent insurrections, provoked by the corruption rife within the disintegrating administration broke out during the last years of the two royal courts. A popular revolution of sorts was in preparation as the peasant insurrections grew to be a force to be reckoned with.

The Tay Son brothers – Nguyen Nhac, Nguyen Lu and Nguyen Hue – seized the day and staged an uprising against the leading Le Lords, easily defeating them. However, Le Chieu Thong managed to flee to China where he called for Chinese protection. In 1788, the Qing court decided to send an expeditionary corps to conquer the divided country.

To save the nation, Nguyen Hue proclaimed himself Emperor Quang Trung in Phu Xuan and overran the Chinese troops in a whirlwind campaign. He pacified the Northern part of the country from the Chinese border to the Hai Van pass in the Center and devoted his energies to national rehabilitation, administrative reorganization and economic development. Significantly, Quang Trung replaced the classic Chinese Han with the popular nom as the official language. Unfortunately, his promising reign was cut short by his premature death not long after in 1792.

The Nguyen Dynasty (1792-1883): Lord Nguyen's successor, Nguyen Anh, was supported by Nguyen royalists who saw him as the legitimate heir in the South.

annexed territory of Dai Viet. The Tay Son suspected they were Nguyen Anh's sympathisers and this suspicion intensified after the leading Tay Son generals, Tap Dinh and Ly Tai, fled to Nguyen Anh's camp. After suffering defeat at the hands of their former generals in the Saigon region, the Tay Son army exacted their revenge and massacred thousands of the Chinese settlers.

The Bishop of Adran saw an opportunity to expand the church's influence in the post Tay Son era and negotiated a promise of military aid for Nguyen Anh from the French Government in exchange for territorial and commercial rights. However, the French were busy with their own internal disputes and the

the legitimate heir in the South. With their backing, Nguyen Anh took up the fight against the Tay Son brothers and after Quang Trung's death, extended his control over the country with the aid of a French missionary, Monsignor Pigneau de Behaine, Bishop of Adran.

The Ming Chinese who had fled the Ching invasion and settled in the Saigon region, regarded Nguyen Anh as the leader who could safeguard their settlement in the newly

Left, traditional dwelling at Hue. **Above**, the earliest European residences in Saigon.

promised aid never materialized. Undaunted, the Bishop organized funds and recruited troops himself. The training in modern military techniques proved invaluable to Nguyen Anh and his army and certainly facilitated his victory when in 1801 he subdued the Tay Son and proclaimed himself Emperor Gia Long.

A power struggle between the French and Chinese factions began within the court. Although Nguyen Anh owed his accession to power to the French, he was nevertheless very suspicious of France's designs on his country and under his reign the court's Chinese faction took precedence. He came to rely more on the assistance of Confucian mandarins than the Catholic missionaries in the consolidation of his empire.

The reunified and newly renamed Viet-Nam extended from the Chinese Frontier to the Camau Peninsula in the South. Serious efforts were made to codify the law and develop the national administration along the lines of Confucian principles. Hue became the country's new administrative capital. Gia Long replaced the Hong Duc Code by a new legislation, which bore his name and served as an instrument to consolidate the monarchic power after thirty years of civil war.

The Nguyen Dynasty's monarchist abso-

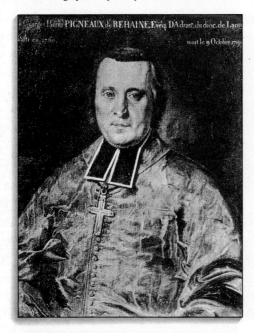

lutism was reflected in the extraordinary development of Hue as the most beautiful city of Vietnam. Elaborate palaces, mausoleums, temples and pagodas were successively built here, all in keeping with the harmony of cosmic order.

The Nguyen kings also extended Vietnam's border into Laos and Cambodia, incorporating these two kingdoms as new vassal states of their Empire. Conversely, they closed the country to Western penetration from the seas. Fearing that the opening of the kingdom and expansion of trade links would undermine the structure of the monarchy, they practised a kind of isolationism vis-a-vis the West.

Meanwhile, Prince Canh, Nguyen Anh's eldest son, had accompanied the Bishop of Adran to France during his negotiations with the French government. The Prince was later educated at a missionary school in Malacca and converted to Catholicism. This made Canh the first Viet prince ever educated by Westerners.

Military leaders within Nguyen Anh's army realized the superiority of modern Western military technology and wished to utilize Prince Canh's knowledge to rebuild the country after the war. The Prince was regarded by many as the one who could modernize Dai Viet and bring it into the era of industrialization.

When the issue of Gia Long's successor was being discussed in court before his death, the power struggle between the French and Chinese factions resumed. The military generals, including Nguyen Thanh, the governor of Thang Long and Le Van Duyet, the governor of Gia Dinh (Saigon), supported the French faction and wanted Prince Canh as the heir. However, most of the court ministers belonged to the Chinese faction and supported Canh's younger brother, Prince Mien Tong.

Again, it was the conservative Chinese faction who triumphed. Prince Canh reportedly died of measles at the age of 21. This prognosis was refuted by missionaries close to the court who reported to the French mission headquarters that he had died of poisoning.

Once Prince Mien Tong was crowned Emperor Minh Mang, the French Chinese divide officially ended. Most of Prince Canh's followers were either demoted or executed. General Nguyen Thanh was forcefully administered poison and General Le Van Duyet's tomb was desecrated.

In the meantime, the Catholic missions had sped up their evangelization of the people. This provoked Minh Mang's anti-Catholic policy which ordered the persecution of Catholic missionaries and their Vietnamese converts.

Vietnam had missed its first opportunity to modernize and industrialize.

Above, Pierre Pigneau de Behaine , the Bishop of Adran. **Right**, Hindu sculpture from Champa.

Un nouveau fait d'armes vient d'être accompli au Tonkin par n...
héroïques soldats. — La place de Lang-Son est tombée entre leurs main...
et le 13 février à midi, le drapeau français flottait au-dessus de
citadelle.

Après la prise du camp retranché de Dong-Song, l'armée fit tro...
jours de marche à travers des gorges presque impénétrables : le 11, ...
brigade de Négrier attaquait et emportait le village de Vanoï; le ...
après de sérieux et sanglants combats livrés au milieu d'un épais brou...
lard, la brigade Giovanelli prenait plusieurs forts d'assaut, repouss...
les Chinois de crêtes en crêtes et bivouaquait le soir à la sortie des gorg...
après avoir fait éprouver des pertes considérables à l'ennemi. — Le 13, un...

arche rapide conduisait toute l'armée devant Lang-Son, et après une
goureuse canonnade, les hordes chinoises étaient mises en déroute,
ssant entre les mains de nos vaillants soldats des approvisionnements
nsidérables et une grande quantité de munitions de guerre.

Les troupes françaises ont été sublimes d'entrain et de vaillance, et ont
pporté avec le plus grand courage la fatigue, le froid et l'humidité
i régnaient pendant ces jours de lutte, du 9 au 13 février.

Nos pertes sont de 99 tués et de 222 blessés; mais c'est par milliers
e l'on a pu constater celles de l'ennemi, qui, au nombre de 20,000
mmes, et malgré une vigoureuse résistance, a dû céder devant la valeur
s soldats français.

The anti-Catholic policy gave the French a pretext to intervene in Vietnam. The landing of a French party in the port of Tourane, (present-day Danang) in August 1858, heralded the beginning of the colonial occupation which was to last almost a century. The French Government wanted to establish a strategic and religious sphere of influence in Indochina, but their demands to install a French Consulate and Commercial Attache in Danang were rejected by the Imperial Court in Hue. The French responded by occupying Danang.

The later Emperors, Thieu Tri and Tu Duc, became more and more entrenched in their Confucian doctrine and the country experienced an era of stagnancy. The court mandarins were increasingly blinded to the development of the outside world and worse still, implemented a policy of isolation that forbade any contact with foreigners.

Seeing the danger of such a policy, the progressive mandarins in Emperor Tu Duc's court launched a movement to modernize the country. Among these were: Bui Vien, the first Vietnamese envoy to Washington D.C. who presented his credentials to President Ulysses Grant; Nguyen Lo Trach, who wrote a discourse on the changing world; and Nguyen Truong To, a Catholic and strong advocate of progressive change. During the persecution under Thieu Tri, Nguyen Truong To had been taken overseas by French missionaries and educated in France and Malacca. On his return to Vietnam a sympathetic mandarin secured him a minor position in the Royal Court where he spent most of his time writing Emperor Tu Duc a proposal on how to modernize the country. However his proposal was rejected by the dogmatic mandarins after a very heated and lengthy debate in the court.

The failure to implement Nguyen Truong To's proposals led the Vietnamese leadership progressively deeper into the dogma of Confucianism. Consequently, when the French navy opened fire in Danang the Court

Preceding pages: Royal transport awaits the king at Hue; French troops overrun local positions at Lang Son. Left, French troops entering Hung Hoa in 1884. Above, Prince Canh.

of Hue was totally unequipped to defend the country against the modern and powerful enemy.

In 1861 the French took Saigon. Six years later the entire southern part of the country, rechristened Cochinchina, was annexed as a French colony. Vietnam lost its independence in 1883 with the extension of French control to the North. The Center of Vietnam, renamed Annam, and the North, Tonkin, became French protectorates. The three regions were each governed somewhat differ-

ently. Cochinchina at first came under a military government, then later a civil governor with a civic council elected by civil servants and naturalized French. The colony sent a representative to the French Parliament. Tonkin was governed in a similar way. In Annam, the Emperor kept his title to power under strong, but more indirect French control.

French efforts to develop the country's natural resources brought no change to Vietnamese thinking. The Vietnamese were no happier living under French domination than they had been under the Chinese. In 1893, Emperor Ham Nghi and Phan Dinh Phung organized a royalist movement "Can Vuong" and staged an unsuccessful uprising at Ha Tinh. The Can Vuong movement survived until one of its leaders was killed by a Vietnamese traitor. Dogmatic Confucian thought was once again the order of the day. Emperor Duy Tan's abortive attempt to form a revolutionary movement in 1916 saw to his rapid replacement by Khai Dinh.

By the beginning of the 20th century, various nationalist resistance movements had formed. Among this was one composed almost entirely of aristocrats, intellectuals and young people led by more radical Confucian scholars such as Phan Boi Chau, Phan Chau Trinh and Prince Cuong De – Prince Canh's

namese revolutionaries and students escape to China.

When the exiled Vietnamese in China witnessed the 1911 Kuomingtang Revolution led by Sun Yat Sen, some young revolutionaries were convinced that the same revolution could take place in Vietnam. They formed the Vietnam Quoc Dan Dang Party, which later became the leading revolutionary party in the struggle against the French.

Meanwhile, a new debate caused a rift between the Westernized reformist Phan Chu Trinh and the nationalist Phan Boi Chau. Phan Chu Trinh opposed Phan Boi Chau's appeal for foreign help to resolve the French occupation.

great grandson. In an effort to break away from the traditional royalist thinking they embraced the new idea of democracy. The new resistance was greatly influenced by the Japanese victory over Russia in 1904. Convinced that Western power was no longer invincible, Phan Boi Chau and Cuong De sought help in Japan. They established the Eastward Movement in 1907 and Vietnamese students were secretly sent to study at institutions in Japan. When the French authorities discovered this they negotiated with the Japanese government for the extradition of all Vietnamese students from Japan. Some Japanese officials, however, helped Viet-

He believed Vietnam could regain independence through the democratic process as purported by the French constitution. In 1915 Phan Chu Trinh went to Paris to rally Vietnamese exiles and radical French politicians to support the Vietnamese struggle.

Nationalist sentiments intensified in Vietnam, especially after World War I, but all the uprisings and tentative efforts failed to obtain any concessions from the French overseers. The Russian Revolution which occurred at this time had a tremendous impact on shaping 20th century Vietnamese history.

Nguyen That Thanh, alias Nguyen Ai Quoc, better known under his later alias of Ho Chi

Minh, a young Vietnamese revolutionary working with Phan Chu Trinh on an anti-colonial petition put forward at the Versailles Conference in 1919 by a group of Vietnamese patriots, was greatly impressed with the Russian Revolution. He became involved with French intellectuals who formed the French Communist Party in 1921.

In 1922 Nguyen Tat Thanh went to Moscow to be trained as a Kominternshik, an agent of the Communist International. As a young revolutionary he enjoyed the special privileges afforded him by his Soviet mentors and wholeheartedly espoused Stalin statesmanship.

In 1924 Nguyen Ai Quoc was sent to China as a delegate in Borodine's advisory team to the Communist Party of China. During this time, he contacted many young Vietnamese revolutionaries, and founded the Association of Vietnamese Youth, which competed with other radical organizations for the liberation of the country. For training purposes, some Vietnamese communist recruits were sent to Moscow and others became affiliated with the Chinese communist party. This situation was to lead to the internal conflict between the pro-Chinese and pro-Soviet factions within the Communist party of Vietnam many decades later.

In the same year, 1924, Emperor Khai Dinh died and his son Bao Dai, then aged 12, mounted the throne. Bao Dai was sent to France for his education and returned to Vietnam in 1932. At this time the Vietnamese were waiting to see the French persuaded to adopt more liberal politics, but it soon became clear that the French had no intention of making any real concessions.

In February 1930, on the Komintern's instruction, Nguyen Ai Quoc successfully rallied several communist groups and founded the Indochinese Communist Party. Under Ho Chi Minh, for the first time in history, a revolutionary party was systematically formed with the unlimited financial and ideological support of an aspiring superpower. Thus the Vietnamese resistance movement was divided into two major factions, greatly influenced by foreign intervention and foreign agents.

Left, French officers are received in Danang, 1831. Above, Father Borie heads off to martyrdom, 1838.

Also in 1930, under the leadership of Nguyen Thai Hoc, the Viet Nam Quoc Dan Dang – a replica of the Chinese Kuomintang, launched a military revolt in Yen Bay. Later, communist groups following the same path of armed revolt, known as the Nghe Tinh Soviets movement, staged a series of peasant uprisings. The French retaliated by taking severe measures against every one of these political movements.

The apparent calm which reigned after the reprisals towards the end of the 1930s shattered with the first battles of World War II in Europe. In Asia, most of the coastal cities of China fell under the advancing Japanese forces, and likewise in Vietnam where the

Japanese rapidly occupied the key regions during 1940.

The Sequels to the Second World War: For Vietnam, the explosion of the World War II in September 1939 was an event as decisive as the French taking of Danang in 1858. When France was invaded the following year, the Vichy Government was formed to govern the country. Vichy accepted the Japanese occupation of Indochina, but as compensation, was allowed to continue administering Vietnam. In March 1945, realizing the allied victory was inevitable, Japan overthrew the French authorities in Indochina, imprisoned their civil servants and rendered Vietnam "independent" under Japanese "protection", with Bao Dai as Chief of State.

The Japanese surrender some months later was an event Nguyen Ai Quoc had been waiting for since the French defeat in 1940. In May 1941, the Central Committee of the Indochinese Communist Party met in Southern China and announced the formation of the Revolutionary League for the Independence of Vietnam, which later became known as the Viet Minh. A longstanding agent of the Communist International, Nguyen Ai Quoc used the Viet Minh United Front as an instrument to apply his revolutionary strategy, which in fact was a pure transposition of the

At first the Chinese Nationalist authorities supported the new Vietnamese nationalist Front, but they later got wise to Nguyen Ai Quoc's new political affiliation. They imprisoned him and created a rival organization. However, they soon realized that Nguyen Ai Quoc's influence and organization were much needed and released him in 1943. They recognized him as the new chief of the Viet Minh Front and Nguyen Ai Quoc soon adopted the new name of Ho Chi Minh.

During this time, Ho's principal collaborator, Vo Nguyen Giap, set up some guerilla units in several regions of North Vietnam and created an intelligence network. Communist cells were organized throughout the

Dimitrov line to Vietnam's conditions. In its creation he finally achieved "the union of diverse Vietnamese nationalist groups under communist direction", a goal that he had been working towards since announcing it as his immediate task to the Komintern Executive Committee in 1924. The nationalists, who later formed the majority in the new Unified Front, had not bargained for their leader's political orientation. Nor did they realize the significance of Nguyen Ai Quoc's words when in 1927 he announced, "I intend to form a national Indochinese revolutionary movement whose leaders will introduce its members to orthodox communism".

country under the supervision of Truong Chinh, the young secretary general of the Indochinese Communist Party. These later became of inestimable value to Ho after Japan's sudden surrender on August 13, 1945. Ho was waiting for the Thoi Co – the opportune moment when all the conditions were met at the end of the war – to launch the general insurrection. Ho's resolute certainty of victory is reflected in the "prophetic" conclusion of one of his poems: "In 1945, the work will be accomplished."

By the end of World War II, Vietnam had become a political void. Bao Dai's Japanese installed Government existed in name only.

Apart from a handful of top French civil servants and troops whom the Japanese had imprisoned prior to their removal, Bao Dai had no allied troops in Indochina. In accordance with an allied agreement, Chinese Nationalist forces entered Vietnam as far as the 16th parallel in order to accept the Japanese surrender. The British assumed control of the South the same month. By the middle of August, chaos and uncertainty reigned once again in Vietnam. Ho Chi Minh wasted no time. Using the clandestine Indochinese Communist Party and the Vietminh Unified Front as intermediates, he worked towards becoming a dominant political force, occupying as much territory as possible before the allies arrived.

The August Revolution began on the August 16, 1945, when the Viet Minh announced the formation of a "National Committee of Liberation for Vietnam". Three days later, Ho's guerilla forces took Hanoi. Hue's turn came four days later on August 23, when Bao Dai's government was besieged and "asked" to hand over the royal seal. Bao Dai abdicated, believing, like most Vietnamese, that the Viet Minh was a true national front supported by the allies. Ho's forces controlled Saigon and practically all the surrounding rural areas. On August 29, Ho announced the formation of a provisional government in Hanoi. On September 2, 1945, Ho Chi Minh proclaimed himself president of the Democratic Republic of Vietnam.

However, Ho Chi Minh found himself in a strategically vulnerable position when the allied forces arrived. He camouflaged the existence of the communist elements within the Unified Viet Minh Nationalist Front and sought support from both the Chinese and the French. In an unprecedented move, the Indochinese Communist Party announced its self-dissolution in November, although in reality it continued to function under the guise of a study group.

Ho Chi Minh then prepared to negotiate Vietnam's future status with France. In the general elections, organized in January 1946, the Viet Minh won the majority of seats in the first National Assembly. Out of a total of 350 seats, 70 were conceded to the opposition parties by prior arrangement. Ho's government was officially approved at the Assembly's first session in March 1946, but at the second reunion in October, only 291 members, including 37 from the opposition, turned up. When asked to explain the poor turnout, one Viet Minh minister announced that the absentees had been arrested for criminal offences! The country's first national constitution was approved by 240 votes to one.

At the beginning of 1946, Ho began negotiating the basis for future relations with France. The French finally recognized the Democratic Republic of Vietnam as a free state within the French Union. A referendum was to be organized to determine whether the

country would be united. However, the relations between the two republics rapidly deteriorated. Hostilities mounted and finally reached a peak with the French bombing of Haiphong port. On December 19, 1946, Ho Chi Minh ordered a general offensive against the French in Hanoi plus the French garrisons in the North and Center. The decade long war for independence had begun.

The Enduring War of Resistance: The war for national independence which began with the Japanese occupation constitutes the most confused period of contemporary Vietnamese history. Thousands of Vietnamese took up arms against the French, yet few knew the

Left, Tonkin mandarin and his escorts. **Above**, His majesty Duy Tan, emperor of Annam.

identity and allegiance of their new leader and his party. The population did not entirely understand the historical events occurring in their country, nor could they imagine the consequences that were to follow. To them, at face value, Ho Chi Minh's new party appeared to consist of nationalists fighting for the common cause of national independence against the known enemy.

On Ho's orders, Vo Nguyen Giap launched a general offensive against the French forces, but in the face of superior fire power Ho's troops were forced to retreat to the countryside and high plateau areas. They soon adopted the concept of "people's war and people's army", the Mao Zedong-inspired

direct contact for the first time. Peking supplied the young republic with military equipment, substantial provisions and further aid to develop the Vietminh army. On his side, Ho Chi Minh attempted to increase his government's base of nationalist support. In the beginning of 1951 it was announced that the Unified Viet Minh Front would gradually merge with the new league for the National Union of Vietnam (Lien Viet), which was supposedly a nationalist multi-party alliance. Ho Chi Minh also announced the formation of the Vietnamese Workers Party (Lao Dong), a disguise for the Communist Party, which although officially dissolved had in fact remained active. The communist nature of the

guerrilla strategy and tactics, which generally consisted of attacking and sabotaging isolated French units, rather than becoming embroiled in any large-scale battles. During this time the French tried to rally support from the non-communist elements, however, they failed to persuade the sceptical nationalists. In 1949, France consented to an autonomous Vietnamese government within the French Union.

The emergence of Communist China towards the end of 1949 favored the communist dominated struggle. After Ho's guerillas had wiped out several French posts on the Chinese border, the two regimes established

Republic's leaders became increasingly evident as the regime's leading members became the leaders of the Workers' Party and in turn occupied the key positions in the Patriotic Front (Lien Viet). The nationalists and non-communists had little choice: either they swore their allegiance to the regime or followed the French.

Vo Nguyen Giap's guerilla forces progressively extended their territory during 1952 and 1953. By the Spring of 1953, several divisions were training in Laos as "volunteers" and had joined forces with the pro-communist Pathet Lao.

1954 began with new communist

offensives menacing South Vietnam, central and northern Laos, and the northeast of Cambodia. On May 8, 1954, the French base at Dien Bien Phu suffered a major defeat after a heavy artillery attack from Giap's forces. The French forces in North Vietnam evacuated to below the 16th parallel. On July 7, 1954, Bao Dai appealed to Ngo Dinh Diem. Bao Dai wished to lead the country with the support of the United States, but a referendum held in October decided to uphold Diem. Bao Dai was deposed on October 26, 1955, marking the end of the Nguyen Dynasty and the beginning of the Republic of South Vietnam.

The North-South Divide: The war for independence officially ended on July 20, 1954, after the long negotiations in Geneva. In finally gaining full national independence, Vietnam lost its unity. The Geneva agreement signed in August 1954, divided the country at the 17th parallel pending general elections previewed for the middle of 1956. The North became the Democratic Republic of Vietnam under the leadership of the Lao Dong party and the South became the Republic of South Vietnam. In April 1956 the last French troops left Vietnam.

The elections for the reunification of Vietnam stipulated by the Geneva Agreement never eventuated. The Republic of Vietnam, which never recognized the document anyway, naturally was not obliged to fulfil its conditions and Ngo Dinh Diem refused to organize the elections cited in the agreement. The conditions predominating in North Vietnam at the time also rendered the general elections impossible.

From 1954 to 1974 the two Vietnams had no diplomatic, cultural, or commercial relations with each other. Almost immediately after the Geneva Agreement and certainly from the end of the 1950s, a virtual state of

One city, two architectural styles: <u>Left</u>, looking down Rue Paul Bert in Hanoi's European quarter and <u>above</u>, the local district.

war existed between the two parts of the country. North Vietnam's intensified armed and revolutionary activities made the prospect of reunification through free elections appear increasingly unlikely. Meanwhile, the United States had reinforced Diem's troops and in three years had transformed South Vietnam into something of an "American protectorate". December 1960 saw the creation of the National Liberation Front of South Vietnam (FNL) which began launching revolutionary activities against the unstable regime in the South, under the banner of national liberation. The Southern communist movement, christened the Viet

Cong by Diem's government, grew considerably during 1961 and 1962.

Facing mounting popular pressures, Diem ordered repressive measures against the Buddhist Church. This move provoked a wave of suicides by Buddhist bonzes who set fire to themselves in protest against the regime. On June 11, 1963, the Venerable Thich Quang Duc, a 66 year old monk, immolated himself on a street corner in Saigon in protest of Diem's anti-Buddhist campaign. The flames which consumed him burnt into the conscience of the Vietnamese, American, and international public alike, as his image blazed across the world's television screens and newspapers. This signalled the begin-

ning of the end for President Ngo Dinh Diem's regime. Diem and his brother were murdered by Diem's own officers following a coup d'etat on November 1, 1963.

The following years witnessed a succession of coups d'etat, which destabilized the nationalist regime in South Vietnam. Several generals and civilian politicians took it in turn to preside over the unstable Saigon regime. On April 1, 1967, the constitution of the Second Republic of South Vietnam was proclaimed and on September 13, General Nguyen Van Thieu was elected president. South Vietnam's principal aim was to gain the free world's understanding and support for its struggle against North Vietnam and its Southern political arm, the National Liberation Front (NLF).

The beginning of 1965 marked the debut of direct U.S. involvement in Vietnam as President Lyndon B. Johnson decided to send troops to Vietnam and to bomb the North. By the end of 1967 there were more than 500,000 American and 100,000 allied troops in Vietnam. 1968 was a year marked by very violent combat and the impact of the Tet offensive, the surprise attack on Saigon and other urban centers throughout the country carried out by Viet Cong commandos at Vietnamese lunar New Year.

The 1968 presidential election campaign in the U.S. triggered a new awareness of the situation after four years of military involvement in Vietnam. President Lyndon Johnson took a decisive turn towards peace and launched an appeal for negotiations to suspend the American bombing of Vietnam. In 1969, Ho Chi Minh died without seeing his work completed.

Between 1968 and 1973, efforts were made at the Paris Conference to try and bring off a provisional agreement. The 1973 Paris Peace Agreement endeavored to: guarantee an end to the hostilities; re-establish peace in Vietnam; ensure the respect of Vietnam's national and fundamental rights; and ensure the South Vietnamese the right to govern themselves. But the agreement failed to end the hostilities. The two Vietnamese parties lost no time in violating the agreement and the fighting intensified.

In 1975 the American Congress refused South Vietnam the military aid demanded first by Richard Nixon and later by Gerald Ford. The Lao Dong leadership chose this moment to launch its final offensive against South Vietnam and on April 30, 1975, the communist army entered Saigon. The communist party's long struggle for power – under the banner of national liberation and reunification – finally ended in their complete victory.

A New Cycle of Conflict and Upheaval: A bright future seemed to stretch before socialist Vietnam after 1975 with the Vietnamese communist leadership making great plans for the rehabilitation of the country. But a series of strategic blunders made – and later admitted – by the Hanoi leaders, shattered all hope for a new era in Vietnam's history. First, the party leadership, under the pressure of the Northern conservative elements, decided to dissolve the Revolutionary Provisory Government of South Vietnam and the National Liberation Front of South Vietnam. In July 1976, Vietnam was officially reunified, thus breaking the fragile balance between the two parts of the country. Second, a radical program of socialist construction was put forward at the Fourth Party Congress in December 1976. It called for the rapid socialization of the Southern economy, with the forced collectivization of agriculture, small industry and commerce. This rapidly led to an unprecedented economic disaster, provoking new waves of refugees.

called "Chinese lesson" were to augur a new cycle of war, which was to absorb most of Vietnam's post-war energies; energies which could have been constructively spent in economic development. Vietnam's all-out alliance with the Soviet Union, who invaded Afghanistan in 1979, did nothing to help boost Vietnam's position on the international scene.

For the whole of the next decade, the presence of Vietnamese troops in Cambodia remained a central issue, around which a coalition of nations – China, Asean and the US – managed to enroll international support to isolate Vietnam. Meanwhile, the Khmer resistance rendered Vietnam's control over

On the international front, as early as 1977, Vietnam found itself in open conflict with Democratic Kampuchea and on a collision course with China. In June 1978, Vietnam decided to join the Comecon and in November, signed a friendship treaty – in fact, a security pact – with the Soviet Union. Once again, Vietnam was entangled in the bloc politics of the communist powers and their proxies. The invasion of Cambodia by Vietnamese troops at the end of 1978 and the so-

Left, General Giap, the North's military mastermind. <u>Above</u>, the military cemetery at Cu Chi.

Cambodia a kind of Sysiph's work. The Coalition Government of Democratic Kampuchea, established in 1982, with Prince Norodom Sihanouk as President and Khmer Rouge participation, received growing support from the international community. They occupied Cambodia's seat at the United Nations, while Vietnam lost most of its hard-earned international reputation. The Cambodian war was becoming a costly stalemate.

At the Fifth Party Congress in March 1982, the old guard, under the guidance of party secretary general Le Duan, obstinately maintained Vietnam's actual course, hoping that against all odds it could consolidate its political and military edge in Cambodia, and at the same time stabilize the socio-economic situation in Vietnam. The new economic policies, introduced at the Sixth Plenum in September 1979, managed to bring some respite on the domestic front, without improving the chronic weaknesses of Vietnam's economy.

It was only at the Sixth Party Congress, in December 1986, which followed the Soviet example of Glasnost and Perestroika, that the party decided to launch the country on an ambitious program of socio-economic renovation. Under the new leadership of Nguyen Van Linh, the motto of the party was then "to change or to die". A new contract-system

was implemented in 1988 to encourage Vietnamese farmers to cultivate their land, and rice production witnessed an immediate upsurge in 1989. Progress was also recorded in the sector of manufactured goods and commodities exports.

Until the end of 1988, socialist Vietnam followed the path of Soviet perestroika, but the Vietnamese leaders were soon to discover the bold and unchartered nature of Gorbachev's "new thinking". The surge of

Above, young campaigner. **Right**, reviewing stand at a veteran's day parade.

turmoil in China and Eastern Europe in 1989 shocked the Vietnamese communist leaders, who feared the impact of these events upon their regime. While reaffirming the party's commitment to the reform agenda, Nguyen Van Linh repeatedly rejected any idea of political pluralism and a multi-party system for Vietnam. Meanwhile, the demise of socialism in the Soviet Union and Eastern Europe contributed to the worsening economic crisis in Vietnam, as former members of the now-defunct Soviet bloc, besieged with domestic crises, were no longer in any position to continue their economic assistance to Vietnam.

It was in this uncertain context that in mid-1990 Vietnam adopted a new course in foreign affairs. In September, Vietnam's top leaders secretly visited China in order to mend fences with Beijing. The earlier withdrawal of Vietnamese troops from Cambodia in September 1989, had cleared the way for the political settlement of the Cambodian conflict. The peace process was a difficult one involving the efforts of all the parties directly and indirectly involved: the Soviet Union, China, Asean, the U.S., Japan, France and Australia.

In September 1990, a U.N. plan was finally endorsed by the Perm-Five – the U.S., the Soviet Union, China, the United Kingdom, and France – which called for the setting up of a Supreme National Council, a ceasefire and the cessation of foreign military assistance to the Khmer factions under a U.N. control mechanism, pending the organization of free general elections in Cambodia.

It is expected that with the final settlement of the Cambodian conflict, the U.S. and Western countries will lift the economic embargo against Vietnam. In the meantime, Hanoi has doubled its efforts to develop its open-door policy.

In early 1991, as the Vietnamese people prepared to celebrate the Tet festival, the party leadership laid the groundwork for a new political agenda, which would set Vietnam's course for the coming decade. A draft strategy for economic development until the year 2000, due to be submitted at the Seventh party congress, promises to bring Vietnam into the modernity of the 21st century. After a long period of great uncertainty, it seems that the dragon is awakening...

Comparative studies of folk songs from the hill region of North Vietnam and the coastal area in the northern part of Central Vietnam, affirm that the Vietnamese originated from the higher land of the Red River Delta in North Vietnam. The most ancient musical traditions so far collected in Vietnam were discovered at the ancient citadel of Co Loa near Hanoi.

These agricultural, fishing and hunting people were probably totemist. Their costume, although unique in Indochina, is found in certain Oceanic islands. The nautical, dance and war scenes depicted on their ancient bronze drums reveal a marked similarity to the mystical traditions of the Dayaks of Borneo and the Batak people of Sumatra.

Throughout monsoon Asia, which includes North Vietnam, a culture existed from a very early era, attested to by its tools, vocabulary and certain essential rites and traditions, such as the blackening of teeth, water festivals, bronze drums, kites, tattooing, use of betel nut and cajeput, pole houses, cock fighting and mulberry cultivation.

From the ethnic point of view, the remains of five races have been found in Vietnam: Malanesians, Indonesians, Negritos, Australoids and Mongoloids; the most predominant of these being the Indonesians and the Mongoloids.

Although the prehistoric Vietnamese may appear to be lost in the midst of time, they are kept alive in the collective memory of the Vietnamese people through numerous tales, legends, and popular songs which recount at length the traditions, customs and manners of this people, including the making of bronze drums and their annual cruise up the Red River. The cruise evoked the homeric battles between the Genie of the Mountain and the Genie of the River in their pursuit of the same Vietnamese princess, which marked the end of a reign, the fall of the spiral citadel and the beginning of Chinese domination.

This long period which extended over several millennium, marked by incessant tribal then war-lord wars, has been brought to light through laborious excavations and continual investigations into the past, and has revealed a series of archaeological, historical and ethnological milestones:

500,000 B.C. Archanthropian – teeth and bones.

300,000 B.C. – Nui Do tools and double-sided objects in basalt.

8000 B.C. – Mesolithic Hoa Binh culture: short axe, gatherers and hunters.

6000 B.C. Early Neolithic – Bac Son & Quy Van Cultures: axes with polished cutting edge, ceramics.

4000 B.C. Middle Neolithic – axes polished on both sides, fishing.

2000 B.C. – Phung Nguyen Culture: quadrangular axes, agriculture (rice), animal rearing, weaving.

1,300 B.C. – Megaliths & bronze-age culture (bronze drums). Slash and burn cultivation, bronze swing ploughs and stone hoes. Totemism, tattooing, the use of betel nut, lacquering of teeth and the crossbow.

690-258B.C. – Hung Vuong Dynasty at Me Linh, ruled by 18 consecutive Hung Kings.

Preceding pages: A mandarin and his family; the emperor's escorts, Hue. **Left**, portrait of a northern delta lady. **Above**, young men near Lai Chau.

257-208 B.C. – An Duong Vuong founds and reigns over the Kingdom of Au Lac, capital at Co Loa, the spiral citadel fortress.

208 B.C. – Trieu Da conquers Au Lac and founds Nam Viet,with capital at Fanyu near Canton.

111 B.C. – Han Wudi conquers Nam Viet to make a link with the Occident. Opening of the route between Burma and India.

106 B.C. – The creation of Giao-Chau, divided into 7 states governed by *thai tu*.

40-43 B.C. – Revolt led by the two Trung sisters and their reign at Me Linh.

43 B.C.– Ma Yuan, re-establishment of imperial Chinese domination.

1st Century – Opening of the sea route between China and Southeast Asia, (the future spice route) with Cattigara (Giao Chi Quan) as the terminus.

2nd Century – Buddhist missionaries arrive at Giao Chi.

982 A.D. – Beginning of Vietnamese expansion into Cham territory and with it the debut of Cham influence on Vietnamese art, music and culture.

The Population: Recent studies on the origins of the Vietnamese people show that the people who installed themselves on the Indochinese peninsula and its bordering regions, came from China, the high plateaus of Central Asia, islands in the South Pacific and various other parts of the world. Thus Vietnam can be considered a "melting pot" where major Asiatic and Oceanic migrations converged and mingled.

The Vietnamese: It is most likely that the first natives of Vietnam originated from several ethnic groups. The most important of these were the Hung or Lac, specialists in wet rice cultivation and inventors of the bronze drums, who inhabited the Red River Delta and central regions and the Muong, from the high wooded plateaus and mountainous regions.

Two major Viet emigrations added to these original ethnic groups. These came from the coastal and Southern provinces of the Chinese Empire which were part of Bac Viet, the 100 Viet Principalities mentioned in the History of China. The first emigration occurred during the 5th century B.C. at the fall of the Viet kingdom of the low Yang Tse Kiang valley and the second, during the 3rd century B.C. when the Au or Au Tay from Kwang Si invaded North Vietnam.

They progressively established themselves in the coastal regions, gradually making their way inland via riverways until they eventually reached the high regions, such as those inhabited by the native Lac people in the Red River Delta and the Muong at Hoa Binh and Thanh Hoa. This is why historians and ethnologists often group the Viet people under the double name of Lac Viet (Lo Yue), while the other ethnic group, the Muong, often called Muong Viet, are considered to be the proto-Vietnamese.

The Vietnamese population's southward expansion from the Red River Delta of North Vietnam brought an important native Malayo-Indonesian element to the fair skinned con-

tingent from the low valleys of the Yang Tse Kiang (Blue River) when they merged with the first native occupants of the Red River Delta towards the 3rd century B.C., founding the Kingdom of Au Lac in 257 B.C.

The many centuries of intermingling between these races has produced the Vietnamese race of today. Their union also resulted in the construction of the citadel fortress of Co Loa, a symbol of the Vietnamese people's spirit of resistance against the Chinese invasions.

In their search for vital living space, this vigorous, tenacious and courageous people crossed the mountain ranges of Central

Indochina and more than 1,800 miles (3000 km) in their expansion towards the South. They crossed through the Gate of Annam into Central Vietnam in 982, reached Hue in 1306, Quang Ngai in 1402, Binh Dinh in 1470, Phu Yen in 1611, Ba Ria in 1623, Nha Trang in 1653, Bien Hoa in 1658, Saigon in 1674, Phan Rang in 1693, Phan Thiet in 1697 and finally Ha Tien in the southernmost province in the Mekong Delta in 1714.

Their expansion was made at the cost of the Kingdoms of Champa and Cambodia. By 1714, the Viet Empire extended all the way from the Chinese frontier to the Gulf of Thailand.

The Ethnic Minorities: More than 54 ethnic

Lon, 6 miles (10 km) from the centre of Saigon, which today flourishes as the Chinese community's commercial centre in South Vietnam. Essentially shopkeepers and traders, they habitually regroup in communities well organized for trade and the research of new markets.

The ethnic minorities living in the mountainous regions in Central and the South of Vietnam form another important group. Called Montagnards by the French, these tribes include Muong, Ra De, Jarai, Banhar and Sedang living in the high plateaus of the West. Totalling around 700,000 people, they have always opposed foreign influence and only recently have begun to integrate more

minorities inhabit the mountainous regions which cover almost two thirds of Vietnam. The Viet or Kinh form the majority, representing about 90 percent of the population. Vietnam's 1 million Chinese constitute another important minority group. Only 3,000 have kept their Chinese nationality, while the rest, referred to as Hoas, have adopted Vietnamese nationality. On the whole, whether naturalised or not, most Chinese remain loyal to the costume and traditions of their country of origin. They settled in Cho

Eyeing the camera. <u>Left</u>, minority Meo tribeswomen and <u>above</u>, Black Thai girls.

into the national life.

The Chams and Khmers numbering around 400,000 constitute two other minorities. Ethnically different to the Montagnards, the Chams inhabit the Phan Rang and Phan Thiet regions, while the Khmers are found in the Mekong Delta. The Chams possessed a brilliant culture which lasted for only a short duration, yet its vestiges can still be seen in the ruins of the Poh Nagar Temple, the shrines and Buddhist monasteries at Dong Duong and the large scale irrigation systems, temples and towers in Quang Nam(Danang) and other sites in Central Vietnam. Most of their architectural and sculptural vestiges relate to their religious life. The Cham's most ancient religious belief, linked with ancient legend, was polytheist. Its prevailing image was that of a woman regarded as the mother of the country who gave birth to the dynasties ruling the country.

Large blocks of vertical standing stones or menhir represented another Cham cult. These symbolized the Genie of the Earth prior to the advent of the linga images which accompanied the propagation of Hinduism and Indian civilization which came later. Mahayana Buddhism reached the Chams a little later but was received at about the same time as Hinduism. The charms belong to the Austro-Asian and Malayo-Polynesian lan-

and midland regions of North Vietnam are home to many ethnic minorities and diverse tribes. Among these are:

The Tay, who number around 870,000, and are found in village groups in the provinces of Cao Bang, Lang Song, Bac Thai, Quang Ninh, Ha Tuyen, and the Dien Bien Phu region of Lai Chau.

Their villages, *ban*, are located in valleys near flowing water where they build their traditional houses, usually on stilts. They cultivate rice, soyabeans, cinnamon, tea, tobacco, cotton, indigo, fruit trees and bamboo higher up on the mountainsides above the *ban*.

That they have been considerably influ-

guage group, and their own script is based on ancient sanskrit.

Apart from records found on epitaphs discovered in the late 19th century and popular legends, Cham national history mainly consists of discontinued Chinese and Vietnamese written records.

Today the Cham people still preserve their traditional customs, language and script with the current religion being a modified form of Hinduism, although a large number have converted to Islam. They still adhere to their tradition of agricultural production and intensive farming.

Minorities of North Vietnam: The highlands

enced by Viet culture is evident in their dialect and customs which distinguish them from the other Tay-Thai speaking groups. Like the Viets, the Tay have been influenced by Buddhism, Taoism and Confucianism, which take their place alongside other local spirits in their temples.

The Nung, in many aspects similar to the Tay, share the same language, culture and customs and often live together in the same villages where they are referred to as Tay Nung. Numbering about 340,000, they inhabit the provinces of Cao Bang and Lang Son.

Their main staple is rice, but maize, millet,

sweet potatoes, vegetables, fruit trees and bamboo are also cultivated. They raise chickens, ducks, geese, pigs and buffalo, and often farm fish in the rice fields. Cotton and indigo are also cultivated for the cloth woven by the women.

The Thai number more than 76,000 and live in the northwest of Vietnam along the Red River, often together with other ethnic minorities. Their bamboo or wooden stilt houses are constructed in two distinctly different styles. The Black Thai build tortoise carapace-shaped homes whereas the White Thai dwellings are rectangular.

The women wear long, black *sarong* style skirts and short tops with silver buttons.

Son, Vinh Phu, Ha Bac and Quang Ninh provinces. They are of the Tay-Thai language group and arrived from China at the beginning of the 19th century. Their agricultural and medical knowledge, religious and superstitious beliefs, have come about through exchanges with neighboring cultures. Their knowledge of nature, moral precepts and social conduct are recorded in their songs, proverbs and verse.

San Chay ritual dances reflect the life of the community. An organized evening when alternating groups of boys and young girls perform their traditional love songs can go on all night and never fails to draw a crowd of singers, musicians and an audience of all

They are very skilled weavers and produce beautiful embroidery using motifs of flowers, birds, animals and dragons.

The Thai hunt and fish to supplement their diet and grow rice in the fertile river basins and valleys. Other crops include maize, manioc, sweet potato, cotton, indigo and beans.

The San Chay, numbering more than 77,000, live in village groups mainly in Ha Tuyen and Bac Thai provinces, but they are also found in certain regions of Hoang Lien

Left, successful end to a tiger hunt. **Above**, 19th century village at Cao Bang.

ages.

The Giay, also of the Tay-Thai language group, number about 28,000, and emigrated from China about 200 years ago. Their villages are often built very close to those of the Tay, Nung and Thai, in certain districts of Hoang Lien Son, Ha Tuyen and Lai Chau. Rice is grown in communal fields and the village is organized very much along the lines of a commune.

Every village has a forbidden forest known as *Doon Xia* where the largest tree is considered sacred. Under it they worship the Village Genie, an entity unique to each village. During the celebration of the cult, strangers are forbidden access to the village and a bamboo pole hung with various animal sacrifices is planted at the edge of the village. If the sight of pig and buffalo ears, chicken feet or a bunch of animal skins dangling from a pole isn't enough to dissuade strangers from entering the village, then perhaps the knowledge that payment, in the form of hens or rice alcohol offerings for the Genie is, and can be demanded from any stranger who chooses to ignore the signs. In some cases the punishment is more severe.

The Giay regard the universe as being composed of three levels, with man in the middle between the highest level of Heaven and the level below, considered a vile place

the Song Ma district of Son La Province, around Dien Bien Phu and Phong Tho in Lai Chau Province. Their homes are built on stilts in the form of a tortoise carapace like those of the Black Thai. Their traditional costume also strongly resembles that of the Thai.

Some Lao women tattoo the palm of the hand in the customary way with insect-like designs, whereas the men's tattoos feature a Buddhist swastika on the wrist and animals on the thighs. Both sexes smoke tobacco in finely carved pipes.

Their elaborate rice growing techniques are similar to those of the Thai. They are also skilled craftspeople, particularly in the fields

inhabited by sinners. An ancestral altar occupies the central position in a Giay home. Each vase of incense arranged on the altar represents the cult of a divinity such as the sky, the earth, the ancestors, or the genie of the home. The Giay's rich cultural background is reflected in the diverse aspects of their traditional life and in their numerous proverbs and maxims which constitute a kind of moral code.

The Lao number about 7,000 and belong to the Tay-Thai language group. They are actually closer to the Thai minority then their Laotian namesakes across the border. They are found along the Vietnam-Laos border in

of ceramics, weaving and embroidery.

Buddhism has had virtually no marked influence on the Lao who only petition Buddha for a good harvest and bring flower and fruit offerings to accompany their request. Every Lao village has its *shaman*, who is both quack doctor and scholar, and a wealth of stories, legends and folksongs besides.

The Lu belong to the Tay-Thai language group. They number around 3,000 and are found in the Phong Tho and Sin Ho districts of Lai Chau Province in well arranged villages of usually 40 to 60 dwellings. They arrived from China and occupied the Dien Bien Phu area as part of the Bach Y settlement in the

1st century AD. The Lu's famous Tam Van Citadel, dedicated to Buddha, was noted by the Black Thais on their arrival in the 11th and 12th centuries.

The women wear embroidered skirts and richly decorated tops. Their menfolk, not to be outdone, wear embroidered trousers, often keep their hair long and tattoo their bodies. Pierced ears and black lacquered teeth are also very common among the Lu.

Their diet consists mainly of glutinous rice eaten with fish and vegetables. Wet rice, maize, manioc, cotton, indigo, vegetables and fruit are cultivated and domestic animals reared for meat, essential for festive occasions, funerals and other religious ceremonies. The Lu believe in a spirit world inhabited by spirits of the mountains, rivers, house, village and countryside. Their literature and folklore comprise many popular tales, proverbs, poems and historical recitations.

The 1,000 or so Bo Y are found in mountainside communes on the Sino-Vietnamese border in Hoang Lien Son Province. They are also found in the Quyet Tien Commune in the Quan Ba district of Ha Tuyen Province. Their ancestors emigrated from China some 250 years ago.

Those living in Ha Tuyen speak a dialect somewhere inbetween Tay-Thai, whereas those near the Chinese border, closer both in location and language to their ancestral land, speak Mandarin.

Bo Y villages are always built near a source of water, from which water is piped into their homes through bamboo. Each house has its own vegetable garden and maize replaces rice as the main crop.

The women are very fond of silver jewellery. Their costume varies depending on location. Those near China wear traditional Chinese costume whereas those further south have adopted the Nung costume.

Buddhism, Taoism and Confucianism have always exerted an influence on the spiritual and everyday life of Bo Y society. They also retain some polytheist and animist superstitions, most evident in their conception of life and death and through some of their rites. They practise ancestor worship and also worship the genies of the sky, the earth, the soil, the forest, *Quan Yin*, *Ha Ba* (Emperor of the Water) plus river and fire spirits.

The Hmong who number more than 400,000 are found in villages known as *giao* throughout the highlands of nine provinces: Cao Bang, Lang Son, Bac Thai, Ha Tuyen, Hoang Lien Son, Son La, Lai Chau, Ha Son Binh and Thanh Hoa.

They emigrated to Vietnam from the Southern Chinese Kingdom of Bach Viet at the end of the 18th and beginning of the 19th centuries due to their wars with the feudal Chinese. Once in Vietnam they installed themselves in Ha Tuyen and Hoang Lien Son provinces.

Maize is their main staple but rice is often grown on terraces irrigated with the aid of a

homegrown hydraulic system. Hemp is grown as the main textile material and cotton is also cultivated in some villages. Poppy and Job's tears are among the plants cultivated for medicinal purposes. Fruit such as plums, peaches and apples, produced by the Hmong, is highly reputed throughout the country, although transport problems make selling their produce very difficult. They collect sticklac, gentian, cardamom, honey, fungi, bamboo and many medicinal herbs from the forests, which constitute a relatively important source of income.

Most families own buffalo, cows, pigs, goats and chickens. The men are keen hunt-

Left, tools of the agricultural trade. **Above**, a century later, little has changed for this Tay girl.

ers and use guns to bring down anything from foxes and wild pigs to tigers, although the chances of bagging the latter these days are rather remote.

Skilled artisans, the Hmong produce a variety of items including handwoven indigo-dyed cloth, paper, silver jewellery, leather goods, baskets, baby carriers, kitchen utensils and beautiful embroidery using traditional motifs.

The Hmong have no written language. Their literature, legends, songs, folklore and proverbs, have been orally passed down from one generation to the next. They have developed a varied and original fund of culture and art, rich in popular knowledge concern-

Lo, the idea didn't really catch on, or last long when it did.

The Dao first arrived from China in the 18th century and belong to the Hmong-Dao language group. They number about 35,000 and are found in the mid and lower regions north of Nghe Tinh living in large villages or small isolated hamlets where they cultivate rice using the slash and burn method. They rear domestic animals such as goats, pigs, hens, ducks, geese and pigeons.

Their homes are built directly on the ground, on stilts or using a combination of both methods.

The Dao are very skilled artisans, the men forge their own tools and make a variety of

ing the nature of society, extolling liberty, justice, charity, the work ethic and virtue and condemning laziness, meanness, hypocrisy and lying.

Totemism is still evident in Hmong culture where spirit worship, animist rites and exorcism are still practised. Buddhism, Taoism and Confucianism have left their mark on some Hmong societies which practise magic, believe in reincarnation and the superiority of men over women.

Catholic missionaries made an all out evangelistic effort to convert the Hmong at the beginning of the century but although some churches were built at Sa Pa and Nghia

bamboo and rattan goods. They even make their own paper which is mostly used for writing family genealogies, official documents and religious books. Certain skills, for example silver smithing and leather tanning, are often a family tradition and passed down from father to son.

The women plant cotton which they weave then dye with indigo. Their beautiful embroidery is worked directly onto the cloth from memory. Their traditional designs are so well fixed in their memory that they have no need to draw the design on the cloth first.

The Dao believe in the existence of another world, the world of the souls. They worship their ancestors and *Ban Vuong*, their mythical ancestor. In their beliefs concerning agricultural production, the soul of the paddy comes first followed by the worship of the genies of the soil, water, then fire. Buddhism, Confucianism and particularly Taoism have greatly influenced the Dao. Taoism's influence is most obvious during their seasonal festivals and prayer imploring divine protection during illness, birth, funerals and natural disasters.

For centuries the Dao have used Chinese characters to record their geneologies, rhymes, folk tales, old stories, humorous tales, fables and popular songs.

Minorities of the Central Highlands: The Jarai

matriachal families, with each family an economically independent unit within the village. A council of village elders under the leadership of a village chief directs village affairs. The chief is responsible for all the village's communal activities.

They cultivate fruit trees, rice, beans and other cereals and raise buffalo, goats, chickens and pigs, primarily to offer as sacrifices to their various genies and spirits. Oxen, horses and elephants are raised as draught animals, and horses are also used in wildboar hunting. Hunting, fishing and particularly gathering are greatly important to the community. The gathering is left to the women and children. Hunting sometimes brings in rare game such

or Gia Ria are located in the provinces of Gia Lai Kontum, Dac Lac and in the north of Phu Khanh. They belong to the Malay-Polynesian language group and arrived in the Tay Nguyen Highlands from the coast during the first centuries AD. They live a sedentary life style in villages known as *ploi* or *bon*. These comprise at least 50 homes, built either in longhouse or "short" style. Jarai villages are built around a central *nga rong*, communal house. The community is composed of small

Tribal diversity: Left to right, Dao, Meo, Pac O and Muong women reflect contrasting sartorial styles.

as tigers, panthers, elephants, rhinoceros, but more often wild boars.

Young girls take the incentive in choosing a marriage partner and make their approach through a go-between. The promise is sealed with the exchange of bronze bracelets and things proceed from there in three stages. The bracelet-exchanging rite, performed in front of the two families and the go-between, is followed by the interpretation of the young couple's dreams, a rite that serves to predict their future prospects and greatly influences the final decision. The rite culminates with the actual wedding ceremony at the home of the girl's in-laws.

The animist Jarai believe in an invisible world inhabited by *yang* or genies, supernatural forces that directly influence both nature and society. Among these are the genies of the mountain, water, village, home, rice, ancestors and war. In this domain ruled by matriachs and ancient agricultural beliefs, the Kings of Fire, Water and Wind are also worshipped by a handful of communities. These kings are none other than the *shamans* who officiate over the rites invoking the rain.

Jarai funerals are extremely complex affairs with endless rites, particularly in connection with the careful construction of the burial house. Inside it are placed carved

wooden sculptures representing men, women and birds. They believe the deceased is transformed into a spirit and joins his ancestors in another world.

The Jarai possess a wealth of folklore, poetry, original traditional dances and an ancient musical tradition which employs a variety of musical instruments.

The Ra De, found mainly in Dac Lac Province and to a much lesser extent in Phu Khanh, number more than 140,000. Like the Jarai, they belong to the Malay-Polynesian language group. Their wooden longhouses built on stilts in villages known as *buon* comprise of between 20 and 70 dwellings.

Each longhouse shelters a large matriachal family under the authority of a *Koa Sang*, the most senior and respected woman. She directs community affairs, settles internal conflicts and is also responsible for the safekeeping of all the communal heirlooms, bronze gongs, the ancient jars used for preparing rice beer, the large seat made from a single tree trunk reserved solely for the *khoa sang*, and special stools that are reserved for the hosts and musicians.

The village's autonomous organization is run by the *Po Pin Ea*, the village chief elected by the village to take care of communal affairs.

The Ra De employ the slash and burn technique to clear the land. They often build a hut on their cultivated land which serves as a rest shelter for the person responsible for keeping the birds and animals off the crops. Rice, the main crop, is cultivated along with aubergines, sugar cane, bananas, melons, cotton, and tobacco.

Almost every village has its own forge to produce and repair farming implements. Basketry, fairly rudimentary pottery and beautiful woven indigo-dyed cloth are produced by the Ra De for their own use.

Being polytheistic, the Ra De worship a varied assortment of deities, the most adored of these are the agricultural genies, *Ae Die* and *Ae Du*. Their annual festivals are linked to worshipping the Spirit of the Rice and the Genies of the Soil, Water and Fire. They also worship the Kings of Fire and Water. These kings have absolutely nothing to do with earthly concepts but belong to the Ra De's own unique world of genies and spirits.

Ra De literature boasts a rich fund of oral traditions, myths, legends, songs, proverbs, sayings, fairytales and epics going back to their origins. Their musical instruments include gongs, large drums, flutes and horns.

Wooden sculpture forms an integral part of their architecture and is used in decorating the funeral houses. They bury their dead with some of their personal belongings and erect a funeral house in the form of a boat over the grave. Offerings of rice to the deceased are placed in this until a special ceremony celebrating the abandonment of the grave is performed.

Above, Meo buffalo boy. **Right**, rice fields have a certain symmetrical beauty.

RELIGION: THE SPIRITUAL AND MORAL UNIVERSE

When men lack a sense of awe
there will be disaster.
Lao Tsu (6th century B.C.)
-The Tao Te Ching

Our karma we must carry as our lot-
let's stop decrying Heaven's whims
and quirks
Inside ourselves there lies the root of good:
the heart outweighs all talents on this earth.
Nguyen Du (1765-1820)
-The Tale of Kieu

Several thousands of years ago the Viet tribes moved from China in the Nam (South) direction to the Song Hong (Red River) Delta and settled in a beautiful land surrounded by high mountains, deep waters, thick forests and narrow plains. Inspired by the wonders of nature, the Viet soon realized that only by blood, sweat, tears and sharp eyes could they preserve their newly acquired Dat (earth) and Nuoc (water). Ever since then, their mission in life has been to build and to defend their country.

To succeed in such a mission, the Vietnamese have had to be conscious of the forces around them, the seen and the unseen, the favorable and the hostile, to understand their nature and intentions, to resist them if necessary and co-exist with them if possible, but never to provoke their anger. To make sense of this immense web of influences and awesome matrix of powers, the Vietnamese have looked to what is in Heaven, on Earth, and among people. To penetrate the mysteries of Heaven, to understand the workings and movements of the Earth, to establish relationships with people, they seek the highest form of education, the way things emerge, exist, progress, disappear and re-emerge.

They seek the religions which in Vietnamese are Ton Giao – the highest, most elevated education, or Dao Giao – the education of the Way, or simply Dao the Way. These words

Preceding pages: Mourners at a funeral; monk at Giac Vien Pagoda, Saigon. Left, an exquiste Buddha. Above, outside Thien Mu Pagoda in Hue.

are actually borrowed from the Chinese who colonized Vietnam in the year 3 B.C. Among the colonizers were tyrants and exploiters, but also compassionate administrators and dedicated teachers who brought with them their religions, philosophies, organizational skills and especially their written characters, the Chu Han or Han characters.

Chinese domination introduced critical new elements to the Vietnamese mission of building and defending their country. It created both grave dangers and possible oppor-

tunities – the dangers of losing their national identity and independence but also the opportunities of assimilating and Vietnamizing the best of Chinese civilization and culture. The testing ground was the Vietnamese village, the Cha, later called the Xa – the Vietnamese usage of the Chinese for "she" which incorporates two components, one representing the earth, the other the spirit.

The traditional village comprises a group of individuals associated with one another in families, clans, or extended families.

Their economic activities, in which all participate, are concentrated on growing food, particularly rice, their major staple. Rice cultivation is an art and a science, requiring constant observation of nature and precise coordination of human labor.

The experience gleaned collectively by the villagers over the years of struggling against the adverse forces of nature, developed certain patterns of work and thought, the basic foundations of culture. Living together in growing communities the peasants evolved a code of public morality, participation and responsibility to ensure peace, order, group cohesion and loyalty. This constitutes the beginning of politics, the aim of which is social order.

However, social order alone does not always provide an answer to the villagers'

and daily life. These beliefs are still held in Vietnam today.

Foremost in their religious hierarchy is Heaven above, which the Vietnamese with their inborn tendency to humanize everything in order to better deal with it, called Ong Troi, the honorable Mr. Heaven. They approach him with food offerings, requests, complaints and prayed to Him. In principle, Ong Troi is the keeper of human fate in charge of all the unseen powers and mysteries of the Universe. Next to Ong Troi is Dat, the Earth, also called Tho, watched over by Tho Cong or Tho Than, the God of the earth whose spirit and power animate the land on which they live, work and bury their dead. He is regarded as the provider

mental anxiety and sense of threat from the unknown. It fails to give meaning to their daily existence or provide them with a sense of belonging to both their human and natural environment, instead it becomes the source of alienation. Thus the adult villagers, elders and leaders formulated a set of interpretations for the felt but unseen powers of the environment which fathered the birth of religion. According to Websters Dictionary, the original meaning of the word religion is "that which binds people together".

Through their polytheist or animistic religion they worshipped all forces which influenced, supported, or threatened their welfare

of food and guardian against wild beasts and deadly snakes. The God of the Earth, the God of the Water and the God of the Mountains together form and transform the geomantic structures which determine the orientation of houses, cities, graves, temples, and fix the good and bad luck of families, communities and nations.

Between Heaven and Earth, but never separate from them, is Man, both male and female, the dead and the living, the ancestors and the descendants. Ancestor worship is considered just as important as procreation for the continuity of the family, clan, nation and human race.

Each of the realms – Heaven, Earth, and Man – inhabited by the Vietnamese, has its own systems, rules, regulations, modes of transformations, elements of good, bad, ugly, beautiful, and above all its own Deities. These Deities are everywhere, in stones, trees, lakes, animals, and are praised, fed, housed and revered with ritual offerings and appropriate behavior. The richness and variety of these worlds and their manifestations has preoccupied, confused and dazzled the traditional Vietnamese, leaving them little space or privacy to "eat, sleep, make love, fart", the basic reliefs of their fleshly demands.

In addition to the pagodas and communal houses found in traditional villages the length of Vietnam, are smaller places of worship where these hosts of benevolent and even malevolent divinities and spirits are worshipped. These include: the Den which is used to commemorate an emperor, a God who particularly helped the village or a national hero or emperor; the Mieu, usually situated on an elevated piece of land or a hill, reserved for the cult of both benevolent and malevolent gods and spirits; and the Ban, where divinities not worshipped in the Den or Mieu are worshipped.

When the Chinese imposed their rule on Vietnam they brought with them not only their modes of exploitation but also their agricultural know-how and books of religion, philosophy and general wisdom, written in one of the most advanced scripts of all time, the Han characters. The Vietnamese loved these characters which represented the picture and meaning and feeling attached to each word.

Although the Vietnamese fought against the Chinese political domination and economic exploitation, they selectively screened and assimilated what they considered the best of Chinese culture. The Chinese teachers, some of whom were administrators, were accompanied by Confucian scholars, Buddhist masters, Taoist wanderers and I-Ching thinkers-diviners.

Confucianism, Buddhism, and Taoism are not religions in the sense of a set of revelations issuing from one God, but the intellectual creations of men. Yet their followers bestow on them the same kind of reverence

and power given to Christianity, Judaism, Hinduism and Islam.

Confucianism – Pillar of the Establishment:
As an ideology Confucianism has lasted longer than any other in the East or West and has crossed many national borders into all parts of the world. It is based on the teachings of Confucius who was born around 550 B.C., and lived at a time of great political turmoil. As a teacher and self-styled, unsolicited adviser to kings, he compiled sets of ideas on relationships between ruler and subject, parents and children, husband and wife, student and teacher. Confucius was more a moral, ethical guide than a spiritual leader. He refused to discuss life after death, the unseen or

the mystical and was primarily interested in social order based on compassion, etiquette (ceremonial), loyalty, knowledge and trust.

Confucianism reached Vietnam through the Chinese over 2,000 years ago. It became the official doctrine of the imperial examinations, the first of which was held in 1706 and the last in 1919.

The Vietnamese monarchy recruited its high officials according to the results of these competitive examinations, were in theory open to anyone except actors and women – many however learned Confucianism at home from their parents. The examinations, which also included knowledge of Buddhism, Taoism or Tan Giao were extremely competitive and for the whole period from 1075 to 1919 only slightly more than 2,000 doctorate degrees were granted. Those who earned their degrees received a hat and tunic from the Emperor, and were welcomed home with great pomp and ceremony by the entire population. Those who failed went quietly home to their villages and earned their living as teachers, and in this way the villagers were introduced to Confucianism.

For over 2,000 years, Confucianism, although imported from China, has remained a pillar of the Vietnamese moral and spiritual establishment.

problems of life and the way to their solution. The Buddha, (Guatama Sidhartha, the Awakened, 563-483 B.C.) perceived these realities or truths and announced the Four Noble Truths in his Sermon of Benares: Existence is unhappiness; unhappiness is caused by selfish cravings; unhappiness ends when selfish cravings end; selfish cravings can be destroyed by following the steps of the eightfold path – Right understanding, right purpose (aspiration), right speech, right conduct, right vocation, right effort, right alertness, right concentration. "Right" means conforming to the Four Noble Truths. Central to Buddhism is the concept of Brahman, the Absolute origin, the equivalent of the

By the time Vietnam regained its independence from China, it possessed a good body of Vietnamese scholars with almost a millennium of Confucian studies behind them. The Vietnamese imperial dynasties adopted Confucianism for its ability to sustain a system of social order without much repression and for its code of social mobility based on merit.

Buddhism—The Four Noble Truths and the Eightfold Path: Introduced across the sea from India and over land from China, Buddhism extended the question of knowledge from the social order to the general human order in an attempt to reach a rational analysis of the

Chinese Tai Chi. To Vietnamese Buddhists, Brahman represents the unknown and unknowable, the source and embodiment of reality, knowledge and bliss. Vietnamese Buddhism is a fascinating blend of three branches: Japanese Zen and Chinese Chan, Tibetan and Pure Land. The Vietnamese have been embracing Buddhism for more than 2,000 years.

Over one thousand years ago a Vietnamese Buddhist master was sent to the Japanese court to teach Buddhist music.

From the 2nd century A.D. to the 10th century, two popular sects, the A-Ham (Agama) and the Thien, (Dhyana in Sanskrit,

Zen in Japanese) peacefully competed for Vietnamese followers. Gradually Thien prevailed, despite its exacting practise, which requires continual training in self-discipline, in mastering the "techniques" of breathing, meditation and right concentration.

Thien is one of the many sects of Mahayana Buddhism widely observed in China, Japan, Korea and Vietnam. Less dogmatic, it is receptive to the diverse cultural and social conditions of different countries at different times. The other branch of Buddhism, Hinayana or Theravada found in Sri Lanka, Burma, Thailand, Laos, Cambodia and parts of Southern Vietnam, is more orthodox, yet co-exists with Mahayana.

do right.

Buddhist practises at village level are not exactly those of Zen, which requires guidance by a well trained Zen master, but a mixture of basic Zen and Amitabha, commonly called Pure Land, devotional faith.

It is believed that Amitabha achieved Buddhahood on the express condition that he receive all who sincerely call upon his name at death and carry them to the Western Paradise, where they may seek ultimate perfection (Nirvana) under happier auspices than on earth. The concept of the compassionate Bodhisattvas (Bo Tat) who postpone their own entrance to Nirvana through loving concern for the salvation of others, is at the heart

Village Worship: In practically every Vietnamese village from North to South, one finds a Chua, (Pagoda), and a Dinh, (Communal House). The villagers worship Buddha in the Chua which is cared for by one or several resident monks. On the first and fifteenth days of the lunar months, the villagers visit the Chua, bringing flowers, joss sticks and fruit to pay homage to the Buddha. They also attend services at the pagoda on the evenings of the 14th and 30th days to repent for wrongs done and to make vows to

<u>Left</u>, muslim community in the South. <u>Above</u>, at mass on Christmas Eve.

of Amitabha. Its practise consists essentially of concentrating the mind through self-absorption and reciting (chanting) the name of Buddha. Those who practise Pure Land must abstain from killing, stealing, banditry, lying, wrong sexual relations, wrong speech and intoxicants. Its adherents are expected to recite the name of Amitabha Buddha, the Amitabha Sutra and perform good deeds to gain merit for self and family. They believe that merits accumulated through good deeds will ensure a happy and joyful present life and a safe delivery to the land of absolute bliss, the Pure Land, after death.

Taoism; The Tao, The Way: The Tao Te

Ching, the Book of the Way and its Power, begins with: "The Tao that can be told is not the eternal Tao". It is the general law of the motion of the universe, of all things. Tao is the highest and most active level of a static consciousness. In Chinese it is represented by a character showing a head in a forward position. It is both energy and matter. It is the moment when the contradictory forces of Yin and Yang fuse in temporary harmony to provide people and things with a sense of direction.

An important book of reference for Taoists and Buddhists alike is the I Ching or The Book of Changes, which uses symbols, simplified and stylized in signs and codes, to

ism, animism and other various forms and places of worship coexisted, Taoist priests were also made welcome. In these villages special places of worship known as Dien or Tinh are found. Introduced to Vietnam at about the same time as Confucianism, Vietnamese Taoism does not have the hierarchy of schools and systems as in China. On the philosophical level, it is expressed in the thoughts and poetry of Confucian and Buddhist intellectuals. However Taoist priests and their places of worship are found in villages among the common people. At this level Taoist practises become a maze of superstitions, magic manifestations, mystic healings – a veritable kingdom of demons

integrate a number of separate communication systems into a seemingly "mysterious" whole. It contains 64 triagrams and hexagrams arranged in broken and unbroken lines, which along with its basic text, represent "the process of vast and never- ending cosmic change. These endless chains of actions and interaction assemble and divide the myriad objects proceeding from and flowing into Tai Chi, the Still Reality underlying the worlds of form, desire and formlessness". In the Chinese characters for I Ching, the word "I" represents a lizard, probably a chameleon.

In villages where Buddhism, Confucian-

and fairies.

Ancestor Worship: Within many Vietnamese homes and all pagodas you will find an altar dedicated to the ancestors. Although many traditional beliefs and superstitions have waned, ancestor worship, a ritual of filial piety, remains of high moral and social significance within Vietnamese society.

On anniversaries of death and traditional festival days, the relatives of the deceased gather together and the deceased's eldest son presides over the ceremonial food and incense offerings for the dead. After these ceremonies, the entire family visit the grave of the deceased. The ceremony ends with the family members prostrating themselves before the altar and burning paper "money" which provides the dead with funds to make their life happier in the other world.

Failing to worship one's ancestors is considered an act of grave filial impiety that condemns the ancestors to a life of wandering from place to place, living on charity.

Other Religious Currents–The Advent of Christianity: To this universe with its rainbow of institutionalized religions and philosophies and kaleidoscope of animist beliefs, came Roman Catholicism. The first Western missionaries set foot in Tonkin (North Vietnam) in 1533 and in Annam (the Center) in 1596, but theirs was only a brief stay. It was not

until 1615 that the first Christian missions were founded by Portuguese Jesuits, in Hoi An, Danang and Hanoi.

Unavoidably, the introduction of this organized and culturally foreign religion generated its share of misunderstanding and conflict. Yet Roman Catholicism contributed two major transformations to Vietnamese culture – the romanization of the language and the modern scientific methods of

Left to right: distinctive Tay An Pagoda in Chau Doc; Khmer monk in the Mekong Delta; religious retreat in the Marble Mountains; temple interior, Hoi An.

Western logic.

Many Vietnamese from all classes of society converted to Catholicism, much to the concern of the mandarins and ruling classes who saw the new religion as an undermining threat to the traditional order of society and its rites, particularly the Cult of Heaven (Nam Giao) and ancestor worship.

Between 1712 and 1720, a decree forbidding Christianity was enforced in the North. In the South, foreign missionaries were sent packing in 1750 and Christianity was forbidden. The attitude towards Christianity varied with the leaders of the day; some were more tolerant than others. Under Emperor Minh Mang (1820-1840), who viewed Christianity as "the perverse religion of Europeans" which "corrupts the heart of men" a decree was enforced in 1825 forbidding the entry of Christian missionaries to Vietnam. Thieu Tri who reigned from 1840-1847, was more tolerant, but his successor, Tu Duc (1848 - 1883), reinforced the prohibition of Christianity and the church underwent another period of persecution. This lasted until the treaty signed between Tu Duc and the French in 1862, which ceded territory and commercial rights to the French and the freedom for Christians in Vietnam to practise their faith.

Between 1882 and 1884, another wave of

persecution hit the Catholic church and many followers paid for their faith with their lives. The persecution ended in 1885, with the French conquest of the entire country.

Many Catholic orders established themselves throughout the country, establishing convents, schools, colleges, hospitals and seminaries.

This religious freedom however was checked by World War II and the Japanese occupation of the country in 1945. After the signing of the Geneva Agreement in 1954 and the division of the country into North and South, 600,000 Catholics fled the North for the South.

Since April 1975, and the reunification of Vietnam (July 2, 1976), the church in Vietnam has lived under the law of the Socialist Republic of Vietnam, whose written law guarantees the freedom of religion or non-religion under an official Marxist-Leninist ideology. All Catholic schools in the country have been nationalized – in the South since 1975 and in the North since between 1945 and 1954.

Despite persecution, the church in Vietnam has continued to grow and today there are an estimated five million practising Catholics throughout the country's thirteen dioceses.

American Protestant missionaries were at work in the Mekong Delta area from the beginning of the 1900s. Their evangelistic efforts were concentrated mainly on the ethnic minority groups inhabiting the high plateaus of Central Vietnam, who today make up the majority of the Protestants in the country. Many Protestant church leaders were imprisoned after reunification, yet despite restrictions the Protestant church continues to grow, although with a much smaller presence than its Catholic counterpart.

Islam: Vietnam's small Muslim community comprises mainly ethnic Khmers and Chams. A 10th century stele inscribed in Arabic, found near the central coastal town of Phan Rang, provides the earliest record of Islam's presence in Vietnam.

Although the Chams consider themselves Muslim, their religious practises are not fully Islamic. They do not make the pilgrimage to Mecca; although they do not eat pork they do drink alcohol; they pray only on Fridays, celebrate Ramadan for only three days and their rituals co-exist with animistic and Hindu-based worship.

Hinduism: Vietnam's Hindus make up a very tiny percentage of the population. The Kingdom of Champa was greatly influenced by Hinduism which was and still is practised by the Cham community. The ancient Hindu god-king Shiva, represented in the phallic form of linga, appears in early Cham religious sanctuaries such as the first temple built at My Son in the 4th century. The influence of Indian art appears strongly in Cham architecture, sculpture and the representations of the Hindu Gods Brahma and Vishnu.

The form of Hinduism practised today in Vietnam, like Islam, is an adaptation which has evolved from the original form which reached Vietnam from India at a very early date.

The Religious, Spiritual and Moral Universe which penetrates and conditions the material and non-material existence of the Vietnamese people is determined by their perception and recognition of the Triad: Heaven (above), Earth (below) and Man (in the middle).

That perception in turn results from their sense of awe for the visible and invisible forces of nature, their observation and interpretation of these forces and the ways and means they have found to compromise and co-exist with or resist them. Above all it is grounded in their intimate relationship with the land in which they live, procreate and bury their dead, in their deep faith in the continuity of the Viet nation and in their sacred mission to defend and build their "land and water" (Dat and Nuoc).

This so-conceived and defined Universe has no room for dogmatism, fanaticism, ignorance and stagnation. It can only be maintained by alert intelligence, shared wisdom, flexibility, creativity, a well developed aesthetic appreciation and a good sense of humor. It is a constant, exacting pressure on the life of every Vietnamese. This is why the secret wish of all Vietnamese is to attain Nhan – a word borrowed from the Chinese meaning "contemplating the moon through a window", laughing off the glory and the burden of the day, immersing oneself in the serenity of a moonlit night.

The eye-catching cathedral interior, Hue.

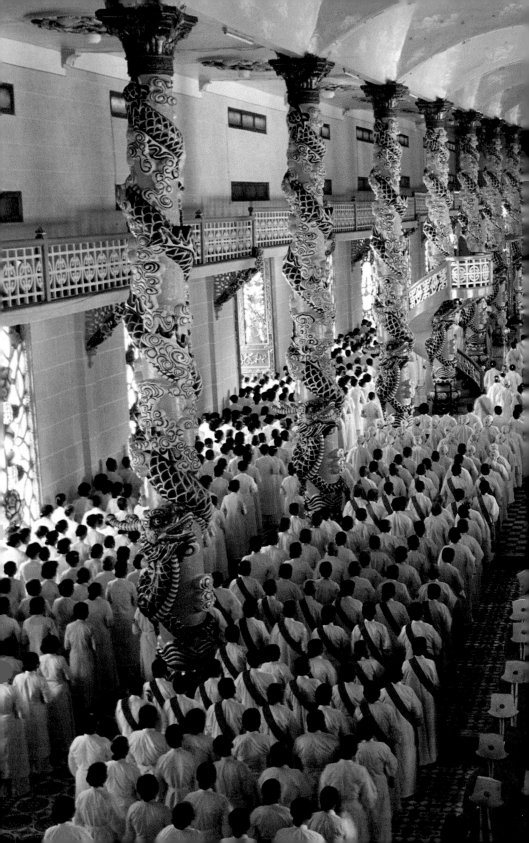

The story of Cao Daism: Hundreds of novels have been written by non-Vietnamese authors about wars and politics in Vietnam, but none have succeeded in capturing the tragicomedy behind the West's arrogant, naive, and brutal attempts to forcibly change the destiny of Asia as Graham Greene's "The Quiet American" (1956).

The "Quiet American" arrived in Vietnam before the French defeat (1954) at Dien Bien Phu to prepare the terrain for the United States involvement. He was interested in him as Cao Dai, literally, High Terrace or Supreme Being. In 1925 Ngo Van Chieu began his evangelization in Saigon. Cao Daism attempted to bring all existing faiths in Vietnam under one single supreme creator, or Cao Dai, Creator of the Universe, beginning first with the three major religions: Buddhism, Taoism, Confucianism, then Christianity, Islam, the Cult of Heaven, the Cult of Ancestor worship and the illustrious Saints of the world, regardless of race, sex or geography. Victor Hugo, Sun Yat Sen, Na-

Cao Daism, a new Vietnamese religion, "a synthesis of the three religions: Confucianism, Taoism and Buddhism". The Cao Dai sect began when Ngo Van Chieu, an obscure official in the French colonial administration, received a message from a "superior spirit" during a seance in 1919, telling him of his future religious vocation and urging him to look hard for the Dao or the Way. Ngo Van Chieu's intense interest in spiritism and occultism led him to devote all his spare time to mystic meditation. He participated in many sessions of spiritism, both in Saigon and the provinces and it was during one of these in 1921 that a "superior spirit" revealed itself to poleon Bonaparte, Joan of Arc, Louis Pasteur and even Winston Churchill are among the host of additional figures revered by Cao Daism.

On Christmas night, 1925, a group of Vietnamese officials in the French administration got together to evoke the spirits and received an announcement from Cao Dai telling them that a new religion was being formed and that Ngo Van Chieu was to be their leader. However Ngo Van Chieu declined to be the head of the new church and Mr. Le Van Trung was chosen as the pope of Cao Daism. On October 7, 1926, Cao Daism became an official new religion recognized by the French colonial administration. Cao Daism's followers fall into three groups: the Religious order who observe strict rules of chastity, simplicity and vegetarianism; Mediums, a group of twelve individuals who receive messages from the spirits; and the Faithful, the followers who obey the directives of the religious order.

The sect's highest authority is the pope and religious practices take the form of prayers four times daily in front of the Altar of the Supreme Being. This can be an elevated table at one end of the main room in the home. In the temples and oratories the altar consists of a paper globe painted with Cao Dai's symbol – an eye surrounded by white and offerings consist of flowers, fruit, tea, alcohol, water and incense.

Cao Daism's pope, administration and Holy See are found in the village of Long Than, in Tay Ninh Province, 53 miles (85 km) northwest of Saigon. Its ornate cathedral, described as the "Disneylike fantasia of the East", by Graham Greene, was built in 1927. Its exotic architecture reflects the influences of an assortment of faiths and cultures. Statues of Jesus, Confucius, Buddha, Brahma, Siva and Vishnu dominate the nave of the cathedral, as do symbols of clairvoyance and human fraternity.

Cao Daism appealed to the peasants, who became its followers in entire village com-

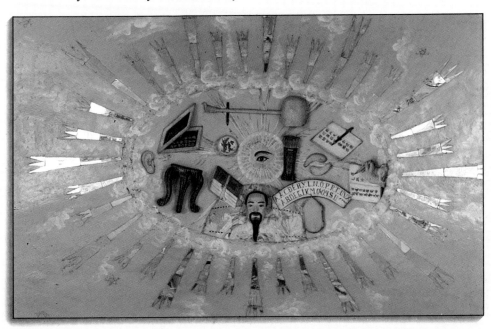

sun rays. Statues of Buddha, Confucius, Lao Tsu, Saints and Genies are placed on the altar around a central spherical glass symbolizing the Primordial Principle, which is kept burning day and night. During ceremonies, the members of the Religious order stand in the center of the Temple. The color of their robes indicates their "branch" of the religion: yellow for Buddhism; purple for Confucianism; and azure for Taoism. The followers dress in

Preceding pages: The spectacular visual impact of Cao Dai. Far left, inside the cathedral in Tay Ninh Province. Left, member of the sect. Above, eye in the sky: ceiling detail.

munities. In the early 1930s, its followers numbered about one and a half million. When Le Van Trung died in 1943, he was succeeded by Pham Cong Tac who turned the religion into a political force. By 1937, Cao Daism had become a "state within a state" and a target of French repression. The French accused the Cao Dai leaders of having contacts with Prince Cuong De, a member of the Vietnamese royal family exiled in Japan. Pham Cong Tac and six of his close aids were arrested and deported to the Comores Islands, a French possession in the Indian Ocean. Pham Cong Tac was allowed to return to Vietnam in 1946 and regained his position as pope of Cao Daism. During the first Indochina war, the French armed the Cao Dai, hoping to use them against the Viet Minh. When President Ngo Dinh Diem came to power after 1954, he signed a modus vivendi with the Cao Dai forces, but soon conflict arose between President Diem and Pope Pham Cong Tac, who was forced to flee to Cambodia where he died in 1958. Mr. Pyle, the "Quiet American" in Graham Greene's novel, was officially a diplomat in the economic section of the United States Legation in Saigon during 1953-54; yet it was obvious to readers that he was working for the CIA. He was particularly interested in the young Cao Dai Chief of Staff, who "took

contacted General Trinh Minh The, the Cao Dai chief of staff, and convinced him to support President Diem in his fight against communism. Trinh Minh The, who was loved and admired by his soldiers for his courage and austerity, fought together with President Diem and defeated other armed religious sects. During one military engagement, General The was killed. Some believe he was liquidated on orders from Ngo Dinh Nhu, President Diem's brother and political adviser, who viewed the Cao Dai General as a rival. The truth will never be known as both President Diem and his brother were murdered by Diem's officers during the November 1963 coup d'etat, in which the U.S. was

to the hills to fight both sides", the French and the communists, thus promoting the Third Force in Third World politics. This concept suited the Unites States policy of the time, which opposed colonialism in theory, and communism. The Mr. Pyle in real life stayed on after the French defeat at Dien Bien Phu and the partition of Vietnam at the 17th parallel. President Diem's government in the South supported the U.S. and vice versa. His efforts to build a national army and unify all the armed religious organizations under his command met with resistance followed by conflict. Mr. Pyle, who by now can be easily identified as Colonel Edward G. Landsdale,

implicated.

Although no reliable statistics are available, the Cao Dai faith has many followers in the South of Vietnam.

Hoa Hao – Return to Purity: Like the Cao Dai, the Hoa Hao sect was created in the South of Vietnam. Its founder, Huynh Phu So, was born in 1919 in the Village of Hoa Hao in Chau Doc province. As a young man he suffered from a mysterious incurable illness. His father, a Roman Catholic peasant, believed he was possessed by a demon and sent him to the Tra Son pagoda near That Son mountain where he regained his health under the teachings of Master Xom. After the

Master's death Huynh Phu So returned to his village, where one night during a violent storm he went into a trance and emerged from it proclaiming himself founder of Phat Giao Hoa Hoa – Buddhist Hoa Hao – meaning Peace and Kindness. Unlike Cao Dai, Hoa Hao avoids glamorous and complicated ceremonies in favor of a return to early Buddhism's essential purity and simplicity through prayer, meditation and fasting. No temple was built, no religious hierarchy was set up, yet the Hoa Hao, a variant of Theravada Buddhism, with its precepts of honoring ones parents, love of ones country and fellow men and respect for Huynh Phu So's interpretation of Buddhism, attracted about one

before a French plan to exile him to Laos could be put into action.

The Hoa Hao opposed both the communists and the French and armed itself to fight both. In 1946 Huynh Phu So created a political party, the Dan Chu Xa Hoi Dang (Democratic Socialist Party). With its clear anticolonial and anti-communist basis, its creation deepened the conflict between the Hoa Hao and the communists.

Huynh Phu So fell into a trap laid by the communist led political organization, the Viet Minh who arrested then executed him in April 1947. By this time other Hoa Hao subsects had sprung up which were far more active and united within themselves than

million followers in only a few years. They called their leader Phat Song or Living Buddha. However, Phat Song was soon caught up in the political climate of the time. The French saw him as a political agitator and detained him, first in a psychiatric hospital, then later under house arrest. This only served to enhance his reputation and he continued teaching his many followers from home. Aided by the Japanese secret police, his followers moved him to Saigon a few days

Left, the cathedral is memorable for its one-of-a-kind architectural style. **Above**, portrait of a Cao Dai follower.

those of the Cao Dai. The Hoa Hao absolutely rejected the bribery and betrayal that had discredited some of the Cao Dai leaders whose sect suffered from disunity and decline after the death of their pope in 1959. By the late 1960s many disillusioned nationalist intellectuals from urban areas had joined the Hoa Hao peasants religious movement.

The rise and fall of the Hoa Hao followed a similar path to that of the Cao Dai, from revelation to evangelization then into politics and armed struggle. After compromise, cooperation and confrontation, it finally became annihilated as a political and military force.

Vietnam's most important and most cherished traditional festival, Tet, is the occasion which unites the Vietnamese, who devote all their creative energy and resources to prepare for it, "eat" it and go all out to enjoy the fun, food and festivities associated with it. The word Tet is a distortion of the word Tiet, meaning festival. The full name, Tet Nguyen Dan, Festival of the First Morning of the Year, refers to the beginning of the lunar year, which falls between the Winter solstice and Spring equinox.

The lunar calendar is divided into twelve months of either 29 or 30 days, but every four years, in order to catch up with the solar calendar, there is a leap of 13 months. Due to this discrepancy between the two calendars, Tet does not fall on the same day every year in the solar calendar.

The Vietnamese twelve year cycle follows the Chinese zodiac: rat, buffalo (ox for the Chinese), tiger, cat (rabbit for the Chinese), dragon, snake, horse, goat monkey, rooster and pig.

Opening of hearts and minds: Tet is the sole time of the year when the usually discreet Vietnamese society opens its heart, mind and cooking skills for all to see. Embodied in both its ceremony and essence is the whole spectrum of Vietnamese mythology, the entire concept of ones' place in the family, the universe and in relation to the ancestors, the dead and the spirits. It is a fascinating mixture of Buddhism, Taoism, Confucianism, the three currents of religion which have blended with the original Vietnamese animistic beliefs and ancestor worship, to form the unique religious fusion adhered to by today's Vietnamese.

Tet is a yearly burst of the latent and deep romanticism nurtured in a rugged and beautiful land over centuries of hard and bloody fighting. A Vietnamese can be a Marxist, an existentialist, a capitalist, an agnostic, or whatever leaning he or she chooses for the rest of the year; but at Tet, will return to his or her true Vietnamese nature. Tet is an occasion when the Vietnamese immerse

themselves in their traditional and national milieu and fill themselves anew with spiritual energy in readiness for the rigors of the coming year.

Vietnam's historical records make no mention of the date Tet was first formally celebrated, but it is accepted that Tet is as old as the Vietnamese nation itself. Under imperial Vietnam, Tet was observed by everyone emperors and commoners alike. During the Ly Dynasty (11th to 13th centuries), the emperor would watch the annual boat race

up the Red River as his imperial galleon glided southwards to Hanoi. He would end the day by offering Buddhist rites at the seven-storied tower of the Doan Mon (Gate of Grandeur), followed by dinner with his court, counsellors and the famous poets and scholars of the land.

The form changed a little during the Tran dynasty (13th to 15th centuries) when the dawn of New Year would find the emperor at the Vinh Tho Dien (Palace of Fame and Longevity) receiving greetings from the crown prince and mandarins. The day before, he and his entourage would attend a play at the national theatre where they were enter-

Preceding pages: Festive season in Saigon. **Left,** altar offerings. **Above,** Tet celebrant.

tained by comedians.

On New Year's Eve, the emperor would pay respects to his ancestors at the Truong Xuan Cung (Palace of Eternal Spring). These same rituals were observed by all Vietnamese monarchs until August 1945, when the last emperor, Bao Dai of the Nguyen dynasty (1802-1945) abdicated in favor of President Ho Chi Minh of the Democratic Republic of Vietnam.

Tet rites begin a week before New Year's Day. On the 23rd day of the 12th month, a ceremony is held at home in honor of the Tao Quan (Gods of the Hearth), where offerings of fresh fruit, cooked food, paper models of a stork, a horse, a car, a pair of mandarin

by and the marriage remained childless. The husband became unhappy, he began to drink too much and mistreat his wife. She, unable to stand him any longer, deserted him and married a hunter in the neighboring village. Lonely and repentant, the woodcutter one day decided to pay her a visit and apologise, but soon after his arrival, the hunter returned. To avoid any misunderstanding, the woman hid her former husband in a small thatched barn near the kitchen. The hunter was smoking his game in the kitchen when a spark from the fire set the small barn ablaze. The distraught woman raced to the barn to save her former husband; the hunter followed suit in an attempt to save his wife and

boots and a ceremonial dress, but no pants, are made to the Tao Quan. The Vietnamese, with their inborn sense of humor and ridicule of the powerful, believe, or at least claim to, that the Tao Quan burnt their pants by staying too close to the kitchen. With or without pants, it is time for the Gods to return to the Kingdom of Heaven and present their annual report on the state of earthly matters and the Vietnamese family to the Emperor of Jade, before returning to earth on New Year's Eve.

The legend behind the Tao Quan derives from the tragic story of a woodcutter and his wife. They lived modestly but happily together but lost their happiness as time went

all three perished in the fire.

Deeply touched by such devotion, the Jade Emperor in the Kingdom of Heaven made them Gods. He assigned them the duty of watching over the welfare of man on earth from the vantage point of the kitchen, where, to this day they are revered as the Gods of the Hearth.

When Tao Quan takes his annual weeklong journey to Heaven, the Vietnamese believe their home has been left without protection and look for ways to guard themselves against an invasion of bad spirits. They erect a Cay Neu (Signal Tree), a very high bamboo pole with a *khanh*, a sonorous clay tablet and a piece of yellow cloth attached to the top, in front of the home.

The origins of this custom are expounded in a story which goes back to the birth of the Vietnamese nation when the Vietnamese were constantly threatened by malevolent spirits. Lord Buddha took compassion on them and one day descended from Nirvana to visit them. He was immediately surrounded by all kinds of devils with whom he struck up a deal for a small piece of land in exchange for precious stones, gold and silver, which he laid before them. When the devils asked him the size of the piece of land he had in mind, Buddha told them it would be as large as his gown. The devils agreed to this thinking they

you while you are enjoying Tet and your union with your ancestors".

The custom of erecting a Cay Neu in front of the house during Tet is still observed in parts of the countryside, but has to a great extent died out in the cities where perhaps T.V. antennas serve the same purpose.

With the malevolent spirits frightened away by the Cay Neu, the Vietnamese set their minds to things material and prepare the Banh Chung, Tet's traditional glutinous rice cakes. With a stock of these and food enough to last a week, the Vietnamese can give full heart and soul to decorating their homes in red and gold.

Another indispensable feature, even for

had struck a very good deal, but when Lord Buddha dropped his gown it spread as far and wide as the territory of Vietnam. The devils were furious, but the deal had been made. Lord Buddha then advised the Vietnamese: "At the end of the year, when you invite your ancestors to your home for Tet, the devils may mingle with them. You must erect a high bamboo pole flying my emblem on a piece of cloth in front of your house to prevent the devils from coming to disturb

Left, Tet is a particularly joyful time for the kids. **Above**, greeting cards for sale at the central market (**left**) and (**right**) roadside dancer.

the poorest families, is a branch of peach tree blossom. During Tet, flower markets selling a wonderful array of flowers spill out into the streets of Hanoi. At this time branches of peach blossom can cost over 100,000 dong (about US$20) – roughly the salary of a high official for two months.

In Southern and Central Vietnam, Saigon and Hue, peach blossom is replaced by Canh Mai, a branch of yellow apricot blossom. The origin of this custom is found in a traditional tale which claims the peach tree was first discovered by the Vietnamese in the mountains of Soc Son in Northern Vietnam. It was then a tree big enough to harbor the benevolent gods, Tra and Uat Ly. The devils were afraid of both these Gods and the peach trees in which the gods made their home. Thus when the Gods of the Hearth and the God of the Earth are away making their annual report to the Jade Emperor in Heaven, the Vietnamese are protected from within their homes by the peach or apricot branches and defended from the outside by the Signal Tree.

For maximum security against any possible intrusion by demons and bad spirits, particularly on New Year's Eve and New Year's day, the Vietnamese fire crackers to thwart the notorious devils Na A and his terrible wife who cannot bear noise and light.

A temporary general truce is declared between human beings and spirits.

All acts performed, all events — whether favorable or unfavorable—which take place on the first day of Tet, are believed to effect the course of one's life for the year ahead.

The first sound heard in the new year is most important and everyone tries to detect it, besides that of the firecrackers. A cock crow signals hard work and bad harvest. The lowing of a buffalo heralds a year of sweat and toil and a dog barking, signifies a year of confidence and trust. Worst of all is the cry of an owl, a warning of coming epidemic and calamity for the whole community.

The first visitor to the home has to be a

With all these precautions taken, the Vietnamese calmly await the arrival of Spring. The first day of Tet is always reserved for the worship of ancestors who are ceremoniously welcomed back from Heaven on New Year's Eve during the Giao Thua, the transition between the old and new year. Elaborately prepared food offerings together with the perfume of burning sandalwood, incense and *thai tien*, a type of fragrant white narcissus which blooms during Tet, await the ancestors at the altar. At midnight on the last day of the old year, all human problems, earthly worries, war, revolution, political intrigue and commercial transactions are left behind.

happy man, a man of virtue. This can be arranged before Tet in a discreet manner, but those who don't want to take any chances will leave home at midnight and return a minute later.

Other superstitious beliefs hold that one should not sew as to do so would mean hardship for the whole year; or sweep the floor, as this could chase away the Than Tai, the God of wealth who just may happen to be on the premises. One must absolutely not curse, get angry, use vulgar words, or break glasses, as all these inharmonious acts attract the malediction of bad spirits.

The timing of the Xuat Hanh (Going Out

Ceremony), which usually takes place on the night of the New Year's Day or the second day of the year, is carefully chosen at a propitious hour in accordance with one's birth date. Young men and women go to a nearby park or forest to gather *loc*, a branch of young leaves which symbolizes hope and good fortune.

During this "Spring promenade" they hope to meet the person of their dreams and return home to compose the first poem of the year on a scroll of flowered paper. With this gesture, they perform the ritual of Khai But (Opening of the pen), one of the most sacred functions of the New Year for poets and intellectuals.

fully to see that their future for the coming year is an auspicious one.

On the third day of Tet, the family bids their ancestors farewell. The fourth day is usually the day for Khai An, Opening the Seal, when government offices reopen for business. However people usually don't feel like working and instead spend the time with their colleagues and friends, drinking cups of tea and chatting about the many festivals they will celebrate during the first few weeks of the month ahead.

On the seventh day, the Cay Neu is taken down as Tao Quan and all the benevolent spirits have returned to earth to watch over the destiny of the human race and the Viet-

One of the most important elements in celebrating Tet, are Cau Doi, parallel sentences written in traditional black Chinese characters on red paper in Vietnamese nom characters, or romanized Vietnamese arranged to look like Chinese calligraphy. These are hung in the center of the home as a good wish for the year. In many families, after gifts of money wrapped in red paper are exchanged, tradition requires that the father read his children's *tu vi*, (horoscope) hope-

Left, happy 'basket cases' in Can Tho. **Above left**, flower sellers do brisk business during Tet and **right**, kumquat plants usher in the new year.

namese people.

The ceremonial Tet of flowers and special foods is now over and the Tet of fun and merrymaking begins. Fairs and festivals of all sizes take place throughout the country, particularly in North Vietnam, until the end of the third month, which marks the beginning of Summer.

A minimum of two weeks is needed to "eat Tet" with the Vietnamese, three days in Saigon to watch people frantically and joyously preparing for Tet, four days in Hue to observe the traditional Tet and one week in Hanoi for the important post-Tet festivities and fairs.

Architecture: The Vietnamese have always placed great importance on the choice and arrangement of buildings and burial sites. Based not only on aesthetics, these must conform to the advice of geomancers who consult the stars and use divining instruments to determine the orientation, form and interweaving of the various elements of any construction. This intricate union with nature and pursuit of harmony endows Vietnamese architecture with a unique charm and a certain sense of mystery.

Chinese colonization which lasted until the 10th century. Once national independence was regained under the Ly Dynasty (11th-13th centuries), Vietnamese architecture reflected a blending of Vietnamese art and Chinese influences together with very strong Buddhist inspiration. The Quynh Lam Pagoda, whose interior could shelter 1,000 statues of Buddha, and the Bao Thien tower, several dozen meters high, were landmarks of that period. Unfortunately all that remains of them today are some stone and wood

Vietnam's most impressive architecture is seen in its palaces and imperial tombs, temples, pagodas and communal houses. Built in wood, stone and brick, these are often beautifully decorated with sculpture and woodcarving. Although the tropical climate has made it necessary to restore some of these old buildings several times, they represent some very ancient architectural styles. The vestiges of Vietnam's oldest capital, (3rd century) Co Loa, with its unique spiralling ramparts, are still visible in Dong Anh district in the suburbs of Hanoi. Like much of Vietnam's most ancient architecture, it was destroyed during the thousand year long

engravings, ceramics, stone sculptures, statues, pillar bases, bricks, pots bowls, plates and tea pots. The dragon of that period winds in harmonious curves, its body progressively thinning to better reveal its inner energy.

In the period that followed, (13th-15th centuries) the artistic expression in architecture became more robust and self-confident. Emphasis was placed on stability and simplicity and greater attention was paid to equilibrium and balance. The Ho dynasty's stone citadel in Thanh Hoa remains a testimony to that period of architectural design. The dragon of this era no longer spreads out in endless convolutions, its body is shorter and its head has fewer details. During the 16th, 17th and 18th centuries, the arts expressed a greater degree of creativity and originality. Serious attempts were made to accentuate the Vietnamese concept of harmonizing construction with nature in the general configuration and particular formations of the earth under geomantic principles. These trends and concepts, designs and decorations were all successfully combined with foreign influences in the grand scale construction of the Nguyen Dynasty's capital of reunified Vietnam in Hue from 1802 to 1945. Its founder, Emperor Gia Long, drew his inspiration from several sources – the Chinese capital, Beijing, the French Vauban

realm to participate in this massive undertaking amounted to a contingent of over 80,000 men. The Vauban-style Imperial Citadel which walls off half the town comprises three concentric enclosures within a square plane. The Thanh Ngoai or External Enclosure measuring 9,186 feet (2,800 meters) long on each side, is defended by a series of bastions with ten gates perforating its periphery. The structure is surrounded in the North, East and West by a large moat which communicates with the River of Perfume and in the South the river serves as a natural defense barrier. Another fortress on the east side of the enclosure, near the northeast corner is known as the Mang Ca (Fish

fortified system and the knowledge acquired over thousands of years of war and defense. The raw materials used in its construction came from all over the country: strong lim wood from Nghe An in the North and Gia Dinh in the South, stone from Thanh Hoa in the North, marble from Quang Nam in the Center, bricks and tiles from Bat Trang in the North and from Hue itself. Skilled workers and decorators drafted from all corners of the

Preceding pages: Comedian troupe at Tonkin; theater performers in traditional garb; sculptor Diep Minh Chau; pagoda by the Perfume River. Left, bronze urns of the Gia Long Dynasty. Above, imperial city from the south gate.

Operculum) fortress. The Thanh Noi or Inner Enclosure, measuring 1,969 feet (600 meters) on each side, has no defense installation but is encircled by a large moat. At the heart of the citadel is the Tu Cam Thanh, Forbidden Purple Enclosure, the private residence of the Emperor and his immediate family. Hue's site on the left bank of the Huong Giang (River of Perfumes) against the background of the Nui Ngu Binh, (Imperial Screen Mountain), which protects it from the winds of the North, was chosen with the utmost care.

Emperor Thieu Tri, a gifted poet and the third monarch of the Nguyen Dynasty, who reigned from 1841 to 1849, explained the reasons behind the choice of Hue as the nation's capital. They are both geomantic and strategic: *"It is protected by natural defenses...It stands at the convergence of the forces of allegiance of the cardinal points... In this enclosure of mountains and rivers, ten men can face one hundred and also the world..."*.

Vietnamese scholars agree that Hue's location follows the configurations of the benevolent Thanh Long (Blue Dragon) and the aggressive power of the Bac Ho, (White Tiger), the two manifestations which to the Vietnamese represent the conflicting- harmonizing forces of good and evil that move

white. Should such a geomantic hemorrage occurs, it would leave Vietnam and Hue powerless against the attacks of the angry White Tiger, characterized by floods and wars and revolutions, misery and bloodshed. In addition to the Imperial Citadel, Hue is famous for its Imperial Tombs built on the pine covered hills to the South of the city. Each tomb has its own unique form of landscaping, architectural style and particular charm, but all share the same general structure: a surrounding area, a flagged wall zone in the middle of which stands the stone tomb, a main forecourt, a pavilion housing the stone stele carved with the Emperor's deeds and virtues, a terrace decorated with statues

heaven and earth and regulate human destiny. Hue's location was also considered to respect the free flow of Long Mach (Dragon Veins), which, according to old geomantic concepts, are the inner textures of the earth. These play a vital role when it comes to choosing a site for a home or burial. These two propitious conditions help nurture the Ngu Hanh, or five elements: metal, wood, water, fire, earth, thus ensuring the happiness and prosperity of the Kingdom.

Much concern has been expressed over the moats dug around the Imperial Capital which geomantically speaking, may have cut the Long Mach and could bleed the Blue Dragon

of the Emperor's ministers, elephants and horses, and a high circular wall surrounding the Imperial Tomb. Emperor Gia Long's mausoleum, considered the most majestic and dignified, exudes an aura of strength, stability and discipline, reflecting the admired qualities of the founder of the Nguyen dynasty.

The burial sites of Vietnam's kings, leaders, heroes and heroines remain for the most part intact despite the devastation of war, thanks to the traditional beliefs preserved in geomancy and ancestor worship.

Until recently, Vietnamese sculpture was mainly of a religious nature as seen in the wood and stone sculptures decorated with symbolic religious motifs which compliment Vietnam's places of worship in a style that has changed little with time. The best examples of traditional sculpture can be seen in the Temples and Pagodas, whose elaborately carved altars abound with wooden lacquered statues of man and animals, representing either mythology or history. The village *dinh* or communal house in each village constitute not only a meeting place for the people, but also for the talents of the artisans, who gave the best of their skills to decorate it. The carved wooden beams and pillars of the communal houses, pagodas and temples are testimony to the skills of sculptors who remain

craft tradition, whole villages were given solely over to block printing. Many families in Ho village in Bach Ninh Province, north of Hanoi, are collectively engaged in producing colored prints of traditional themes. The village craftsmen make their own paper and natural colors and prepare the blocks in variations of classic models depicting good luck signs, historical figures, scenes of historical battles, spirits, popular allegories and social comment. Good fortune is symbolized by a corpulent pig decorated with garlands often accompanied by a litter of suckling piglets. A hen surrounded by chicks symbolizes prosperity. The rooster, herald of the dawn, is the symbol of peace and courage. Social

the anonymous craftsmen of a bygone era.

Folk Art: Vietnamese folk art went into decline with the advent of French colonization at the end of the 19th century. In recent years, visible attempts have been made to revive it. The best examples of this revival are the Tranh Lang Ho or Ho village paintings, mostly woodcuts. The woodcut art form existed from as early as the 11th century under the Ly Dynasty. It was at first limited to black and white but after the 15th century, color was introduced. In accordance with the

criticism is expressed by caricatures of mandarins represented by croaking frogs and rats marching with drums and trumpets. Warriors are shown together with apes, tigers and other animal spirits, all in splendid colors. These prints truly reflect major aspects of peasant outlook with its blend of solid humor, optimism and a canny ability to ridicule the corrupt and the powerful.

Lacquer (Son Mai): Objects made of lacquered wood found in tombs dating from the 3rd and 4th centuries A.D., reveal that lacquer has been produced in Vietnam since very early times. Today, lacquer goods including paintings, screens, boxes, vases, trays and

Left, the multi-tiered Thien Mu Pagoda. **Above**, Temple courtyard in Saigon.

chessboards, are fast becoming one of the country's main export items. Their quality is a result of the meticulous attention given to the preparation of the lacquer and the designs of a thousand year old tradition. Two types of lacquer are used: varnish lacquer, which is obtained by mixing lacquer resin with mu oil: and the higher quality and more durable pumice lacquer which is produced by mixing lacquer resin with pine resin. Unlike varnish lacquer, pumice lacquer is rubbed and smoothed in water after painting to bring out the gloss finish. Lacquer is prepared from the resin of the cay son (lacquer tree) which is collected in the same way as latex. After being stored for a while, the resin is diluted

hues of red; pure gold or silver applied as thin sheets or strips; blue goache; several kinds of aniline dyes which produce carmine red or green; and the yellow dye obtained from the seeds of hydrangeas are also used. Egg shell fragments yield the purest white color and fragments of mother-of-pearl, mollusc and snail shell produce a blue and violet sheen.

Lacquer artists painstakingly select and prepare the boards for their pictures. These must be smooth, dry and free of the smallest crack, scratch or imperfection before they are coated with several layers of lacquer. This is followed by a thin layer of cotton fabric or silk followed by another layer of lacquer. The board is then left in a damp

with water and the dark brown surface layer known as oil lac is skimmed off. With the addition of various ingredients this is used for the upper layer of lacquer paintings. This high quality lacquer is poured into a bamboo or wooden vessel and stirred vigorously with a wooden pestal for eight to ten hours. A small amount of colophony is added to render it more elastic and suitable for polishing. If lacquer is poured into a vessel made of porcelain or fired clay then stirred with an iron pestle, it turns black. Normal paint added to lacquer will also produce a black or grey color. Special paints are needed for lacquer pictures: cinnabar which produces various

place for two or three days until dry, then coated with another layer of lacquer, a layer of lacquer putty, sawdust and kaolin, which render the board uniformly smooth. The dried surface is rubbed with wet pumice before another two to four layers of lacquer are applied and left to dry for several days between coats, then painstakingly rubbed for hours. Only after all this preparation is the board ready for painting. If the artist uses egg or mollusc shells, he cuts the shape in the upper layers of lacquer covering the fabric, smears the depression with black lacquer, which acts as a glue, and taps the shell into position with a tiny hammer. More lacquer is applied, then tinted with the desired dye. When this is quite dry, the picture is rubbed down thoroughly to bring out the texture of the shell with its numerous tiny cracks. If the artist uses gold or silver sheets, he glues them to one of the lower layers of lacquer and leaves them to dry for 24 hours. These yield a wide gamut of colors and tints depending on how much dye the artist has added to the lacquer and how long he has rubbed it. To add lustre to the painting the artist polishes its surface with very fine soft powder and straw ashes until the lacquer surface begins to glow. He will continue rubbing the picture with the palm of his hand to remove the half dry ash particles until the contours become perfectly outlined and the lacquer acquires the transparency and sheen he desires.

In the old days lacquer craftsmen had a very limited choice of paints at their disposal – black, red, brown, gold and silver. Of these, only the black paint could withstand polishing – the others were destroyed by rubbing and apt to develop cracks. In 1926 several students at Hanoi's Higher School of Arts undertook a study of artisan technology. Their findings expanded lacquer's artistic potential. Instead of vegetable oil they began adding colophony to the lacquer resin which produced brown lacquer suitable for polishing. They also pioneered the use of eggshell which enriched the lacquer palette with white and grey colors. Further research and experiments have yielded new techniques which have contributed to making Vietnamese lacquer the most sophisticated and original in the world.

The Performing Arts: Art in Vietnamese is My Thuat, which literally translated means beauty skill. Vietnam's artists use traditional art to communicate their ideas through the mediums of music, poetry, dance, theater, painting, sculpture and architecture.

Vietnam with its 4000 year old civilization has no great monument like Cambodia's Ankor Wat. Many of Vietnam's ancient monuments have fallen prey to the ravages of war and the climate.

However, despite centuries of foreign invasion and destruction, nothing has succeeded in destroying the vast legacy and love of poetry which is a great testimony to the

Left, temple detail. **Above**, cultural show appeals to the masses.

culture and spirit of the Vietnamese people.

Poetry (Tho): Above all else poetry dominates the Vietnamese arts. The Vietnamese language is a natural tool for poetry as each of its syllables can be pronounced in six different tones to confer six different things. By simply combining these tones and modulating certain words, a sentence turns into a verse and plain speech becomes a song. Another group of Vietnamese words made up of repeated syllables can cast an indefinable shade on the meaning of words, conjuring up a particular color, movement, attitude or mood.

Vietnamese poetry falls into two major categories, the popular or Ca Dao, folk song,

oral in origin but collected and transcribed in written form; and Tho Van, literary poetry written by kings, scholars, Buddhist monks, mandarins, Taoist recluses, political dissidents, feminists, revolutionaries, even Marxists, old and young, men, women and children. Poetry has become such an important medium of communication that even present-day political slogans have to be in verse to be effective.

Traditional Music: According to Confucius, *"Personal cultivation begins with poetry, is made firm by the rule of decorum and is perfected by music"*.

· Before Western domination and influences

penetrated Asia, music played an integral part in religious ceremonies, but was not used for public entertainment.

The Dong Son drums, which depict dancers performing to the accompaniment of musical instruments, and the lithophone of Ndut Lien Krat in the southern Highlands of Vietnam, testify to the existence of musical and dance traditions in Vietnam since the Bronze Age. Along with the other arts, music received its share of Chinese influence during the millennium of Chinese colonization. It was also influenced by the music of the Hindu Kingdom of Champa in the South, which Vietnam gradually absorbed during its long Southward march. Court Music had

for helping the sun and moon during an eclipse; Dai Trieu Nhac, music for ordinary audiences; Dai Yen Cuu Tau Nhac, music for large banquets and Cung Trung Chi Nhac or Palace music.

Between the 15th to 18th centuries, Vietnamese leaders took great interest in reorganizing and unifying diverse orchestral groups. These varied from complete orchestras represented by the Phuong Bat Am, a popular ensemble of eight instrumental timbrels, to various theatrical orchestras.

Ceremonial and Religious Music: In the coastal provinces of Central Vietnam, songs known as Hat Ba Trao – songs for worshipping the Sea spirits – are very much a popular

its beginnings during the Le Dynasty (1428-1788) when a Vietnamese mandarin was asked to establish a system of court music inspired by the Chinese Ming Dynasty. He organized the following categories of music to be played at different religious and social occasions: Giao Nhac, played as an offering at the Esplanade of Heaven during the Vietnamese Emperor's triennial celebration of the Cult of Heaven; Mieu Nhac, played during ceremonies at the Court of Literature in honor of Confucius and anniversary commemorations for deceased Vietnamese emperors; Ngu Tu Nhac, music of the Five Sacrifices; Cuu Nhat Giao Trung Nhac, music

tradition. The most popular is the Hat Chau Van, a kind of incantation used in hypnotizing a person estranged from the spirits through musical tunes, rhythms and lyrics.

Buddhist Music falls into two styles, the Tan or melismatic chant and the Tung or sutra prayers. The Tan is accompanied by a string and percussion orchestra in syncopated rhythm, while the Tung is a cantillation on knowledge and enlightenment recited by a monk and punctuated by strokes on a wooden slit drum.

Chamber Music, performed by small instrumental ensembles for selected audiences of intellectuals was confined to major cities.

The most popular, known as A Dao, takes its name from a story of national importance which recounts an event that took place at the beginning of the 15th century during the Ming invasion. During the military struggle all manner of weapons were used, including on one occasion a combination of female beauty and music. A country girl from Dao village in Hai Hung province, North Vietnam, used her charm, dance, song and music to distract the Ming soldiers and gain precious time for her countrymen to organize a guerilla attack against the enemy. She became a heroine of that war and the Hat A Dao, the Song of the Lady from the Dao village, was composed by a group of manda-

drum in a specific way. This form of music has enriched Vietnam's large treasury of poems with many works by famous poet statesmen. However, by the beginning of the 20th century it had gradually became a refuge for pleasure rather than a center for song and poetry. Its counterparts, although lacking the same importance and influence, are the Ca Hue, Music-Song of Hue and the Dan Tai Tu, music of the amateurs, in Southern Vietnam. Each region of Vietnam has its own musical tradition and expression as do each of its 54 ethnic minorities, but on the whole, Vietnamese music falls into two basic groups, the Dieu Kach or Northern tune with its more Chinese influence and the Dieu

rin scholars to commemorate her beauty, talent and patriotism. Essentially Hat A Dao is sung poetry performed at the home of a songstress where the audience enjoy famous old poems or poems they compose themselves, sung to a rhythmic accompaniment on the Phach, a bamboo instrument beaten with two wooden sticks and the Dan Day, a long-necked lute with three strings. The audience express their appreciation and comment on the singer's talents by beating a

Left, traditional instruments at the Hanoi Conservatory of Music. Above, child prodigy in the making?

Nam or Southern tune, influenced by slower tempo and more sentimental musical tradition of Champa.

Folk Music takes the form of songs sung and composed by villagers which illustrate their life in the countryside from birth to death in lullabies known as Hat Ru in the North, Ru Em in Central Vietnam, and Au O in the South and Ho or work songs and Ly or love songs. Each region has its own Ho and Ly, as does every season, every type of work and every leisure activity. Ho means, to call people to work in a rising and prolonged voice. To begin, one person leads the chant which is then taken up by others in the same working party. The most cherished of these is the Ho Mia Nhi, usually sung by young boatwomen on the Perfume River in Hue. Structured like a poem, its four lines express deep thoughts and feelings. Ho are often composed by famous poets who wish to remain anonymous. The most interesting characteristic of Vietnamese culture is the osmotic communion and communication between the literati and the common people. An invisible but active red thread seems to exist between the spontaneous creativity of the peasants and the sophisticated learning of the scholars.

Theater and Theater Music: Vietnamese theater embraces all the major theatrical

Tieu – Chinese for laughter. Cheo's origins can be found in the religious and social activities depicted on the engravings of Bronze Age drums and urns. Developing from animistic customs, mime, dance, song, prayers and poetic extemporization, Cheo reached its present form by the 10th century. Performances are usually staged in front of a village community house or Buddhist Pagoda. The troupe's equipment is carried from village to village in a single box which also serves as a unique part of the stage setting, representing whatever is required of it. The themes of Cheo plays provides a framework within which the players have unlimited scope for improvization. The troupe is judged

forms. Vietnam's oldest form of theatrical performance recorded is the Tro He or Farce, created by Lieu Thu Tam under the Tien Le Dynasty (980-1009). During the Tran Dynasty (1225-1400) two new types of theater emerged, the Hat Giau Mat or masked performances and the Hat Coi Tran or coatless performances. A blend of various theatrical forms including Court theater, folk performances and assimilated foreign influences, today's Vietnamese theater presents three types of performances: the Cheo, the Tuong and the Cai Luong. Cheo, Vietnam's oldest form of theater, is as old as the Vietnamese nation itself. The word Cheo is a distortion of

according to its ability to vary and renew a known theme. The musicians sit to the right of the playing area with their drums, gongs, rattles, a couple of stringed instruments and a flute. To start the play, someone from the audience versed in the Cheo art beats the big drum reserved for the use of the audience. When a performer sings well, this drum will be beaten by a member of the audience to show appreciation and approval, however when the performance is poor the wooden part of the drum is struck. Performances last according to the amount of time paid for which is calculated in the time it takes an incense stick to burn. When special approval is marked by the drum, incense tapers are laid in a pile in honor of the player, thus increasing the fee paid. The play begins with a series of beats ending in three single beats, whereupon the orchestra strikes up the opening chorus in which the female lead sets the mood for the play. The audience knows the rules of Cheo down to every last detail and throughout the performance the players explain events, question and receive replies from the audience. The ground rules for Hat Cheo were laid down as early as 1501. Melodies known to all symbolize certain events; marriage, birth, death and all gestures, including movements of the eyes and mouth, have a specific meaning. The chorus and the

expose the injustices of those in power. Under some dynasties, Cheo was forbidden and its performers prosecuted.

Unlike Hat Cheo, which is uniquely Vietnamese and part of Vietnam's traditional culture, Hat Tuong theater arrived from China in the 13th century under the Tran Dynasty after their defeat of three Mongol invasions. Among their prisoners was a master of Chinese theater, Ly Nguyen Cat, who later became a Vietnamese citizen and taught Chinese drama to the Vietnamese court. From the Chinese came the red, rosy and black face makeup, the ceremonial costumes, masks, stylized gestures and speeches, the majestic percussion and wind instrument music and

clown, indispensable in all plays, express emotional high points. The clown with his black makeup interrupts the players to comment on their lies and tricks, make fun of them and praise their good deeds. The audience often stops a player to demand a replay of an interesting or intriguing detail. Alert, critical and interested, they participate fully in the play.

Cheo is the most democratic form of popular theater. Essentially anti-establishment, it indirectly educates the peasants in how to

Left, creating at the Academy of Fine Arts. **Above**, pop group performs in a Saigon restaurant.

the emphasis on the heroic and the noble. A Hat Tuong begins with a sung introduction spelling out the drama's story line. Each player describes his character and role to the audience. The stage is almost empty except for special props representing the landscape or objects of common use indicated by a few basic elements: a branch for a forest, a painted wheel for a cart. The action, always dramatic, is guided by Confucian moral virtues and concepts: loyalty to Kings, devotion to parents. The orchestra sits at the side of the stage, accompanying not only the singing but also, details of the movement on stage.

With the passing of time, in typical Vietnamese fashion, the Hat Tuong, although a copy of Chinese drama was adapted to the Vietnamese character. Women replaced men in the female roles and the orchestra was enlarged, incorporating some Indian influences from the Champa culture. Today, Hat Tuong's orchestra includes cymbals, gongs, drums, tambourines, flutes and an arsenal of stringed instruments; the Dan Nguyet, a moon shaped lute; the Dan Nhi, a violin with a high register played by drawing two strings tight over a drumskin; the Thap Luc, a zither-like instrument with 16 strings plucked with the fingers and the Dan Bau, or monocord, a uniquely Vietnamese instrument whose single string stretched over a long lacquered

free dialogue.

Mua Roi Nuoc – Water Puppet Theater: Puppetry (Mua Roi) has been known for the last thousand years in Vietnam; yet apart from Mua Roi Can or land puppetry, Vietnam is the home of another form of puppetry found nowhere else in the world, Mua Roi Nuoc or Water Puppetry. Like most Vietnamese traditional arts, the Water Puppet Theater began in Northern Vietnam. From there it has spread to all parts of the country. It reached the peak of its popularity in the 18th century when many Mua Roi Nuoc companies presented a very diverse repertoire to their audiences. The stage of this unusual puppet theater is the surface of the water. Puppeteers hidden

sound box, is both bowed and plucked to produce a variety of vibrato effects and long resonances of great subtlety. Hat Tuong began as a theater for the elite, it allows criticism and flexibility, but in the end it is still very much a theater for the moral and social status quo.

Cai Luong or renovated theater made its first appearance in Southern Vietnam in 1920. It interprets classical Chinese stories in a more accessible style. Influenced by the European stage, Cai Luong has evolved into its present spoken drama form, abandoning the cumbersome epic style in favor of shorter acts, emotional and psychological play and

behind a long screen manipulate the puppets with bamboo rods while standing chest deep in water.

A Mua Roi Nuoc show can take the form of a two-hour realistic enactment of the main aspects of Vietnamese life and history – the building and defending of their country against the major forces of nature and man, the meticulous rice-growing work of the Vietnamese peasants and how they enjoy their moments of rest between harvests, the return of the laureate from the imperial examinations to his village. These shows reveal the artistic qualities and historical values of the Vietnamese people.

THE ALLURE OF THE AO DAI

The national dress of Vietnamese women, the ao dai (which literally translates as long gown) is a close-fitting high-collared knee-length or longer gown, split to the waist and worn over trousers. Both alluring and provocative, the ai dai covers everything but hides almost nothing.

Considering the country's long history, the ao dai is a relatively recent creation. It replaced the traditional dress whose color and design were dictated and regulated by ceremonial requirements, social class and pro-

less along the lines of the Chinese style of the time. Buttoned coats and trousers replaced the skirts and split coats tied in the front. Emperor Minh Mang, the Nguyen Dynasty's second monarch, imposed the wearing of trousers on the entire female population from the South to the North.

In the 1930s, an artist from a liberal political and cultural reform group, the Tu Luc Van Doan, attempted to modernize the Vietnamese women's dress through employing a greater variety of colors and designs. His

fessional hierarchy. Yellow was solely reserved for emperors who were also entitled to wear a five claw dragon design. White was for mourning and blue was worn by officials only on formal occasions. Before the mid-18th century, Vietnamese women wore long skirts, still worn in some villages in North Vietnam, but never trousers. In 1744 Lord Vu Vuong of Hue's Nguyen Dynasty, which ruled from Central Vietnam southward, ordered a change in Vietnamese dress more or

new creation, a longer coat, used different materials and colors and could even be bare shouldered, although it was not overly popular with the modest Vietnamese. His innovations, gradually tempered with some moderation, evolved to become today's ao dai.

After the end of the war in 1975 and reunification, Vietnam entered a period of severe austerity. The graceful and feminine ao dai practically disappeared and was replaced by a uniform dress of blouse and trousers.

Since 1987, traditional aspects of life that were temporarily forbidden have slowly returned, among them the ao dai.

Left, cigarette break for the Dragon Dance Troup.
Above, ao dais on parade.

Writers and poets have always occupied a place of very high esteem in Vietnamese society. Their writings reveal the spirit of the Vietnamese, as a nation and as individuals, who, well acquainted with struggle, tribulation, and hardship, find their rich literary heritage a source of comfort, hope and inspiration.

A seemingly endless wealth of traditional oral literature, consisting of myths, songs, legends, folk and fairy tales, constitutes Vietnam's most ancient literature. Later Viet-

writers, influenced Vietnamese prose and poetry with new literary forms which expressed ideas in novel ways and also reflected the mounting nationalism of the time.

The Tale of Kieu: Nearly every Vietnamese reads and remembers a few chapters of a 3,254 verse-story published 200 years ago. Considered the cultural Bible and window to the soul of the Vietnamese people, "The Tale of Kieu" has also been acclaimed by non-Vietnamese and translated into other major languages. One may wonder how "The Tale

namese literature, written in Chinese characters (chu nho) was penned by scholars, Buddhist bonzes, kings and court ministers who were also talented writers and poets. This was greatly influenced by the Confucian and Buddhist thought of the Han.

Many poems and literary works were written with the advent of Chu Nom. However the Vietnamese found Quoc Ngu's simpler written form a more accessible means of communicating their thoughts and ideas. Through it, Vietnamese literature was enriched with new ideas of Western thought and culture. European literature, translated for the first time by famous Vietnamese

of Kieu" came to occupy its special position in Vietnamese literature and why the complicated tale of a woman's personal misfortunes has come to be regarded by a whole people as the perfect expression of their essential nature, their national soul.

To the Vietnamese, regardless of age, gender, geography or ideology, Kieu is the heart and mind of their nation, the mirror of their society, past and present. To them, its author, Nguyen Du is the faithful interpreter of their hopes and the discreet confidant of their misfortunes. Born in the village of Nghi Xuan, Ha Tinh Province, Nguyen Du came from an old aristocratic family of mandarins and scholars. His father was Prime Minister in the Court of Emperor Le in Thang Long. He grew up in a country torn by civil war under the nominal rule of the Le Dynasty. In reality Vietnam was ruled by two rival regimes, the Trinh in the North and the Nguyen in the South. When he was 24 years old, the Le Dynasty his family had faithfully served for generations, was overthrown by a peasant-based revolution led by the Tay Son brothers. The Tay Son emperor, Nguyen Hue, unified the country for a short while and liberated Hanoi from the Manchu occupation forces in 1789. The Tay Son brothers were eventually defeated by a descendant of the Southern Nguyen warlords, Nguyen Anh,

the height of fame and power, Nguyen Du was not happy. His nostalgia for the Le Dynasty was even noticed by Emperor Gia Long, who valued his service and respected his personal feelings.

Having reunited Vietnam, Emperor Gia Long then had to tackle the important problem of national security: the establishment of cordial, diplomatic relations with China. All Vietnamese envoys to China were chosen from the cream of Vietnamese literati, as it was by intellectual, rather than military might that Vietnam sought to impress China. Nguyen Du, already recognized as a great poet and writer, was a natural choice for the post of Ambassador to China. After five

who became Emperor Gia Long in 1802 and brought Vietnam back under a single administration after almost two hundred years of partition.

Under Gia Long, Nguyen Du became the district officer of several provinces in the North, and distinguished himself as an honest and able administrator. In 1806, at the age of 41, he was summoned to the capital of Hue to serve as High Chancellor. He rose rapidly to the position of Court Minister. Yet even at

Left, gateway to the Temple of Literature. Above, those who made the grade became members of officialdom.

years in China he returned, more familiar with Chinese culture, but also more convinced of the greatness of his own country's intellectual heritage. He then devoted most of his time to literary pursuits until his death at the age of 53 in 1820.

For a Confucian scholar to describe in detail "the difficulties of the art of pleasure", took great courage and Nguyen Du's boldness endeared him to his readers.

But literary beauty and diversity alone cannot wholly explain the immortality of "Kieu". What makes "Kieu" as pertinent today as it was two centuries ago, is Nguyen Du's ability and courage to lay bare the whole spectrum of Vietnamese society. The vices, virtues, ugliness, beauty, noble acts, vile tricks, intrigues, all entangled in a seemingly hopeless tragi-comedy reflect the true face of Vietnam. Kieu also personifies the inherent contradiction between talent and misfortune or disaster, the cause and effect relationship between Tai (talent) and Menh (fate) as illustrated by the tales opening lines:

"Within the span of a hundred years of human existence, what a bitter struggle is waged between talent and fate", and the conclusion, *"When one is endowed with Talent, do not rely on it"*.

Deep in their hearts and behind their smiling

they committed. From the 1960s until 1975, the United States bombed North Vietnam, to stop international communism, and also bombed South Vietnam to save it from Vietnamese communism, leaving the Vietnamese peasants, the victims of the B52s and napalm, probably wondering why they received the bombs and not Moscow, the citadel and source of communism since 1917. After 1975, the most visible victims of the anti-communist crusade, big power politics and manoeuvres, were the hundreds of thousands of Vietnamese who fled their homeland to live in exile as refugees in nearly all parts of the world.

The best English translation of "The Tale

modesty, the Vietnamese know they are not lacking in Tai. At the same time they do not understand why this Tai which has helped them preserve their independence against formidable foreign invasions and enabled them to develop and nurture a respectable culture and civilization, has failed to bring them the lasting peace and durable prosperity they deserve.

Without an adequate answer to this question most Vietnamese believe they are *oan*, a word meaning wronged, that recurs throughout "The Tale of Kieu". The Vietnamese, like Kieu, see themselves as victims, punished for crimes they are not aware

of Kieu" was made by Mr. Huynh Sanh Thong, a Vietnamese scholar at Yale University. In his introduction he explains Kieu's significance to the refugees: *..."Often psychologically and socially estranged in a host country whose language they do not understand, many derive spiritual comfort from Nguyen Du's masterpiece. They know most of its lines by heart, and when they recite them out loud, they speak their mother tongue at its finest. To the extent that the poem implies something at the very core of the Vietnamese experience, it addresses them intimately as victims, as refugees, as survivors..."*.

LANGUAGE

The origin of the Vietnamese language remains a subject of debate but it is generally accepted to be a mixture of Austro-Asiatic languages sharing many similarities with the Mon-Khmer, Thai and Muong languages.

Vietnamese is not recognized as having its origins in the Chinese language, although present-day Vietnamese incorporates thousands of Chinese words, which has come about through the years of Chinese domination and influence of the Chinese classics.

One thing is certain, present day Vietnamese is not a pure language but rather a blend of several languages, ancient and modern, which has evolved through Vietnamese contact with other races. In addition to Vietnamese, Vietnam's many ethnic minorities speak their own distinct languages and dialects.

Vietnamese is essentially a monosyllabic tonal language. Each syllable can be pronounced in six different tones to confer a totally different meaning. The tones are expressed by five diacritical accents and one atonic, where the syllable has no accent. For example the syllable "ma", depending on the tone, can mean ghost, mother, horse, tomb, a term of relationship or a rice shoot. Obviously that leaves a lot of room for confusion for anyone unfamiliar with the language. These tones give spoken Vietnamese a musical quality and although the same language is spoken throughout country, as in most countries, regional variations and a marked difference in accent exist between the North, South and Center.

Written Vietnamese: The Chinese influence during the first centuries of Vietnam's history led to the extensive use of Chinese characters known as Chu Nho, which replaced an ancient written script of Indian origin conserved and used today

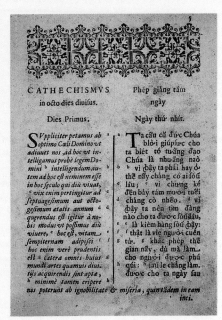

only by the Muong minority. Even after their independence in the 10th century, all Vietnamese books, government and official documents were written in Chu Nho, which continued to be used by scholars for some decades.

From the first centuries of independence, Vietnam's scholars realized the need and advantages of developing a separate written Vietnamese language. Several tentative attempts were made to modify the original Chinese characters, but it was a 13th century poet, Nguyen Thuyen, who managed to incorporate the previous efforts into a distinct, but very complicated script known as Chu Nom.

Although standardized for popular literature and non official documents, Chu Nom never received official recognition and most Vietnamese writers continued using the Chinese calligraphic script used since the first century A.D.

The Vietnamese alphabet was phonetically romanized in 1548 by a French Jesuit missionary, Alexandre de Rhodes, who published the first Vietnamese-Portuguese-Latin dictionary using the latinized script, Quoc Ngu, in 1651.

Quoc Ngu was at first used only by the Catholic church and the colonial administration. Its widespread use only became popular a century ago. In 1906, the study of Quoc Ngu became compulsory in secondary schools and two years later the Royal Court in Hue directed the Ministry of Education to establish a new curriculum entirely in Quoc Ngu. After the triennial literary examinations were abolished, with the last examination taking place in the imperial city of Hue in 1919, Quoc Ngu became the national written language. Of the foreign languages spoken in Vietnam, French, Russian and English are the most widespread. French is spoken by those of the colonial generation; English, which many Vietnamese are clamoring to learn today, is spoken by those lucky enough to avail themselves of the limited opportunities offered in the country and those who had contact with the Americans. Russian, although dwindling in popularity, was introduced after reunification and is spoken quite widely, particularly in the North.

Left, noted historian Dr Le Van Khoi. **Above**, opening page of Alexandre de Rhodes' Latin-Annamese religious text.

VIETNAMESE CUISINE

*In Food as in Death, we feel
the essential brotherhood of Mankind.*
— A Vietnamese saying.

Vietnam's cuisine is very much a reflection of its culture and contacts with other cultures. Rice, *com* in Vietnamese, is the main staple of the diet and the basis of the country's agriculture. The years of Chinese influence and occupation is evident in the use of chopsticks and the tendency to eat plain white rice separately with other foods, rather than mixing them together. However, the similarities end there. The extensive use of *nuoc mam*, fresh herbs — lemon grass, basil, coriander, mint, spear parsley, *laksa* leaf, fresh lime — and practically all the spices used in Southeast Asia, in Vietnamese cuisine, lend it a subtlety of flavor which sets it apart. Virtually every meal is accompanied by a delicious soup.

The later French influence brought with it the baguettes and *pate* sold in the markets and roadside stalls today and an appreciation of French food, shared by visitors and locals alike in the country's numerous Vietnamese-run French Restaurants. Vietnam's 3,000 kilometers of coastline, innumerable rivers and waterways provide an ample and varied supply of fresh fish and seafood all year round. Fresh and salt water fish, shellfish and crustaceans are eaten as the main source of protein in delicious dishes such as *cha ca*, barbecued fish and various minced fish meat cakes. The national condiment, *nuoc mam*, a fermented fish sauce, imparts its fine piquancy to practically every dish and to a large extent replaces salt, which lacks *nuoc mam*'s nutritive and flavor-enhancing properties. By adding a few other ingredients, *nuoc mam* is transformed into a delicious sauce — *nuoc cham* — that accompanies and complements every meal. Every cook has his or her own formula, but usually it consists of fresh chilli, fresh lime juice, garlic and sugar. This is used as a dipping sauce for a variety of snack type foods, for example the popular *cha gio* – small rolls of minced pork, prawn, crab meat, fragrant mushrooms and vegetables wrapped in thin rice paper and deep fried until crisp. Before eating, the *cha gio* is rolled in a lettuce leaf with fresh herbs and dipped in the *nuoc cham*.

Many South Vietnamese delicacies are served with raw, leafy vegetables, bean sprouts and herbs and wrapped up in a do-it-yourself manner. This custom, far from being Chinese, is probably indigenous to the area. The southerners, living in a tropical

area, use more coconut milk in their cooking and traditionally prefer their food spicier than people in the colder north. But despite their differences, North and South Vietnam share many tastes in common.

The Vietnamese have created very innovative dishes using pork, chicken and beef, sometimes combining meat together with fish and seafood.

Whether it be boiled, barbecued, grilled, stewed or fried, Vietnamese cuisine is a skilful and deliciously different blend of many unique flavors, textures and influences. Variety is certainly the spice of life and cuisine in Vietnam.

Left, no doubt as to the message, even if you can't read Vietnamese. **Above**, local spring rolls feature raw vegetables.

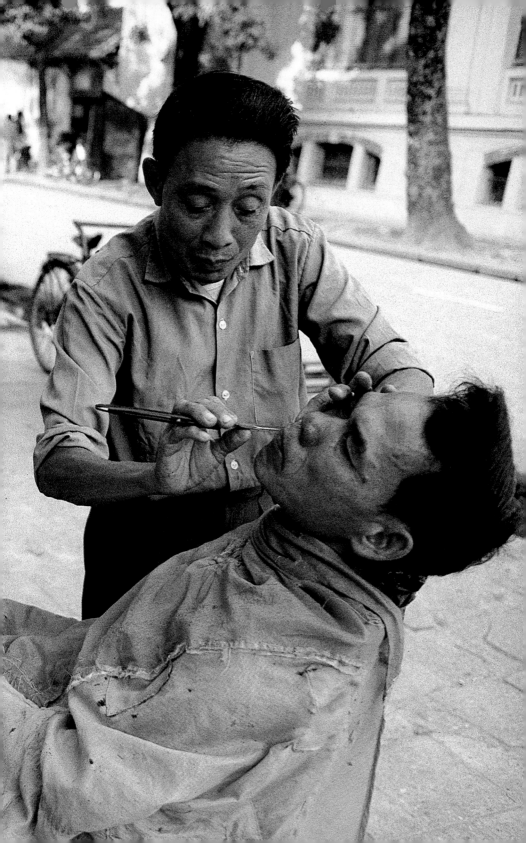

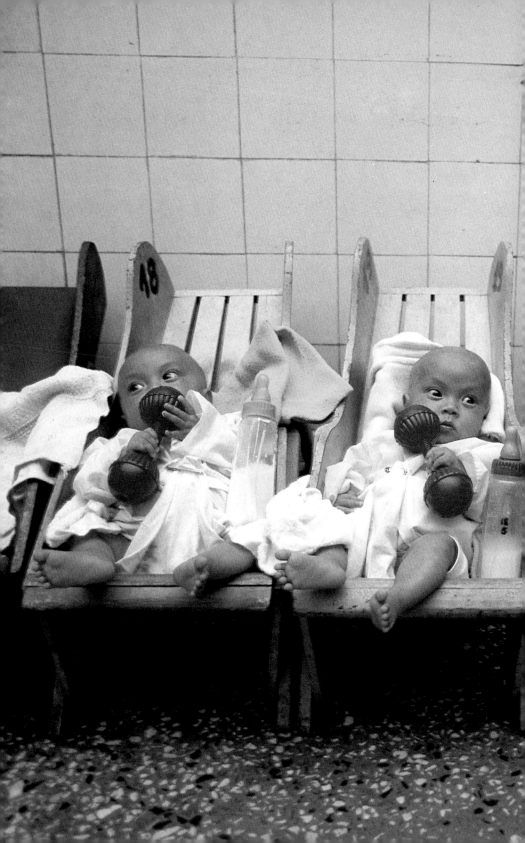

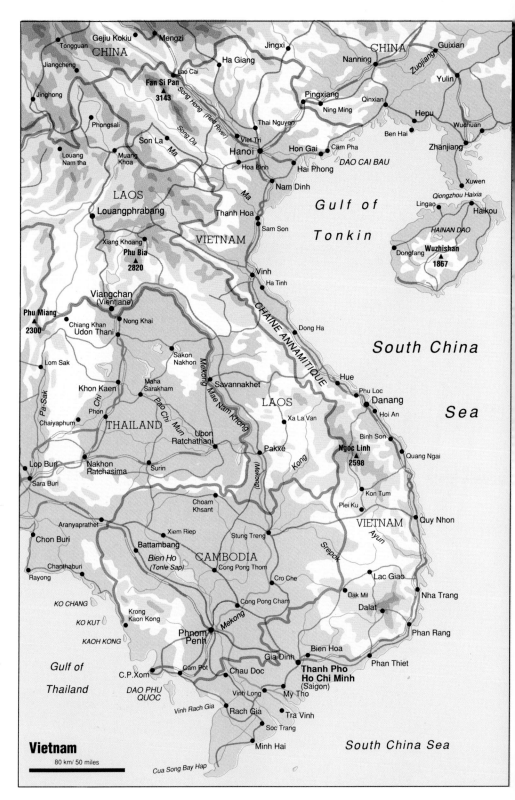

Vietnam

80 km/ 50 miles

JOURNEY THROUGH THE LAND
OF THE ASCENDING DRAGON

A journey through Vietnam is an unforgettable encounter with a land of remarkable and unexpected unspoilt beauty. Arriving in Hanoi, the ancient capital of Thang Long established by King Le Thai To in 1010 A.D., today's political capital, is like stepping back in time. The last 50 years of this century seem to have passed it by.

Further afield, the provinces of the vast northern Red River Delta reflect the traditional agricultural culture on which the economy is based, in lush inundated rice fields, and ponds where mauve water hyacinth and lotus bloom in profusion. Beyond the plains, the cooler forested mountainous regions rise towards the western border with Laos and the northern border with China.

An overwhelming sense of the past pervades Hue, the old imperial capital of the Nguyen Dynasty who moved the capital to the Center and ruled the country from the beginning of the 1800s until 1945. The old citadel and Imperial Enclosure surrounding the Forbidden Purple City occupy the left bank of the Perfume River and the "new city" with its predominantly colonial architecture. The tombs of the Nguyen kings lie scattered on the hillsides, surrounding the south of the old city.

To the north and south of Hue, a chain of coastal provinces washed by the South China Sea, links the immense rice growing deltas of the Red and Mekong rivers. To the south lie the lands of the ancient kingdom of Champa, whose sanctuaries, temples and towers stand as a landscape of Central Vietnam. To the west the mountainous Tay Son region stretches across the country to the Central Highlands.

Saigon, outspoken and cosmopolitan, as far removed in character as in physical distance from the more reserved and traditional cities of Hanoi and Hue, lies in the heart of the South. The beaches of Vung Tau and Nha Trang to the north and the vast rice bowl of the Mekong Delta to the south offer some welcome respite from the constant flow of traffic and humanity of Vietnam's most populous city.

It is impossible to come away from Vietnam untouched by its beauty, its richness, its poverty, its history and its people. Although the visitor will depart, the impressions and images of the journey will remain for a lifetime.

Preceding pages: Market day; rush hour in Hanoi; barbershop quartet; a day at Vung Tau beach; twin peeks: new arrivals in a Saigon hospital ward.

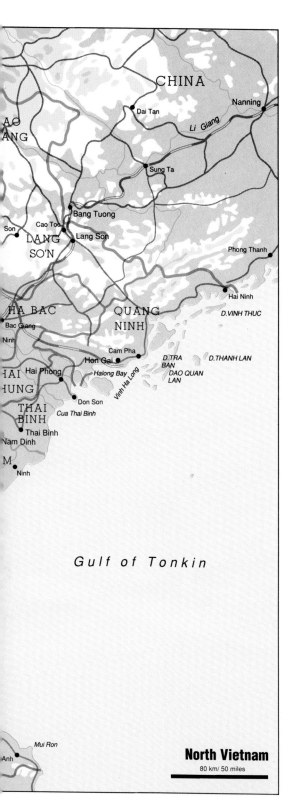

Our journey through North Vietnam begins in Hanoi, the ancient capital of Thang Long, today's political capital. Visitors to Hanoi will encounter the cultures of both east and west.

In this bustling city, the changing fortunes of history are reflected in the architecture of its many traditional temples and pagodas, and the lingering presence of the French remnants of its colonial past.

Leaving Hanoi and its populous suburbs we enter the picturesque provincial regions with their chequer-board patterned paddy fields. Green belts of trees and bamboo enclose villages where traditional communal houses, pagodas and temples remain hidden from view beyond the roadside fields.

Little mechanization is evident. Men, women, children and buffalo toil together in the fields seven days a week in all weathers. The scene is one of tranquil beauty, but the hardship of this life is obvious.

The eastern tour explores the rural landscapes, ancient temples and pagodas of Hai Hung and Thai Binh provinces, the busy port of Haiphong and the stunning scenery of Halong Bay in Quang Ninh Province.

The tour west of Hanoi begins in Ha Son Binh Province with its many beautiful old pagodas, sanctuaries and grottoes, and encompasses the plateaus and mountains of Son La and Lai Chau provinces.

The northern tour from Ha Bac, a province full of historical sites, temples and pagodas, continues into Vinh Phu Province, the cradle of the ancient Hung Lac civilisation and Kingdom of Van Lang.

Further north lie Bac Thai Province and the provinces of Hoang Lien Song, Ha Tuyen, Cao Bang and Lang Son bordering China in the north. This mountainous region is home to many minorities, yet remains largely inaccessible to foreign visitors due to border disputes between China and Vietnam.

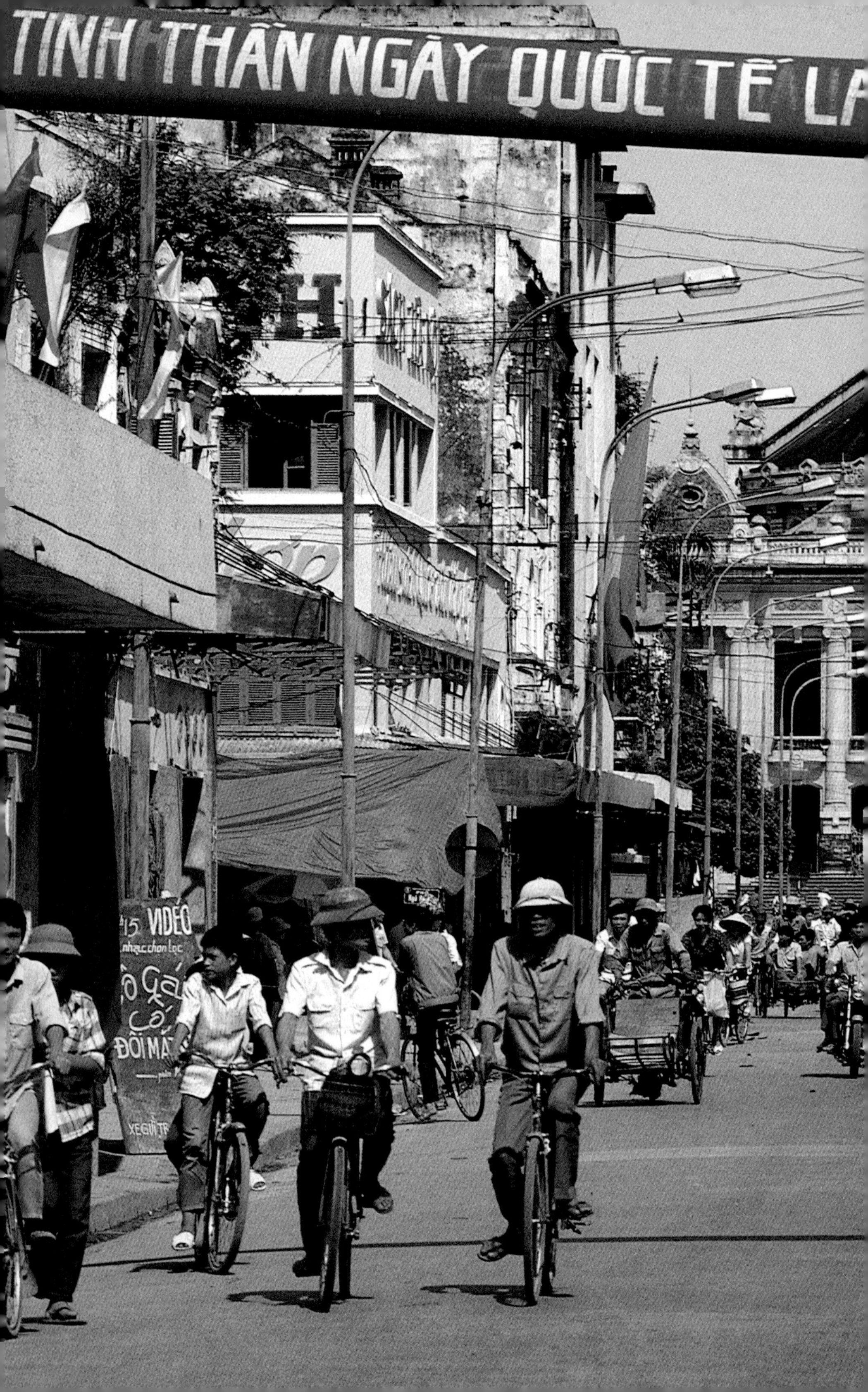
TINH THẦN NGÀY QUỐC TẾ LA
VIDEO

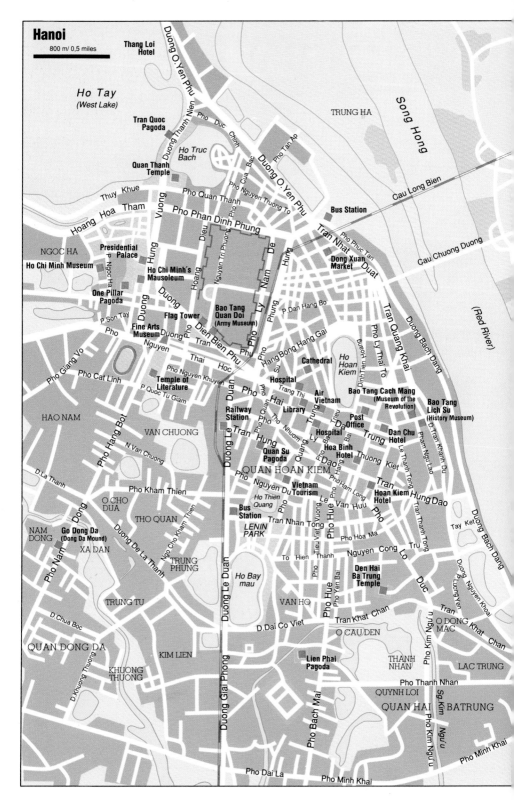

Hanoi

800 m/ 0,5 miles

Ho Tay
(West Lake)

TRUNG HA

Song Hong

Thang Loi Hotel

Tran Quoc Pagoda

Duong Thanh Nien

Pho Duc Chinh

Chua Bac

Pho Tan Ap

Cau Long Bien

Cau Chuong Duong

Ho Truc Bach

Quan Thanh Temple

Thuy Khue

Pho Quan Thanh

Pho Nguyen Truong To

Duong O. Yen Phu

NGOC HA

Hoang Hoa Tham

Dieu

Vuong

Pho Phan Dinh Phung

Nguyen Tri Phuong

De

Hung

Tran Nhat

Pho Phuc Tan

Bus Station

Ho Chi Minh Museum

Presidential Palace

Ngoc Ha

Duong Hoang

Ho Chi Minh's Mausoleum

Duat

Dong Xuan Market

(Red River)

One Pillar Pagoda

P. Son Tay

Flag Tower

Bao Tang Quan Doi *(Army Museum)*

Pho Ly Nam

Phung

P. Dan Hang Bo

Tran Quang Khai

Duong Bach Dang

Fine Arts Museum

Pho Nguyen

Duong

Dien Bien Phu

Tran Phu

Thai

Hoc

Hang Bong Hang Gai

Su

Hang Bao

Pho Ly Thai To

Pho Giang Vo

Pho Cat Linh

Pho Nguyen Khuyen

Temple of Literature

P. Quoc Tu Giam

Cathedral

Ho Hoan Kiem

HAO NAM

Pho Hang Bot

N. Van Chuong

VAN CHUONG

Duong Le

Duan

Hospital

Trang Thi

Tho Nhuom

Air Vietnam

Library

Trung

Trieu

Bao Tang Cach Mang *(Museum of the Revolution)*

Bao Tang Lich Su *(History Museum)*

D.Tran Khanh Du

Pham Ngu Lao

Railway Station

Pho

Pho

Hai

Ba

Ba Trieu

Post Office

Dan Chu Hotel

Le Thanh Tong

D.La Thanh

Pho Kham Thien

O CHO DUA

THO QUAN

Ngo Cho Kham Thien

Tran Hung

Quan Su Pagoda

Ly

Dao

Hospital

Hoa Binh Hotel

Thuong Kiet

Tran

Hung Dao

Tran Thanh Tong

NAM DONG

Go Dong Da *(Dong Da Mound)*

Dong

Duong De La Thanh

QUAN HOAN KIEM

Vietnam Tourism

Pho Ham Long

Hoan Kiem Hotel

Pho Nam

XA DAN

Nguyen Du

Ho Thien Quang

Van Huu

Pho

Tay Kuong

Duong Bach Dang

TRUNG PHUNG

Bus Station

Tran Nhan Tong

LENIN PARK

Le Van

Pho Hoa Ma

Duong Nguyen Khoai

P. Luong Yen

D.Chua Boc

Ho Bay mau

To Hien Thanh

Nguyen Cong Lo

Tru

Duc

Tran

Khat Chan

O DONG MAC

QUAN DONG DA

KIM LIEN

VAN HO

Pho Hue

Den Hai Ba Trung Temple

THANH NHAN

LAC TRUNG

KHUONG THUONG

D.Khuong Thuong

Duong Giai Phong

D.Dai Co Viet

Tran Khat Chan

O CAU DEN

Lien Phai Pagoda

QUYNH LOI

Pho Thanh Nhan

Sg.Kim

Pho Kim Ngu

Ngu'u

QUAN HAI

BATRUNG

Pho Dai La

Pho Bach Mai

Pho Minh Khai

Pho Minh Khai

HANOI

Built on the former site of the ancient city of Dai La, on the right bank of the Song Hong (Red River), **Hanoi**, the historical and political capital of unified Vietnam, was the name Emperor Minh Mang gave to the ancient capital of Thang Long founded in 1010 by King Ly Thai To. According to legend, on his arrival in Dai La the King saw an enormous golden dragon emerge from the lake and soar into the sky above the site of the future capital. On the strength of this he decided to move the capital from Hoa Lu to Dai La which he renamed Thang Long (Ascending Dragon). Hanoi's later less inspired name, Dong Kinh (Capital of the East) became Tunquin after Alexandre de Rhodes Latinized written Vietnamese. The name finally became Tonkin courtesy of the French colonial administration who used it to refer to the entire North of Vietnam during the colonial era.

In Vietnamese, Hanoi is usually written as two words, *Ha* meaning the river, in reference to the Red River and *Noi* meaning this (inner) side.

Hanoi's history dates back to the neolithic era when the ancient Viet people settled in the Bach Hac and Viet Tri regions (present-day Vinh Phu province). They settled at the confluence of the Red and Lo rivers at the summit of the triangular North Vietnamese delta.

In the 3rd century after a bloody decade-long war against the Chinese invaders, King Thuc Phan descended from the 100 Viet Principalities (a region of 100 separate states encompassing all of Southern China south of the Yang Tse Kiang River) and founded the State of **Au Lac**. He installed his capital at **Ke Chu**, the site of the vast spiral citadel of Co Loa (the Old Conch).

After regaining independence, from the middle of the 10th to the beginning of the 11th century Vietnam's more or less brief Ngo, Dinh and Le dynasties installed their capitals at Hoa Lu, 60 miles (100 km) from Hanoi in Ha Nam Ninh province. There it remained, until

King Ly Thai To moved the capital to its present site in the Spring of 1010. He found the surrounding countryside too flat for defense purposes so by royal decree dykes and artificial hills were built. Even today it is still possible to make out the contours of these ancient earth works.

Initially Hanoi was a small lakeside village built on stilts over the To Lich River. The royal capital grew from a small village to a town. The area between the West Lake and the citadel became the civil city (Kinh Thanh) where the mandarins, officers, soldiers and general public lived. In the heart of this was the Royal City (Hoang Thanh) where the royal court resided behind high walls. This enclosed the Forbidden City (Cam Thanh) where the King, Queens and concubines lived protected by a royal guard.

Three of the four city gates are still visible: the South Gate, Dai Hung (Prosperity) near the **Cua Nam Market**; the North Gate, Dieu Duc (Wonderful Virtue) by the West Lake and the East Gate, Tuong Phu (Good Omen) near Sail Street (Hang Buom). Only the West Gate, Quang Phuc (Great Happiness) has not survived.

In 1010, the center of the royal city contained eight palaces and three pavilions. Eight new palaces were built during 1029 and further additions were made in 1203. The Temple of Literature, the One Pillar Pagoda and the Tran Quoc Pagoda were built during that era.

In 1400 the capital was transferred to Thanh Hoa by the usurper Regent Ho Qui Ly who took over from the Tran Dynasty. His capital, **Tay Kinh** (Capital of the West) lasted until the Le Dynasty restored the capital to Hanoi in 1428.

From the 16th century on, few new buildings were constructed in Hanoi. Gia Long built a smaller Vauban style citadel but its walls and gates were torn down during the colonial era and all that remains of it today are traces of the flag tower.

The royal city was destroyed twice in less than 50 years, first in 1786 when King Le Chieu Thong ordered the de-

Preceding pages: 19th-century panorama of Hanoi's European quarter; Hanoi's Opera House on the former Rue Paul Bert (see photo on page 64).

struction of the Trinh Palace, then in 1820 by Gia Long's son, Minh Mang, in his fury at the Chinese Emperor's recognition of Thang Long and not Hue as the capital. In 1848 Tu Duc had most of the remaining palace destroyed and its valuable contents removed to Hue, the 19th century capital of the Nguyen Emperors.

The beginning of the 17th century marked the arrival of Western traders: Dutch, Portuguese, French. Hot on their trail came missionaries from the Company of Jesus followed by the Paris Foreign Missions. The great influx of newcomers and diverse merchandise from Europe brought many changes and new animation to the capital of Thang Long. The French presence and influence grew and eventually changed the course of Vietnamese history.

When Hanoi fell into the hands of the French in 1882 the city underwent considerable transformation and modernization. The face of Hanoi acquired an appearance reflecting a harmony between progress and tradition, although this harmony did not extend to the relations between the Vietnamese and their French overseers. In the wake of new roads and buildings tradition suffered some casualties as it was forced to make way for progress. The Ba Tien Pagoda was knocked down to make way for the Cathedral and the Bao An Pagoda was replaced by the Post Office. Today all that remains of the pagoda is a small shrine beside Hoan Kiem Lake.

The substantial architectural legacy left behind by the French includes the Doumer bridge, the cathedral, Dong Xuan market, the French School d'Extreme Orient, the Louis Finot Museum, Hanoi University, several hotels, many beautiful colonial villas and an opera house.

Unfortunately the combined effects of war, climate, lack of finance and materials have taken their toll on the state of Hanoi's historical buildings. Apart from the colonial buildings used by the government or foreign missions, most of these are in a very sorry state.

Today, with a population of about 3,057,000, Hanoi extends over 825 square miles (2,139 square km). The city center comprises four districts: Hoan Kiem (the Restored Sword), Hai Ba Trung (the Two Trung sisters), Dong Da (where King Quang Trung defeated the Manchu invasion in 1789) and Ba Dinh. It also incorporates eleven recently integrated suburban districts (quan): Thanh Tri, Tu Liem, Dong Anh, Gia Lam, Ba Vich, Thach That, Phuc Tho, Hoai Duc; Dan Phuong, Me Linh and Soc Son. The city suffers from a severe housing shortage.

The city center has evolved little since 1955, leaving Hanoi's original character very much intact, preserved in its traditional pagodas and temples, colonial architecture, tree-lined streets, lakes, and the ancient heart of the old town center. The soul of the old Thang Long city rests in the ancient town center which dates from the 15th century when it was known as the city of 36 streets and guilds. Here streets bear the names of the trades and commodities plied in them for generations. The main artery and tramway of the old town, Hung Dao (Silk Street), extends up to the **Dong Xuan Market** from where many small streets branch off, in the east towards the ancient dykes and the Red River and in the west towards the old citadel of Co Loa.

West of Hanoi relatively high hills extend up to the 4,060 foot (1,237 meter) summit of **Mount Ba**, 40 miles (65 km) from the city. In the north a much higher range of hills and mountains leads to the mountainous regions of **Viet Bac**. The city is bordered by the West Lake (Ho Tay) in the northwest.

Hanoi is accessible from the north by three bridges: Long Bien, (formerly Doumer Bridge), the more recent Chuong Duong Bridge nearby, and the Thang Long bridge.

The 5,520 feet (1,682 meter) **Doumer Bridge** was built by the French and inaugurated in February 1902 by Governor General Doumer. It suffered some damage from American bombing but was continually repaired and until 1983, all northbound road and rail traffic passed over it. These days it is reserved for cyclists, pedestrians and trains.

Discovering Hanoi: We begin in the

north of the capital at the **West Lake** (Ho Tay), formerly known as the Lake of Mists. This 1440½ acre (583 hectare) lake, the largest in Hanoi, lies in an ancient bed of the Red River. Royal and warlord palaces once graced its banks but these were destroyed during the feudal battles.

During an uprising against the occupying Chinese in 545, the national hero Ly Bon built a wooden and bamboo citadel at the mouth of the **To Lich River** and at the same time built the **Khai Quoc** (Foundation of the Country) **Pagoda** beside the Red River. In the 17th century the pagoda was transferred to its present site on the tiny peninsula of the West Lake and renamed **Tran Quoc Pagoda** (Defense of the Country). The Tran Quoc is one Vietnam's most ancient pagodas, its stele, dating from 1639, recounts the pagoda's long history.

According to legend the lake was previously the site of a huge wood, the lair of a wicked fox with nine tails. The creature terrorized the neighbourhood until it was drowned by the Dragon King, who in the process of unleashing the waters to get rid of the beast created the lake. Hardly less fantastic is another legend which tells the story of an 11th century bonze, and a golden buffalo. The bonze, Khong Lo, had an enormous bronze bell made. When its sound first reached the ears of the golden buffalo, the confused creature, believing he heard his mother's voice, rushed immediately towards the south and in his stampede transformed the site into a lake. Take your pick!

Separated from the West Lake by Thanh Nien Street is **Lake Truc Bach** (White Silk). This was the ancient site of Lord Trinh's Summer palace which later became a harem where he detained his cast off and wayward concubines. The lake derives its name from the beautiful white silk these concubines were forced to weave for the princesses.

The ornate **Quan Thanh Pagoda** beside the lake was originally built during the Ly dynasty (1010-1225). It houses a huge bronze bell and an enormous four ton bronze statue of Tran Vu,

Left, Ho Chi Minh's mausoleum and **below**, pottery works by Long Bien (Doumer) Bridge.

guardian Genie of the north, to whom the temple is dedicated. It was Tran Vu who helped King An Duong dispose of the devils and ghosts which plagued the building of Vietnam's ancient capital at Co Loa.

Not far from here looms the imposing grey stone bulk of **Ho Chi Minh's Mausoleum** in Ba Dinh Square. His embalmed corpse lies in a glass casket within this monumental tomb (contrary to his wish to be cremated). The place is usually closed for two months while his body is packed off to Russia for an overhaul. Rumour has it that despite this yearly checkup the corpse is decomposing. The construction on the mausoleum began in September 1973 and finished in August 1975. Ho Chi Minh's embalmed body lies on top of a platform in a cold room within.

The strictly guarded mausoleum, inaugurated on September 2, 1975, is built of marble, granite and precious wood gathered from all over the country. It was from this square that Ho Chi Minh read his declaration of independence speech on September 2, 1945.

Around the corner from the mausoleum is the unique **One Pillar Pagoda** (**Chua Mot Cot**). Built in 1049 under the Ly dynasty, this beautiful wooden pagoda rests on a single stone pillar rising out of a lotus pool. The banyan tree behind the pagoda was planted by President Nehru in 1958 during an official visit to the young Vietnamese Republic.

Legend has it that in a dream King Ly Thai To saw the goddess Quan Am seated on a lotus leaf offering him a male child in her outstretched arms. Shortly after his dream he married a young peasant girl who bore him the male heir he had dreamed of. The King is said to have built the pagoda as a sign of his gratitude. The small **Dien Huu Pagoda** shares this lovely setting. Unfortunately this tranquil traditional scene is overshadowed by the recent Ho Chi Minh Museum.

Behind the **Army Museum** (Bao Tang Quan Doi) on Dien Bien Phu Street is one of the symbols of Hanoi, the flag

Classy colonial: the former governor's residence in Hanoi.

HOW MANY STREETS IN HANOI?

Hanoi was, and still is, locally referred to as the city of **Ba Muoi Sau Pho Phuong**,36 streets and districts. In fact there are more – some 160 of them – so the question arises: why the number 36?

The discrepancy arises from two sources. First of all, the words: *Pho*, which refers to commercial streets and *Phuong*, meaning districts, which refers to both professional guilds and administrative districts, helped to cause the initial confusion.

This was later compounded by two folk poems popular throughout the country in the late 19th century. These both praised the beauty of Thang Long, (Ascending Dragon) Hanoi's ancient name, referring to it as the city of Ba Muoi Sau Pho Phuong, 36 streets and districts, although at the time Hanoi already had 60 commercial streets, 60 professional guilds and 40 administrative districts.

However this misrepresentation was not simply a casual error. Many people believed that 36, the exact number of streets in Hanoi from the 15th to 18th centuries, was a lucky number and nobody among the superstitious Vietnamese, particularly the poets, who further propagated the discrepancy, wanted to change it.

Today, walking through the streets in this ancient heart of the old city, you will find they still bear the names of the trades and commodities plied in them many generations ago and in some the tradition carries on to this day: Cotton, Sail, Rice, Sugar, Vermicelli (*Hang Bun*), Jute (*Hang Gai*), Fish products, Jewellers (*Hang Bac*), Mat, Votive Paper (*Hang Ma*), Traditional Medicine, and Grilled Fish (*Cha Ca*) Streets, but a few of the 36.

Thus the name, Ba Muoi Sau Pho Phuong, like the names of the old streets recalling the professional guilds, national heroes and heroines, historic places and political leaders, remains unchanged to this day.

Crammed tram on Silk Street.

tower, **Cot Co**. Built in 1812 under the Nguyen Dynasty as part of the Hanoi citadel, the hexagonal 197 foot (60 meter) tower is more or less all that remains of the citadel that was destroyed at the end of the 19th century.

The **Fine Arts Museum**, (Bao Tang My Thuat) a short walk away at 66 Nguyen Thai Hoc Street features an expensive collection of artefacts. Exhibits cover some of Vietnam's ethnic minorities and prehistory, beautiful wooden statues of Buddha dating from the 17th century, the Dong Son bronze drums and examples of Vietnamese art, both ancient and contemporary. Closed on Mondays, opening hours are from 7.30-11.30 a.m. and 1-4.30p.m.

Just next door is the **Temple of Literature** (Van Mieu). Built in 1070 under the reign of King Ly Thai Tong of the Ly dynasty, the temple is dedicated to the cult of Confucius. In 1076 the temple was adjoined by the **School of the Elite of the Nation** (Quoc Tu Giam), Vietnam's first national university. Under the Tran dynasty the school was renamed the **National College** (Quoc Hoc Vien) in 1235. The Van Mieu became known as the Temple of Literature when the capital was transferred to Hue at the beginning of the 18th century.

Above the main entrance gate is an inscription requesting visitors to dismount from there horses before entering the gate.

The large temple enclosure is divided into five walled courtyards. After passing through the Van Mieu Gate and the first two courtyards one arrives at the Khue Van Cac (Pleiade Pavilion) where the men of letters used to recite their poems. Through the Dai Thanh Mon (Great Wall Gate) an open courtyard surrounds a large central pool known as the Thien Quang Tinh (Heavenly Light Well). Here under the trees on either side, 82 stone stelae, survivors of the original 117, rest on the backs of stone tortoises. The stelae are inscribed with the names, works and academic records of the laureates who succeeded in the three year doctorate courses between 1442 and 1779.

The Dai Thanh (Great Success Gate)

Spices for sale in the old city.

leads to the temple itself. Facing it is the Bai Duong (House of Ceremonies) where sacrifices were offered in honour of Confucius. Behind it are the Eastern gate and the Great Success Sanctuary. The last part of the temple, the **Khai Thanh Sanctuary**, on Nguyen Thai Hoc Street, is in ruins.

Behind **Thu Le Park** in Thu Le village in the northwest of the city is the 11th century **Temple of the Kneeling Elephants** (Voi Phuc). It was built by King Ly Thai To in honour of his son, Prince Linh Lang, who distinguished himself during the resistance against the Sung invaders by charging the enemy with his squadron of elephants. The simple lakeside temple houses statues of the Prince and his generals. In front of the temple are stone statues of kneeling elephants from which the temple derives its name.

In the very heart of the old town of Hanoi lies the **Lake of the Restored Sword** or **The Little Lake** (Ho Hoan Kiem). If you are up early enough, around 6 a.m., you'll catch the locals

seriously engrossed in their morning exercises, particularly *Tai Chi Kuan*, before going off to work.

A legend, with innumerable variations, sounding like a Vietnamese version of *Excalibar*, tells of how King Le Thai To received a magic sword which he used during his 10 year resistance against the Ming domination (1418-1428). After liberating the country the king took a boat to the center of the lake to return the magic sword given to him by the Divine Tortoise. The tortoise is said to have snatched the sword from his hand and disappeared into the lake. Thus the lake acquired its name. Near the middle of the lake stands the small 18th century tower, Thap Rua, **Tortoise Tower**.

Perched on a tiny islet (Jade Island) in the lake not far from the tower, is the Ngoc Son Temple (**Temple of the Jade Mound**). The national hero Tran Hung Dao and three saints: Van Xuong – a man who dedicated himself to the development of literature, Quan Vu – a martial arts expert and La To, a physi-cian. The temple is reached from the shore via the brightly painted, red arched bridge, known as the **Sunbeam Bridge** (The Huc). On the small hillock at the end of the bridge stands a stone column in the form of a brush next to an inkstand inscribed with three Chinese characters, *"Ta Tien Qing"*, meaning "written on the blue sky". Also on the islet are the remains of a small communal house known as Tran Ba Dinh.

From Lake Hoan Kiem many streets lead to Hanoi's ancient quarter and the oldest church in the city, **Hanoi Cathedral** (Nha Tho Lon), which was consecrated on Christmas night 1886. It was built on the site of the **Bao Thien Pagoda** which had to make way for its Christian counterpart. Two other churches open in Hanoi can be found in Bac Son Street behind the citadel and near the evening market **Cho Hom** at the corner of Ngo Quyen and Le Van Huu streets.

A narrow passage way off the street facing the cathedral leads to the **Ba Da Pagoda**. This charming pagoda was built

The Army Museum on Dien Bien Phu Road.

in the 15th century after the discovery of a stone statue of a woman during the construction of the Thang Long citadel. The statue, which was thought to have magic powers, disappeared and has since been replaced by a wooden replica. The pagoda's modest exterior belies its exquisite interior and atmosphere. An impressive lineup of gilt Buddha statues forms the central alter. Worth visiting.

At 42 Ly Trieu Quoc Su Street, to the right of the cathedral is the small **Ly Quoc Su Pagoda**, also known as Chua Kong, the Pagoda of Confucius. It was founded under the Ly dynasty in the 11th century and later restored in 1855. The pagoda contains some attractive wooden statues and an old bonze who is said to have lived there for over 60 years without ever leaving the building.

The **Bach Ma Temple** (White Horse Temple) on Hang Buom Street is dedicated to the genie Bach Ma. Originally built during the 9th century, it was reconstructed in the 18th and 19th centuries. Although no longer in use it remains in a good state of repair.

Part of Hanoi's charm lies in the pagodas, temples and *dinhs* (community houses) that you may discover quite by chance. Some are still used for worship although others have been transformed into schools or meeting places. The **Hoa Loc Dinh** at number 90 Hang Dao Street was once a communal house for people from the village of Hai Duong. According to records discovered on a stele, these villagers settled here towards the end of the Tang dynasty era and founded the artisanal district of Thai Cuc which became Hang Dao (Silk) Street. Also in the same street is the **Phu My Dinh**. Nearby in Hang Tien Street is the **Nhi Khe Dinh** and at 133 Hue Street, the **Dong Ha Dinh**.

Another old pagoda is the 12th century **Chieu Thien Pagoda** or **Lang Pagoda**, near Giang Vo Road. It is dedicated to King Ly Than Ton and was reconstructed in the 17th century.

Near Nam Dong Street is the sacred **Dong Da Mound** (Mound of the Multitudes). According to legend it was formed by the bodies of Chinese sol-

Below, lakeside trim and right, Soviet newlyweds pose with Lenin.

diers killed after Quang Trung's victory. Very little remains of the temple that was constructed on the site.

The area around the **Dong Xuan Market** at the end of Silk Street is an interesting place to explore. The state market displays a rather limited array of fixed priced goods, often very dated, but behind it is the spice market and the market selling plants, fish, birds and animals.

The private covered market sells a variety of goods such as baskets, wickerwork, small carpets, soup, vermicelli and rice. In the streets behind the market farmers squat on the pavement selling their produce directly to passersby. Keep an eye out for caviar, French wine, champagne and Russian vodka as they are surprisingly cheap in Hanoi, and the genuine article no less.

In front of Dong Xuan Market florists add a welcome splash of color with their fragrant blooms. Nearby a traditional medicine shop sells all manner of dubious and otherwise cures, including snake wine and lizards preserved in alcohol. Do not be put off by appearances, the Gecko Elixir is excellent.

Southwest of Hoan Kiem Lake the Quan Su or **Ambassadors' Pagoda** is located at 73 Quan Su Street. In the 17th century the site was shared by a house used to accommodate visiting foreign ambassadors and envoys from other Buddhist countries. The pagoda was reconstructed in 1936 and again in 1942. Visiting hours are between 7.30-11.30 a.m. and 1.30-5.30 p.m.

Behind the Municipal Theater at 1 Pham Ngu Lao, the **History Museum**, (Bao Tang Lich Su) formerly the Louis Finot Museum, occupies the old archaeological and history research institution of *L'Ecole Francaise D'Extreme Orient*. The museum opened in 1910, was rebuilt in 1926 and reopened in 1932. Exhibits displayed here cover every era of Vietnam's fascinating and complex history. It houses an excellent archaeological collection dating from the Paleolithic and Neolithic eras including, relics from the era of the Hung Kings, neolithic graves, bronze age im-

Constables make curbside comparisons.

168

plements, the beautiful bronze drums of Ngoc Lu and Mieu Mon, Cham relics, stelae, statues, ceramics and an eerie sculpture of the goddess Quan Am with her one thousand eyes and arms. One room features an ornate throne, clothes and artefacts belonging to the thirteen kings of the Nguyen Dynasty. Open from 8.30-11.45 a.m. and 1-3.45 p.m., closed Mondays.

Near the History Museum, the **Revolutionary Museum** at 25 Tong Dan Street, documents the struggles of the Vietnamese people from the era before Christ up until 1975. Among the exhibits are some of the long wooden stakes used to cripple the Mongol fleet during the battle of Bach Dang in Halong Bay and an enormous bronze war drum dating from 2,400 B.C.

In the south of the city on Pho To Lao is the **The Temple of the Two Sisters** (Den Hai Ba Trung), also known as the Dong Nhan temple after the village that surrounded the site at the time of its construction in 1142. The temple is dedicated to the two Trung sisters who

organized an uprising against the Chinese Han invaders in 40 A.D. – the first uprising against foreign invaders in Vietnamese history.

The temple has since been restored and contains some of the sisters' belongings. Two unusually formed stone statues said to represent the two sisters kneeling are kept in a small room and brought out once a year during February for a procession which evokes their battle against the Chinese. Outside the central court are several small temples dedicated to the first buddhists who constructed the temple.

A little further south on Bach Mai Street, the **Lien Phai Pagoda** and the Buddhist monastery, Lien Phai Tu or Lieu Khai, shelters in an attractive garden. The temple was built under the Le Dynasty and reconstructed by one of the Trinh Lords in 1732. The temple was restored in 1884 and again more recently. Three statues, two representing good and evil, occupy the pagoda's main room.

Further west on Tran Nhan Tong

Sharing duck tales at a Hanoi market.

Street lies **Lenin Park**, formerly known as Thong Nhat Park. It is said to have been built by local voluntary workers on marshy land used as a rubbish tip. This attractive park is designed around a large central lake. In it, rather incongruously, stands a statue of Lenin. This statue is the brunt of an oft-quoted piece of popular local humor:

Mr. Lenin, you are from Russia

Why are you standing here in this garden

With your right hand on your front pocket

And your left hand on your back pocket?

In the Dong Anh district of Hanoi's western suburbs lie the remains of the citadel fortress of **Co Loa**. Recent excavations in the area have uncovered quantities of ancient arms and many bronze arrowheads. Co Loa dates from the year 257 B.C. when it served as the capital of the Thuc Dynasty under King An Duong. Of the nine ramparts which covered an area of more than 2 square miles (5 square km), remnants of three

are still visible. Some architectural and sculptural works remain in the center of the citadel. Within the citadel's gateway an historical banyan tree shades the shrine dedicated to Princess My Chau. Inside is a rough stone statue of a headless woman thought to be the princess. Further on is the upper temple dedicated to King An Duong which is thought to have been built on the site of an ancient palace. People gather here on January 6 every year to celebrate the festival commemorating King An Duong Vuong's efforts against the foreign invaders.

The Vietnamese, with their irrepressible talent for blending history and legend, will tell you that King An Duong of Tay Au invaded Lac Viet after his request to marry the King of Vietnam's daughter was unceremoniously refused. He managed to annex the country of his coveted princess without too much difficulty and amalgamated the territories of Tay Au and Lac Viet to form the kingdom of Au Lac. Well aware that this expansion would antagonize his great northern neighbor, China, King An Duong wasted no time in building the walls of his new capital. But for some mysterious reason his efforts were frustrated and the walls repeatedly collapsed. The mystery was finally revealed when the golden tortoise, *Kim Quy,* appeared to the king in a dream and disclosed that occult forces were responsible. Aided by the tortoise the king was able to defeat the evil forces and complete his indestructable fortress. China, however, wanted the fortress destroyed and a certain General Trieu Da was picked for the task. However, the repeated attempts of his powerful forces proved futile. The Golden Tortoise again appeared to King An Duong and this time provided him with a magic crossbow. The following day the Chinese forces suffered heavy losses from the arrows of the crossbow. Seeing this, General Trieu Da realized that all was not as it appeared and called for peace. He asked for and was granted the hand of King An Duong's daughter, the Princess My Chau, for his son, Trong Thuy. During the honeymoon, Trong Thuy asked his young wife to show him her

A popular streetside stall.

father's crossbow. The unsuspecting My Chau obediently did so, but Trong Thuy took the magic crossbow and substituted another in its place. The king was so furious when he discovered this that he beheaded the princess. Her inconsolable husband is said to have drowned himself in the well in front of the temple dedicated to King An Duong.

Although this tale is surely no more than a legend, archaeological discoveries made at the site reveal that a protracted struggle did take place here during that time in history.

Co Loa was not only Vietnam's very first capital but also something of an architectural marvel. Three earth walls, 13 to 16 feet (4 to 5 meters) high, and at certain strategic points, 26 to 39 feet (8 to 12 meters) high, enclosed the capital. The 5 mile (8 km) outer wall was reinforced with thorny bamboo hedges and surrounded by a deep moat which allowed troops and boats to circulate.

Watchmen scrutinized the horizon from watchtowers built at the eight cardinal points of the citadel's ramparts.

They continued their vigil throughout the night, kept permanently awake by gongs which resounded every half hour until dawn. A marine conch shell was used to sound the alert. Due to the citadel's spiral form any sound from within it was rapidly amplified and carried not only all around the city but also to the surrounding villages.

The **Tay Dang Communal House** in Hanoi's Bay Vi suburb is worth visiting for its beautiful architectural structure and carving. It is not known exactly when it was built but inscriptions on one of its beams reveal that it was extensively restored in the 16th century and further repairs were again carried out in 1808, 1926 and 1942. Built entirely of hardwood, it comprises five partitions and four roofs whose curling tops are decorated with the *tu linh* – dragons, unicorns, tortoises and the phoenix – the four animals which according to folklore bring happiness. Many valuable woodcarvings grace the interior. Bas reliefs depict detailed scenes from everyday life in this beautiful old wooden building.

Magazine vendor at the railway station and right, specialist shop.

EAST OF HANOI

Heading east from Hanoi will eventually bring you to fine white sand beaches washed by the China Sea, a sea which remains a constant source of contention between Vietnam and China but in the end is lost in the waters of the Pacific Ocean.

Before reaching the coast the road passes through the relatively flat province of **Hai Hung**, famous for its beautiful orchards whose fruit, particularly longan and lychee, reputedly the best in the northern delta, supplied the royal court in days gone-by.

The **Kiep Bac Temple**, 37 miles (60 km) from Hanoi in Hung Dao commune dates from the 13th century. It is dedicated to the national hero Tran Hung Dao who vanquished the Mongols in the 13th century and was made a saint by the people. During the 13th century his army encamped here in the Kiep Bac valley. His statue, plus those of his two daughters, General Pham Ngu Lao and the Genies of the Northern Star and Southern Cross, are venerated in this temple. The temple festival falls on the 20th day of the eighth lunar month. This very beautiful site is shared by an old garden of medicinal plants formerly used in the army's medical service.

Con Son, 6 miles (10 km) further on is the home of another national hero, Nguyen Trai (1380-1442). He helped King Le Loi chase out the Ming invaders and free the country from Chinese domination at the beginning of the 15th century. At the foot of the hill, the well-maintained **Hung Pagoda** contains statues of Nguyen Trai, his maternal grandfather and the three superior bonzes who founded the *Truc Lam* Buddhist sect. Some 600 stone steps lead up to the summit, where there is a superb view of the mountain ranges.

The porcelain factory in the provincial capital, Hai Duong, is the largest of its kind in North Vietnam.

Further east is **Thai Binh Province** which has the highest population den-

Preceding pages: Boats by Halong Bay. **Below**, collecting salt.

sity in the country – 3,318 people per square mile (1,106 per square km). Salt fields cover extensive areas on the coastal shores. In addition to rice, jute, rushes, mulberry, sugar cane and ground nut are cultivated here. Among the crafts found in Thai Binh, rush and jute carpet making, silk weaving, wickerwork and embroidery are the most common.

The **11th century Keo Pagoda**, located some 4 miles (10 km) from Thai Binh township in Vu Thu district, is considered one of the finest examples of traditional Vietnamese architecture in the northern delta. It is dedicated to Buddha, his disciples and the bonze superior. No metal nails were used in the construction of this impressive wooden pagoda with its three-storey bell tower. Today, only 107 of its original 154 rooms remain.

Many traditional rituals and diverse forms of traditional entertainment are performed here, particularly during the period of Tet.

Dong Chau Beach in Tien Hai district is an ideal spot for a swim and if you wish to stay overnight quite a number of small hotels provide adequate accommodation.

The town of Thai Binh was badly damaged during the war and doesn't have a great deal going for it except a small wool carpet factory and the museum which contains some prehistoric exhibits. The road from here passes through many fishing villages and ever-present paddy fields before reaching **Haiphong**, Vietnam's second most important port and third largest city.

Haiphong occupies the right bank of the busy **Cam River** 75 miles (120 km) from Hanoi in the northeast of the Bac Bo delta. The city, built in 1888, is crossed by 16 rivers, the most famous of these is the Bach Dang River where in 938 the national hero, Ngo Quyen defeated the large southern Han fleet. The Sung invaders suffered a bitter defeat here in 981 and the Mongols suffered the same fate in 1288.

Haiphong Port, 8 miles (20 km) inland from the eastern sea, constitutes an important gateway for Vietnam's for-

Paddy field fishing.

eign trade.

The first of the French warships arrived in Haiphong in 1872 and the last units of the French expeditionary forces left the same way in May 1955.

Today, many industrial plants, engineering factories, glass, brick and cement works, and lime kilns are evident from the main road into Haiphong. The city's industrial area sprung up after the French left and more recently local industry has grown to meet the demands of the construction and rebuilding underway in the area.

Haiphong was very badly damaged by bombing during the war, but thousands of new residences have been built and today the city is thriving.

More a busy port than a tourist attraction, a brief stop is long enough to take in the sights. The architecture surrounding the market, city center and the river betrays the former colonial presence. The fish market is worth a visit early in the morning when the fishermen are arriving with their catches as they land some rather unusual sea prod-

ucts.

In the shops opposite the Dien Bien Phu Street Theater Square a variety of handicrafts including mats, brass and cast iron figures, tortoise-shell, horn, lacquer and mother of pearl inlay articles, can be bought at very reasonable prices.

Like every city in Vietnam Haiphong has its temples. The **Du Hang Pagoda** in the south of the city at 121 Hang Kenh Street was built three centuries ago. The **Nghe Temple**, built in 1919, in the city center at 51 Ngo Nghe Street is dedicated to Le Chan, the valiant woman warrior who aided the Trung sisters in the uprising against the Chinese in 39 A.D. The **Hang Kenh Pavilion**, located at 53 Nguyen Cong Tru, houses a surprising 500 wooden sculptures representing the themes of everyday life.

The **Cung Chuc Communal House** in Cung Chuc village, Vinh Bao district, is worth visiting for its unique architecture, and clay statuettes. The traditional entertainment staged here during local and traditional festivals includes **Downtown Haiphong.**

water puppetry, water buffalo fights and firecracker contests.

The **Cat Ba Archipelago**, 50 miles (80 km) from the coast can be reached by boat from Haiphong. Its 366 islets and islands cover a total area of 50,000 acres (20,000 hectares). The area is known for its beautiful beaches and interesting grottoes. The largest island, Cat Ba, occupies 73 square miles (188 square km). Its beautiful landscape features forested hills, coastal mangrove and freshwater swamps, lakes and waterfalls. Some 42,000 acres (17,000 hectares) of the island is covered in forest, 3,500 acres of this is primeval forest. Some 1,400 acres (570 hectares) have been reserved as a National Park.

The Park's rich diversity of flora and fauna includes 21 species of birds–among these the hornbill–reptiles, and 28 species of mammals including wild cats, wild boar, porcupines, monkeys, deer and gibbons.

Human remains and stone tools from the neolithic era have been discovered in some of the caves on the island.

Submerged vegetation, hot springs and limestone lakes add to the diverse attractions here.

Boats from Haiphong also leave for **Cat Hai Island** and the **Do Son Peninsula** 12 miles (20 km) east of the city where palm-fringed sandy beaches set against pine forested hills stretch far out into the clear blue waters of the Tonkin Gulf. In the past Do Son was exclusively reserved for the French and privileged Vietnamese holding high positions in the colonial administration. Today, Do Son is a popular weekend spot with the locals and a more picturesque and recreational alternative to the busy port of Haiphong.

Other possibilities here are visits to the **Nguyen Binh Khiem Temple**, the museum, the ancient **Hang Kenh communal house**, a carpet weaving workshop and the small **Den Ba De** on Doc Mountain.

The **Elephant Mount**, 6 miles (10 km) from Haiphong warrants a visit. Here you can visit the **Long Hoa Pagoda** and vestiges of a citadel fortress

Hon Gai, a coal mining center in Halong Bay.

dating from the Mac era of the 16th century. Halfway up the mountain, the Chi Lai Communal House has been converted into a museum where Neolithic bronze artefacts are displayed.

Caves within the mountain served as guerilla base camps during the resistance war against the French.

From Haiphong you can also visit the **Bao Ha woodcarving village**. The village has earned a reputation for its high quality wood carving since it was founded by the master craftsman Nguyen Cong Hue in the late 17th century. After his death his students carved his likeness and built a temple in his honor. One of his most famous statues can be seen in the **Ba Xa Temple** at Bao Ha. Most of the work produced by the village craftsmen is of a religious nature, however they also turn out a variety of carved animals. The fragrant jackwood is the wood most preferred by the craftsmen who value its beauty, lightness, and softness.

Quang Ninh Province and Halong Bay: No trip to North Vietnam could be con-

sidered complete without a trip to **Quang Ninh Province**. This province shares a common border with China in the north, and harbors one of the wonders of the world (according to the Vietnamese), probably the most stunning scenery in Vietnam, **Halong Bay**. The bay's tranquil beauty encompasses 1,500 square miles (3880 square km) dotted with well over 1000 limestone islands and islets, many of them named. Bizarre rock sculptures jutting dramatically from the sea and numerous grottoes have created an enchanted, timeless world. The sails of the junks and sampans gliding on the bay add further to the timeless beauty of the scene.

A boat trip on the bay includes stops at some of the grottoes – the *Bo Nau* **(Pelican) Cave**, the 1.2 mile long **Hang Hanh Tunnel** and the **Trinh Nu (Virgin) Cave**.

Folklore claims that the Virgin Cave was named after a young girl whose parents were poor fishing folk. They could not afford to own a boat of their own and had to rent one from a rich man.

Waiting for their boat to come in.

178

When they could not pay what they owed him, the rich man demanded their beautiful daughter in lieu of their debt and forced her to marry him. The poor girl refused all his advances and he had her beaten, but still she would not submit to him so he had her removed from the house to a grotto where she starved to death. Her body was found by fishermen who buried her. She was immortalized in stone by a rock that emerged from her burial site in her form.

The most spectacular of all the bay's grottoes is the beautiful **Dau Go Cave** with its stalactites and stalagmites resembling beasts, birds and human forms. It was christened the *Grotte des Merveilles* (Wonder Grotto) by the first French tourists who visited it in the late 19th century.

Halong Bay has been the setting of many historic battles against invasions from the north in the past. It is believed that the sharp bamboo stakes General Tran Hung Dao planted in the Bach Dang River to destroy Kublai Khan's fleet were stored here in these caves.

The name *Ha Long* means the Landing Dragon, evoking some ancient dragon which in the mists of time is said to have descended in the bay.

In such a place it comes as no surprise to hear that certain individuals claim to have seen the Vietnamese equivalent of the Loch Ness monster, a black creature resembling a snake about (feet) 30 meters long which is supposed to inhabit the bay. More plausible are the other inhabitants of the bay: lobsters, crabs, abalones, prawns and cuttlefish which provide a wide variety of excellent sea food all year round.

Within view of Halong Bay is the beautiful site of **Mount Yen Tu**. Minorities such as the San Chi, Dao, Tay, San Chi, Hoa and Tay live in the vicinity.

Perched on the summit of this mist-shrouded mount is the 13th century pagoda built by King Tran Nhan Tong. After vanquishing the Mongols, the King abdicated in favour of his son, Tran Anh Tong and retired to a retreat at Mount Yen Tu where he founded the Thien Tong Sect (Vietnamese Zen) of Truc Lam Dhyana (the bamboo forest), a unique form of Buddhism.

Forty-five stupas containing the bones of bonzes lie scattered amidst shady pine forest on the mountainside along the rather tortuous route up to the pagoda. The climb to the summit is well worth the effort on a clear day for the fine view over Halong Bay.

Another excellent view of the bay can be had from the coal mining town of **Hong Gai**. The high quality anthracite coal from Quang Ninh's mines makes up about 90 percent of Vietnam's reserves. In colonial times under the French, thousands of men from the surrounding countryside were brought in to work the mines. The intolerable working conditions they were forced to endure sparked off an uprising against their French overseers.

The island of **Tra Binh** off Vietnam's northernmost coast harbours the beautiful beach resort of **Tra Co**. It is possible to stay overnight in one of the many beach houses available for rent. A 15th century temple on the island features some interesting wooden carvings.

Halong Bay is positively picturesque.

WEST OF HANOI

Leaving Hanoi and traveling westwards the plateaus and mountains once inhabited by the Lac Viet people of the prehistoric era, the road enters **Ha Son Binh Province**. Many relics from the Hoa Binh Culture of the ancient Lac Viet people have been discovered in the province. A number of ethnic groups, including Muong, Hmong, Thai, Tay and Zao, make up the local population. The province's diverse landscape comprises plain, midland and rugged mountainous regions. **My Duc** district, 40 miles (65 km) southwest of Hanoi, harbors one of the country's most beautiful landscapes, **Huong Son**, The Mountain of Perfumes. Pagodas, shrines, sanctuaries and grottoes nestle in Huong Son's limestone relief surrounded by tropical forest, their architecture harmonising perfectly with nature. The trip to Huong Son can be made either by road or by boat. If you have the time, the leisurely boat trip is the way to go. The boat follows the meanderings of the **Yen Vi River** through an idyllic rural setting of rocky limestone mountains and tranquil paddy fields before arriving at the landing near the **Thien Tru Pagoda** (The Pagoda Which Leads to Heaven). From here, a steep mountain path runs for 1½ miles (2 km) past many pagodas and grottoes such as the Tien Son and Hinh Bong, and the **Giai Oan Chua**, (The Pagoda of Purgatory) where souls are reputedly purified and sorrows healed, Anyone who makes it this far aims for the highest point, the **Huong Tich Grotto** (Traces of Perfume Grotto), regarded by many as the most beautiful spot in all Vietnam. Huong Son's main pagoda, the **Pagoda of Perfumes** (Chua Huong Thich) is found in this immense grotto which can be explored by boat. Ornate characters above the entrance proclaim it "The first grotto under the Southern sky". The pagoda, dedicated to the goddess of mercy, was classified the most important in all the kingdom by Lord Trinh Sam (1767-1782). According to tradition, it was at Huong Son that the Hindu bodhisattva, *Avalokitecvara*, transformed himself into female form and became *Quan Am*, the Goddess of Mercy, to whom this sanctuary is dedicated. Legend has it that this grotto was discovered more than 2,000 years ago, but work on the pagoda began only in 1575. An inscription on a stone stele reveals that the main statue within the pagoda, that of Quan Am (Kuan Yin), was first cast in bronze in 1767, then during the Tay Son uprising, Tay Son troops removed the statue and melted it down to make cannon balls. In 1793 the bronze statue was replaced with one of stone.

It is not difficult to understand why this beautiful setting remains an important Buddhist center, drawing thousands of Buddhist followers from all over North Vietnam on their annual pilgrimage to the pagoda every Spring.

About 25 miles (40 km) from Hanoi, in **Sai Son Village**, the **Chua Thay** (Pagoda of the Master) nestles against the Sai Son hillside. Built in 1132 by

Preceding pages: curious gaze of a White Thai woman. Below, boats for pilgrims to Huong Son.

King Ly Thai To, the pagoda is dedicated three ways: to the venerable bonze Dao Hanh (the Master) of the Ly dynasty; to King Ly Than Tong - king of the Ly dynasty from 1127 to 1138; and the cult of Sakyamuni Buddha and his 18 disciples (*arhat*).

Dao Hanh was a great herbalist who had been a medical man in his native village before entering the pagoda. He was also very fond of the choreographic arts, particularly the traditional water puppet theater. This he taught in the artificial lake in front of the pagoda which is still used today as the setting for water puppetry. The two arched covered bridges spanning the lake date from 1602. The pagoda's official name is **Thien Phuc** (Heavenly Bliss). Within the pagoda is a large, white sandalwood statue of Dao Hanh which can be moved like a puppet using cleverly intertwined strings. Wooden statues of Buddha and various guardians are also housed in the temple's enclosures. A climb up the hillside will bring you to another two small shrines and a superb view of the picturesque setting of the pagoda, the lake, the village and surrounding countryside. This idyllic setting is an excellent spot for a picnic. Several limestone grottoes are worth exploring in the vicinity, notably the one known as **Hang Cac Co** (The Mischievous).

Nearby, in the picturesque village of **Thac Xa**, 25 miles (40 km) from Hanoi, the **Tay Phuong Pagoda** (West Pagoda) perches on the top of the 50 meter Tay Phuong hill. The pagoda dates from the 8th century and is famous for its 73 wooden lacquer statues, which are said to illustrate different stories from the Buddhist scriptures. Their facial expressions reflect the different attitudes and faces of human nature. The pagoda is reached by climbing 262 laterite steps where incense and fan sellers will be hot on your trail hoping to be rewarded for their efforts, if not on the way up, then while you're catching your breath at the top.

Built of ironwood with walls made of unplastered bricks, the pagoda with its round windows is built in three parts:

Small tobacco patch and <u>right</u>, grave of a young Meo girl.

the **Bai Duong** (Prostration Hall), the **Chinh Dien** (Central Hall) and the **Hau Cung** (Back Hall), which together form the **Tam Bao** (Three Gems). The overlapping roofing of the halls is richly decorated with engravings and terracotta figures of dragons, phoenixes, flowers and various animals. Many valuable examples of traditional Vietnamese sculpture are preserved here. The collection includes some beautiful wooden statues of *arhats* dating from the 18th century which are considered to be the best examples of Vietnamese 18th century sculptural art.

The **Dao Pagoda**, 19 miles (30 km) from Hanoi, dates from the 13th century. It is a bit off the beaten track but the trip is well worth setting some time aside for as it passes through some very picturesque countryside and affords a glimpse of traditional village life at close range. The pagoda houses two lacquered statues contain which the mummified remains of two bonzes, the brothers Vu Khac Minh and Vu Khach Truong, who lived at the pagoda three centuries ago.

If the effects of the incredible roads and last minute *kami-kasi* manoeuvers of the fascinating assortment of traffic that careers over them leave your nerves shattered and your body aching, then a trip to the **Kim Boi Thermal Springs** would be in order. Located 60 miles (100 km) from Hanoi, these springs produce hot water at a constant temperature of 36°C and are reputedly therapeutic in treating anything from muscular pain to stomach troubles and tension. A bottling plant and sanatorium have been recently built here.

The village of **Nhi Khe**, about 7 miles (16 km) from Hanoi, is the birthplace of one of Vietnam's national heroes, Nguyen Trai (1380-1442), the great statesman, poet, philosopher and military strategist who served King Le Loi, the king famous for liberating Vietnam from Ming rule. Nhi Khe is also noted for its craftsmen who are skilled wood turners and sculptors in wood and bone.

The Mai Chau district of Ha Son Binh is home to the Thai minority. Visits can be arranged to a village where you can partake of the home brewed rice wine through long reed straws while acquainting yourself with some of the other customs of your hosts.

Further west the province of **Son La** shares a common southern border with Laos. The region is home to many ethnic minorities including Thai, Mnong, Tay, Muong, Mun, Kho Mu, Zao, Xinh and Hoa. Forests and mountains cover 80 percent of the province which is one of the largest cattle breeding centers in northern Vietnam. Two distinct seasons are experienced here, the rainy season which lasts from May to September and the dry season from November to April. During the coldest months, January and February, the temperature can fall to 3°C below zero.

The deep **Mai Chau Valley** in Son La Province, is the main area settled by the Black Thai minority. They live in villages known as *ban* which may comprise up to 50 individual dwellings. For more than a century, gold panning in the streams hereabouts has provided the locals with a better livelihood than can be had in the city. Between May and

Poppies near Lai Chau.

October the road beyond Son La is often washed away or impassable due to mountain slides caused by the excessive rains monsoon. January and February are the recommended months to make the trip, bu even climate permitting there are no guarantees.

The provincial capital, Son La, is situated 375 feet (600 meters) above sea level on the southern bank of the Nam La River. The prison built in 1908 by the French to hold revolutionaries, still stands, a grim reminder of the long years of war, on Khau Ca Hill in the middle of town.

Further west, **Lai Chau Province** shares a border with China in the North and borders Laos in the West. Among the ethnic groups here are the Thai, Hmong, Xa, and Ha Nhi.

Seventy-five percent of the province is covered in forest containing valuable timber, and rare animals such as tigers, bears, bison and pheasants.

The former military Muong Thanh Airport is only an hour's flight from Hanoi, providing that you can get on a flight. Fifty miles (80km) south of Lai Chau township on the route to Laos, the famous battle site of **Dien Bien Phu** lies in an immense gorge 12 miles (20 km) long and half a mile (3 km) wide, which opens onto the **Muong Thanh Valley**. Bordered by mountains to the West and in the East by the 6,160-foot (1,897-meter) **Phu Xam Xan**, it forms a natural barrier blocking the valley off from Laos. It was here that the French met their defeat at the hands of General Vo Nguyen Giap's Viet Minh forces on July 20, 1954.

For anyone interested in Vietnam's minorities Dien Bien Phu has much to offer. Among the groups in the area are the Thai, Hmong, Meo, Zao, Tay, Khmu, Ha Nhi and the Luy. If you wish to visit any of the minority villages you are required to acquire permission and a guide familiar with their location and language, so count on staying in the area for at least two days.

Permission is not easily acquired but if you have both the time and the patience there is no harm in trying.

A patchwork quilt of paddy fields.

NORTH OF HANOI

The Northern circuit from Hanoi to the Chinese border begins in **Ha Bac Province** and the key region of **Bac Ninh**. This area is full of historical, cultural and religious vestiges. Among these are the remains of the ancient **Luy Lau Citadel** and the temple and mausoleum of Si Nhiep, the governor of ancient Giao Chi.

The **Phat Tich Pagoda** (Relic of Buddha) on Mount Lan Kha in Phuong Hoang village was built in the 11th century under the Ly dynasty. It has been badly damaged by the ravages of time and war but a 120 feet (37 meter) stone statue of Amitabha Buddha dating from the 11th century remains intact within the pagoda.

A typical example of Buddhist architecture, the **But Thap Pagoda**, built under the Tran dynasty in the 13th century and renovated in 1647, is found on the bank of the Duong River in Dinh To Village, Tien Son district. It incorporates a collection of both everyday and religious buildings including a stone tower 42 feet (13 meters) high (Bao Nghiem) which stands in front of the pagoda. The pagoda houses over fifty Buddhist statues, including one of the Goddess of Mercy, Quan Yin, the Asiatic metamorphosis of ancient India's Bodisattva *Avalokitecvara* with her thousand eyes and arms. Those who worship her believe her many eyes and arms have supernatural power; the eyes to see and the hands to help those in need. The pagoda also contains statues of the two Trinh princesses and Thi Kinh, yet another goddess of mercy.

Dong Quang Village, also in Tien Son district, is the site of the spectacular Dong Ky firecracker festival which takes place on the 4th day of the first lunar month. **Lim Village** in the same district is the site of yet another popular festival, the Lim Festival which is held every year soon after Tet. For three days, from the 13th to the 15th of the first lunar month, people from all over the region

Preceding pages: Traditional gowns add color to the Dong Ky Firecracker Festival. Below, on the way to Lang Son.

converge on the village for the competitions of popular *quan ho* folksongs sung alternately by groups of young men and women. Here you can also visit the Lim Pagoda and hill. More seasonal and traditional festivals are celebrated in Bac Ninh than in any other part of the country. Dancing and the popular *quan ho* always feature in the festivities.

The traditional theater at the **Dinh Bang Communal House** in Dinh Bang Village is something of an architectural marvel on stilts. Built of ironwood in 1736, the building is one of the largest of its kind in Vietnam and even if there is nothing happening on stage the building alone is worth a visit.

Dong Ho Village, in Bach Ninh is famous for its communal production of woodcut prints. The prints depict traditional themes and their preparation is as traditional as their subjects. The various stages in production, such as carving the wood block, preparing the paper, obtaining natural colors from plants and minerals, are tasks mastered and shared by different family members.

Cam Son Lake in Luc Ngan district covers an area of 6,500 acres (2,600 hectares), surrounded by limestone mountains. This tranquil and picturesque setting offers accommodation in the form of rest houses on some of the small islands in the lake. Other places of interest in the province are the 16th century **Mac Citadel**.

The neighboring province of **Vinh Phu** is the cradle of the pre-Vietnamese **Hung Lac** race of the Middle Ages, the ancestral land of the Viet people, who first settled here before moving into the Red River Delta. Bronze relics 4,000 years old have been discovered in the region.

The area still bears the mark of their presence in the remains of the **Hung Temples**. These were built by the founders of the **Van Lang Kingdom** between the 7th and 3rd centuries B.C., when a line of 18 successive Hung kings graced the throne of Vang Lang. In all there are three Hung temples built on **Mount Nghia Linh** in Phong Chau district. The lowest temple, **Den Ha**, is

Shrine for highway travelers.

reached by climbing 225 steps. Below the temple at the foot of the hill is an arched portal flanked by two huge stone columns engraved with two parallel sentences glorifying the origins of the Vietnamese people. A further 168 steps lead up to the middle temple, **Den Hung** from where another 102 steps must be climbed to reach the superior temple **Den Thuong**. The temple is dedicated to the cults of Heaven, Earth, the Rice Genie (Than Lua) and also Than Giong, the infant hero, who in the third century B.C. is said to have chased out the Chinese Han invaders assisted by a genie in the form of an iron horse. It was here that the last of the Hung kings transferred his power to the Thuc king at the end of the third century.

People from all parts of the country congregate here every year on March 10th, the anniversary of their ancestor's death, to celebrate the Hung Temple festival.

For those who prefer mountain resorts and cooler temperatures the **Tam Dao Resort**, established in 1902 at an altitude of 2,844 feet (879 meters), is today considered one of the country's best. It is set on a large plateau within a valley 54 miles (90 km) northwest of Hanoi in the Tam Dao mountain range. These mountains stretch from the northwest to the southeast, separating Vinh Phu from Bac Thai Province in the north. The name Tam Dao, meaning Three Islands, derives from the three mountains, Thien Thi (4,468 feet/1,375 meters), Thach Ban (4,511 feet/1,388 meters) and Phu Nghia (4,500 feet/1,400 meters), which dominate the landscape, appearing from a distance like three islands jutting above a sea of clouds. Rare trees and plants cover the mountainsides and the forests harbor many species of wild animals, butterflies and flowers. The resort's calm atmosphere is complemented by an average temperature of 10°C. A stream known as Suoi Bac (Silvery Stream) meanders its way past the foot of Mount Thien Thi creating languid pools perfect for swimming. A waterfall cascades in three stages forming a beautiful lake beside which stand several pagodas.

Meo girls on the go.

190

In Lap Thach district in the northwest the **Binh Son Tower** of the **Vinh Khanh Pagoda** rises 49 feet (15½ meters) into the sky. Built under the Tran dynasty in the 13th century, the 11 tiered baked clay tower is remarkably decorated with many diverse sculptures.

You may be interested in visiting the **Vinh Son Snake Farm** in Vinh Lac district. Established over 10 years ago, it breeds snakes and produces snake wine and an ointment (Najatox) containing snake venom which is used to relieve muscle and joint inflammation.

Vinh Phu's diverse scenic beauty is enhanced by a range of flora, the extensive green tea plantations and in winter by the beautiful white blooms of sasanca flowers.

Lying to the North of Vinh Phu is **Bac Thai Province**, a region intimately linked with the anti-colonial resistance. Its mountainous terrain rendered the region virtually inaccessible to colonial troops. The climate here is both tropical and subtropical, with an average temperature of 27.6°C during the hottest

Spectators at the Firecracker Festival and right, on the way to the market.

month and 13.6°C during the coldest. Travelers palms with their wonderful fan shape leaves and varieties of bamboo abound in the province.

Located on a mountain top 470 feet (145 meters) above sea level, **Lake Ba Be** in Cho Ra district, is the largest lake in the country. This impressive lake, over half a mile (1 km) wide and six miles (9 km) long, reaches a depth of 98 feet (30 meters) and offers an opportunity for a spot of sailing. The surrounding forests harbor many birds and animals. Another diversion in the vicinity is a visit to a Zao minority village.

Hoang Lien Son Province, to the North, shares a northern border with China. Here Vietnam's highest summit, the 10,311 foot (3,143 meter) **Fan Si Pan** towers above the rest. Valuable timber, precious essences, rattan and rushes are obtained from the forests. Cinnamon and tea are the local specialities. The Red and Chay rivers supply the province with hydroelectric power.

The **Sa Pa Resort** in the northwest of the province was established by the

French in 1922. It rests on a plateau at an altitude of 4,921 feet (1,500 meters) in a locality famous for its forests of precious woods and peach orchards. You can hire horse and cart to visit Hmong and White Tay minority villages, the Bac Falls, the May Bridge, and other scenic spots nearby.

East of Hoang Lien Son, the highland region of **Ha Tuyen Province** shares a 168 miles (270 km) common border with China in the North. Three large rivers, the Lo, Gam and Pho Day, flow through this province where a primal forests provide a valuable source of timber and over 1,000 species of medicinal plants. Heavy mists shroud the mountains during the winter months when snow sometimes falls on the peaks in the higher regions.

Dong Va village, located on a plateau 3,362 feet (1,025 meters) above sea level, is home to the Tay and Hmong minorities. On market day Dong Va comes alive as people gather to buy and sell, socialize and often, celebrate local traditional festivals. Specialities of the area include peaches, pears and plums.

In 1945, during the resistance war against the French, Ho Chi Minh arrived in Tan Trao, a region 24 miles (39 km) northeast of Tuyen Quang township in the southwest of the province, and set up the headquarters of the Central Committee of the party and later the provincial government. The 1945 August Revolution was launched from the Tay minority village of **Kim Long**, 93 miles (150 km) from Hanoi. The village is also known for its huge banyan tree which has shaded many historical and political events. The roots of this old survivor cover several acres.

Cao Bang Province to the East shares a 195 miles (314 km) border with China. Forest covers 90 percent of the province and the climate is cool, particularly in Winter when snow caps the high peaks. The picturesque **An Giac Falls** in Trung Khanh district are formed by a stretch of the Quy Xuan River falling from a height of 99 feet (30 meters). Many wild orchids grow in the region. Limestone mountains and forests surround another

Spectacular scenery on the Ho Chi Minh Trail.

of the province's beauty spots, **Lake Thang Hen** in Quang Hoa district.

Southwest of Cao Bang, **Lang Son Province** shares a common border with China's Guangxi Province. Mountains and forests cover 80 percent of the province's land area. Tigers, panthers, bears, deer, pangolins, chamois and monitor lizards are among the animals found here. Here, provincial specialities include forest products, jews ears and fragrant mushrooms, anise from the Chinese anise tree and fine flavoured Lang Son tobacco. Tay, Nung, Hmong, Zao, Hoa and Nghia are among the minorities found in the province. The Ky Cung River which flows through the province is unique in that it is the only river in the region flowing northwards into China.

The narrow **Chi Lang Gorge**, a series of passes connected by tortuous tracks forged between high mountains 36 miles (58 km) South of the Sino-Vietnamese border, is the battleground where the Vietnamese have fought many major battles against the Chinese invaders throughout every era of history. In 1076 the Vietnamese defeated 300,000 Song troops here and in 1427, 100,000 Ming troops received the same treatment. The gorge's northern entrance is known as Quy Quan Mon (The Barbarian Invaders Gate) and the southern exit is called Ngo The (the Swearing Path). The almost incessant fighting on this northern border has forged the temperament and galvanized the resilient character of the Northern Vietnamese people.

The provincial capital, Lang Son, lies about 95 miles (154 km) from Hanoi. The Ky Lua Market, held in the mountainous region nearby, is a popular gathering place for members of the region's many minority groups. **Thanh Grotto** and the beautiful **Tan Thanh Pagoda** are well worth visiting.

The **Waiting Lady Mountain**, another well known site in the province, is a stone outcrop at the summit of a limestone mountain. Popular legend attributes its form to a woman who waited so long for her husband to return that she turned to stone.

Unofficial trade at the border with China.

SOUTH OF HANOI

The old Mandarin Route which heads South from Hanoi was renamed National Highway 1 after independence in 1945. It stretches the length of the Indochinese eastern coast for more than 1,240 miles (2,000 km), from **Nam Quan** at the Chinese border to **Ha Tien** in the Gulf of Thailand.

The richly varied landscape of **Ha Nam Ninh Province**, the southernmost province of North Vietnam, contains every terrain imaginable – mountains, limestone hills, low lying plains, ricefields and long stretches of sand. Nam Dinh, the provincial capital lies 60 miles (90 km) from Hanoi. Under the French it became a center for the textile industry which flourishes today as the largest in the country.

The Ancient Capital of Hoa Lu: The picturesque site of **Hoa Lu** was once the ancient capital of Vietnam, or Dai Co Viet as it was then known, under the Dinh, Le (10th century) and Ly (11th century) dynasties. Remains of the ancient citadel bordering the Hoang Long River are visible over an area of 740 acres (300 hectares). An enormous stone column engraved with Buddhist sutras dating from 988 was recently discovered here. Although the original palaces have long since disappeared, temples have been built on the original sites.

After the capital was transferred from Hoa Lu to Thang Long, two temples were built, one dedicated to King Dinh Tien Hoang and the other to his successor Le Dai Hanh. King Dinh Tien Hoang's temple, first built in the 11th century was reconstructed in 1696. Statues of mythical animals stand guard outside the temple where King Dinh Tien Hoang is worshipped at a central altar. The large Vietnamese characters written in ancient Vietnamese script translate as "From this day onwards we have our independence". Also written on the pillars in ancient Vietnamese is *Dai Co Viet*, the name King Dinh Bo Linh gave Vietnam. In the temple's back room are

Preceding pages: Highway 1, Central Vietnam. Below, ploughing by the light of the evening sun.

some rather dusty statues representing King Dinh Bo Linh and his three sons.

The Dragon Bed, once an area used for sacrifices, lies in the center of the courtyard in front of the main building. These days gifts and food offerings are placed on the slab during festivals.

The **Le Hoan Temple** is a miniature of the **Dinh Hoang**. The statues in the back room are those of King Le Hoan, his Queen, Duong Van Nga and his sons, Le Long Dinh and Le Long Viet.

Less than two miles (3 km) to the north of **Nam Dinh** lies **Mac Village**, and the ancient Tran remains. These ruins are all that remain of the palaces built by the kings of the Tran dynasty who defeated the Mongol-Yuan invaders three times in the 13th century. Among these are the **Thien Truong Temples** which were dedicated to the 14 Tran kings and the **Co Trach Temple** which was dedicated to General Tran Hung Dao. The only buildings left intact are the beautiful **Pho Minh Pagoda** and the 13-storey Pho Minh Tower, built in 1305, which contains the remains of King Tran Nhan Tong.

Another scenic spot well worth visiting in Hoa Lu district is the **Chua Bich Pagoda** in the **Hanh Son Range** 62 miles (100 km) from Hanoi. Built in 1428 the pagoda is renowned for its beautiful bronze and marble statues and huge bronze bell. From the same area a leisurely boat ride will take you to the three magnificent grottoes of **Tam Co**. These wonderfully decorated caverns with their huge stalagmites and stalactites, recede into the depths of the mountain.

About 62 miles (100 km) South of Hanoi, National Route 1 crosses three mountains via the **Tam Diep Pass**.

Located about 62 miles (100 km) southwest of Hanoi, the **Cuc Phuong Forest**, a national park since 1962, is one of the few remaining tropical primeval forest reserves in the world. The park shelters 64 species of fauna and nearly 2,000 species of flora, including trees no longer found many other parts of the world. The fauna is particularly remarkable. Flying lizards, yellow monkeys and other bizarre animals akin to those found in the Galapagos Islands roam amidst the park's more than 61,000 acres (25,000 hectares), three quarters of which are covered by limestone mountains. These mountains form two parallel ranges enclosing a valley with a micro climate quite different to that of the surrounding region. Many caves and grottoes lie within the mountains. Three tombs excavated in one of the grottoes in 1966 contained shells, animal teeth, rudimentary stone tools and human remains.

For a therapeutic warm dip try the park's thermal springs. These remain at a constant temperature of 37°C and contain more than 20 chemical elements believed to have healing properties.

Accommodation in the form of wooden houses on stilts in traditional Muong style, is available in the park.

The **Phat Diem Cathedral**, built in 1865, today remains an important center for Christian pilgrims from all over Vietnam. This remarkable cathedral, built of ironwood in Sino-Vietnamese style, was one of the earliest Catholic churches to be built in North Vietnam.

Catholic church on the road to Nam Dinh.

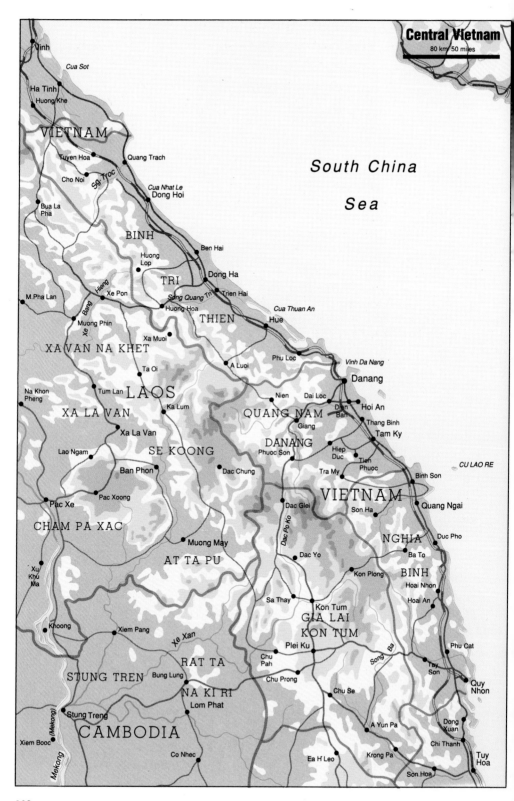

THE CENTER

A long string of coastal provinces linking the vast rice growing regions of the Mekong Delta in the South and the Red River Delta in the North, forms the region of Central Vietnam. At the heart of the Center lies Hue, the imperial city of the Nguyen kings with its majestic citadels, fortresses and imperial mausoleums. We begin our journey through the Center among the vestiges of this ancient capital. The region of Hue became part of Vietnam in 1306 when the king of Champa, Jaya Simhavarman III (Che Man) offered two districts of his kingdom, O and Ri, to the Tran king of Dai Viet in exchange for the Viet Princess, Huyen Tran. This diplomatic marriage served to ensure peaceful coexistence between the two kingdoms and the peaceful acquisition of new territory by the kingdom of Dai Viet. When Che Man died a year later his unfortunate widow was expected to join him on the funeral pyre, in keeping with Cham custom. However, thanks to the strategy and speed of the Viet King such was not to be the grisly fate of the young princess. She was whisked away by the king's general and taken by boat back to Thang Long.

The two former Champa districts were later renamed Thuan Hoa, *Thuan*, meaning allegiance or submission and *Hoa* meaning transformation. The name Hue is believed to have come about through the common mispronunciation of Hoa. The area stretching from the Thach Han River, in former Quang Tri Province, to the Cloudy Pass, (Hai Van) corresponds to ancient Thuan Hoa.

From Hue we continue our journey through the central coastal provinces to the North, Nghe Tinh, Binh Tri Thien, before entering Quang Nam Danang Province and the ancient Kingdom of Champa, South of Hue. The distinctive red brick Cham Towers and sacred sites built between the 8th and 12th centuries stand as silent testimony to the kingdom which flourished here before its absorption by the Vietnamese. Another unique feature of the province is the charming 15th century town of Hoi An, which was the biggest sea port and most important center of trade in the country during the 17th and 18th centuries. Its beautifully preserved communal houses, pagodas and other places of worship, reflect the presence and influences of the Vietnamese, Chinese, Japanese and Westerners who later settled in the region. In the West lies the Central Highland area, the provinces of Gia Lai Kontum, Dac Lac and Lam Dong, home of many ethnic minorities and the beautiful mountain resort of Dalat. We then continue down the central coast South of Hue to the scenic seaside resort of Nha Trang and the provinces of Nghia Binh, Phu Khanh and Thuan Hai.

HUE

Hue, the ancient imperial city of the Nguyen kings is located seven miles (12 km) from the coast on a narrow stretch of land not more than 50 miles (80 km) wide in Binh Tri Thien Province, which shares a border with Laos in the West.

The Nguyen Lords administered the whole region with the agreement of the Trinh Lords. In the beginning everything went more or less smoothly, but rivalry flared up as the territory was extended southwards and bloody battles broke out between the two rival families. Each side was fiercely determined to consolidate and assert their own sovereignty, but eventually the Nguyen Lords gained the upper hand. As a result Hue became a new kingdom, independent of the North under the reign of Lord Vu Vuong (1739-1763).

The first Lord to reach Hue was Lord Nguyen Hoang (1524-1613) in the Spring of 1601. He found a particularly good location to build a capital and erected the **Phu Xuan Citadel**.

He also built the **Thien Mu Pagoda** which remains intact on the left bank of the Perfume River. The seven tiers of the temple's octagonal tower each represent a different reincarnation of Buddha. Six genie statues guard the Buddhist pagoda which contains a gilt statue of the laughing Buddha, happy in his prosperity, and three superb statues of Buddha enclosed in glass. Many generations have heard the tolling of the pagoda's enormous 4,617 lb (2052 kg) bell since it was cast in 1701. The main temple, **Dai Hung** is found in an attractive garden of ornamental shrubs and trees. A bronze statue of Maitraya Buddha presides over the first room. Behind this temple is the **Quan Vo Temple** (God of War Temple) and behind that another, the **Quan Am Temple**, dedicated to the goddess Quan Am.

Lord Nguyen Hoang was the first in an uninterrupted succession of 10 feudal lords to rule over the area of Hue between 1558 and 1802. In 1802, after quelling the Tay Son uprising, the 10th

Nguyen Lord proclaimed himself Emperor Gia Long and founded the Nguyen Dynasty which was to last for 143 years. Some 33 years later Hue was invaded by the French. During their rule a quick succession of emperors graced the throne. The considerable unrest, anti-French demonstrations and strikes of the colonial era were followed by the Japanese occupation in 1945 and the abdication of Bao Dai, the last of the Nguyen emperors, on August 24th 1945.

The relative peace that reigned after 1954 when Hue became part of South Vietnam was shattered when the Diem regime's repressive anti-Buddhist propaganda sparked off a series of demonstrations and protest suicides by Buddhist monks in 1963.

Hue's imperial city suffered extensive damage during the Tet Offensive of January and February 1968 and although many priceless historical monuments and relics were bombed out of existence, many have survived.

Always an important cultural, intellectual and historical city, Hue remains

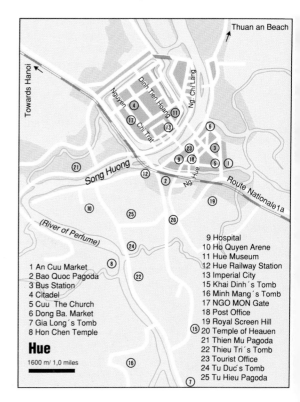

Hue

1600 m/ 1,0 miles

1 An Cuu Market
2 Bao Quoc Pagoda
3 Bus Station
4 Citadel
5 Cuu The Church
6 Dong Ba. Market
7 Gia Long's Tomb
8 Hon Chen Temple
9 Hospital
10 Ho Quyen Arene
11 Hue Museum
12 Hue Railway Station
13 Imperial City
15 Khai Dinh's Tomb
16 Minh Mang's Tomb
17 NGO MON Gate
18 Post Office
19 Royal Screen Hill
20 Temple of Heauen
21 Thien Mu Pagoda
22 Thieu Tri's Tomb
23 Tourist Office
24 Tu Duc's Tomb
25 Tu Hieu Pagoda

one of Vietnam's main attractions. The charm of this timeless old city lies not only in its historical and architectural value but also in the natural beauty of its location along the banks of the Perfume River.

Legacy of the Nguyen Emperors: The **Imperial City** (Dai Noi) is made up of three different walled enclosures. The **Yellow Enclosure** (Hoang Thanh) and the **Forbidden Purple City** (Tu Cam Thanh) are enclosed within the **Kinh Thanh** (exterior enclosure). Stone, bricks and earth were used to build the exterior wall which measured 26 feet (8 meters) high and 65 feet (20 meters) thick and was built during the reign of Emperor Gia Long. Ten large fortified gates topped with watch towers were built at various points along the wall.

The Yellow Enclosure is the middle wall enclosing the imperial city, with its palaces, temples and flower gardens. Access to it was via four richly decorated gates: Ngo Mon (South or Noon Gate), Hoa Binh, Hien Nhan and Chuong Duc. The Ngo Mon Gate, first built of granite in 1834 during the reign of Emperor Minh Mang, was repaired in 1921. The gate is topped by the **Lau Ngu Phung**, the Five Phoenix Watch Tower, with its roofs brightly tiled in yellow over the middle section and green on either side. From here the emperor used to preside over formal ceremonies and with special permission it is possible to climb the stairs and enjoy the same view.

Once through the Ngo Mon Gate, the **Golden Water Bridge**, at one time reserved solely for the emperor, leads to the **Thai Hoa Palace** (Palace of Supreme Peace) the most important place in the imperial city. Here the emperor received the high dignitaries of the land and foreign diplomats, and the royal court organized important ceremonies. Built in 1805 during Gia Long's reign, the palace was renovated first by Minh Mang in 1834 and later by Khai Dinh in 1924. Today it stands in excellent condition, its ceilings and beams highly decorated in red lacquer and gold inlay. The emperor used to rest in the **Truong**

Sanh Palace (Palace of Longevity) and read the classics in the Van Palace or the Co Ha Garden. The temples within the enclosure are dedicated to various Lords: the **Trieu Mieu Temple** to Nguyen Kim, the **Thai Mieu** to Nguyen Hoang and his successors, the **Phung Tien Temple**, to the emperors of the reigning dynasty and the **Hung Mieu** to Nguyen Phuc Lan, emperor Gia Long's father. The well-preserved **The Mieu**, dedicated to the sovereigns of the Nguyen dynasty, houses the shrines of seven Nguyen emperors plus the stelae of the revolutionary emperors: Ham Nghi, Thanh Thai and Duy Tan, which were added in 1959. In front of the temple, completely undamaged, stands the magnificent **Hien Lam Cac** (Pavilion of Splendor) with the nine dynastic urns lined up before it. The urns, cast in 1822 during Minh Mang's reign, are decorated with motifs of the sun, moon, clouds, birds, animals, dragons, mountains, rivers, historic events and scenes from everyday life. Hundreds of artisans from all over the country were involved in their casting. Each urn represents an emperor of the Nguyen Dynasty and weighs between 4,275 and 5,625 lb (1,900 and 2,500 kg).

The **Dien Tho Palace** built by emperor Gia Long in 1804 served as the Queen Mother's residence.

In the first enclosure of the Royal City, towards the Chuong Duc Gate are the **9 Genies Canons** (Sung Than Cong). Five on one side represent the five elements: metal, water, wood, fire and earth, the other four represent the seasons. Each canon weighs 12 tons.

The Forbidden Purple City (Tu Cam Thanh) was reserved solely for the Emperor and the royal family who resided here behind a brick wall 3¼ feet (1 meter) high and 13 feet (4 meters thick). Seven gates set into the wall each had a special function and name glorifying the ancestral virtues. Unfortunately this area was extensively damaged and more or less destroyed during the Tet offensive.

The main building in the enclosure is the **Can Thanh Palace** (Celestial Perfection). The other once grand palace, **Can Chanh**, now sadly in ruins, was used by the emperor to receive dignitaries and settle the affairs of the kingdom. Its remaining walls, riddled with shell and bullet holes, stand as a crumbling reminder of the weapons that wrought such destruction to this once grand complex. Beyond lies an empty stretch of ground where the royal apartments once stood. The most modern palace in the enclosure was the **Kien Than Palace** which Emperor Khai Dinh (1916 – 1925) had built complete with all the western comforts. Unfortunately this too was a casualty of the war and completely destroyed.

Another world lies beyond the walls of the citadel which is surrounded in the South and East by Hue's commercial area. This is confined mainly to the area around the arched **Trang Tien Bridge**, which spans the Perfume River and the **Gia Hoi Bridge**. Both bridges lend their names to the areas surrounding them. Located in Gia Hoi, with its mainly Chinese and Minh Huong (Vietnamese Chinese) population is the lively **Dong**

Stone guardians on the esplanade of a royal mausoleum.

Ba Market. The market has been around since the beginning of the century and offers a great variety of local products and gastronomic delights.

Vy Da District on the other side of the river, is renowned as a popular refuge for artists, poets, scholars and mandarins. Of an entirely different character is the district of Phu Cam, best known for its cathedral and the fervor of its predominantly Catholic community. For those who like to look around old cemeteries, there are two rather interesting family cemeteries in Hue, one belonging to the Ngo Dinh and the other to the Ho family.

The Hue Museum, built in 1845 under Emperor Thieu Tri, was formerly the Long An Palace. It was dismantled and moved to its present site where it was reconstructed to house the treasures bequeathed by the royal family and nobility. Sadly many objects have disappeared without trace in the course of revolution and war since December 1946.

The Royal Tombs and Pagodas: Unlike the other dynasties, the Nguyen Dynasty did not bury its members in their native village, Gia Mieu, in Thanh Hoa Province. Instead their imperial tombs lie scattered on the hillsides either side of the Perfume River to the West of Hue. Although the dynasty had 13 kings, only seven of them reigned until their deaths; thus only Gia Long, Minh Mang, Thieu Tri, Tu Duc, Kien Phuc, Dong Khanh and Kai Dinh have been laid to rest in this valley of the Nguyen Kings. Their tombs more or less follow a set general pattern. Each has a large brick paved courtyard (Bia Dinh) containing stone figures of elephants, saddled horses, soldiers, civil and military mandarins. In front of this stands the Stele Pavilion (Bia Dinh) containing the tall marble or stone stele engraved with the biography of the deceased king written by his successor. (Except in the case of Tu Duc who wrote his own). Beyond this is the temple (Tam Dien) where the deceased king and queen are worshipped and their royal belongings displayed. The king's widows would keep incense

Dynastic urns in the royal citadel.

and aloe wood perpetually burning before the altar until their deaths. Behind and on either side of the temple are the houses built for the King's concubines, servants and the soldiers who guarded the royal tomb.

In certain mausoleums, Gia Long's and Thieu Tri's for example, a special pavilion was built in the center from where the emperor himself would direct the construction work on his tomb or simply relax on hot days. Tu Duc's tomb is something of an exception as it comes complete with a lakeside pavilion which served as both a bathroom and somewhere to relax for a spot of fishing. The emperor's body is laid in a concealed place (Bao Thanh), enclosed by high walls behind well locked bronze doors.

Setting foot in any of the tombs, one feels a sense of admiration for the noble grandeur and elegant simplicity of the architecture. This sense of awe is described by one of Vietnam's celebrated writers, Pham Quynh, a former minister of national education:

"This tomb is the general blending of all the colors of the firmament and of all the tints of water: it is an amalgamation of high mountains, of thick forests, of wind blowing through foliage. This tomb is a spectacle of nature, a marvel of great beauty, added to another sight, created by the hand of man, of a beauty no less marvellous. It is the patient and inspired work of the artist whose intention was to color the countryside to awaken the awaiting soul, soaring in the silence of this mournful place or whispering in the top of the lone pine tree. There are not the words to express the bizarre sensation, both gentle and of tender exhilaration, which grips one with an eagerness for poetry in this scenery charged with depth and mystery."

Minh Mang's Mausoleum can be reached by hiring a small motorboat from any of the local owners opposite the Perfume River Hotel. Alternatively take a car to **Ban Viet village** and from

Dramatic entrance to Emperor Khai Dinh's tomb.

there take a boat across the Perfume River. Minh Mang was Gia Long's fourth son and the Nguyen dynasty's second king. He built the Imperial City and was highly respected for his reforms in the sphere of customs, traditions and agriculture. His mausoleum is located where the Ta Trach and Huu Trach tributaries of the Perfume River meet. Its construction was begun a year before his death in 1840 and was finished by his successor Thieu Tri in 1843. The setting blends the beauty of nature with the majestic architecture and superb stone sculpture created by its many anonymous craftsmen. The setting is at its best in mid-March when the **Trung Minh** and **Tan Nguyet** lakes bloom with a mass of beautiful lotus flowers.

Tu Duc's Mausoleum, 4 miles (7 km) southwest of Hue can be reached by a very pleasant cycle ride through pine forests and lush hills. The mausoleum begun in 1864, took three years to complete. The end result resembles a royal palace in miniature and harmonizes beautifully with the natural surround-

Inside the grounds of the imperial city.

ings. A work force of 3,000 men was used in its construction. Tu Duc, the son of Thieu Tri and the Nguyen dynasty's fourth king, reigned for 36 years, the longest reign of any of the Nguyen kings. He spent his leisure hours in the two pavilions beside the lake, **Luu Khiem**. Here he wrote poetry, no doubt inspired by the beauty of his surroundings, fished and enjoyed the fragrance of the lotus. The more popular of the two lakeside pagodas is the **Xung Khiem Pavilion** which dates from 1865.

A staircase leads to the **Luong Khiem Mausoleum** which contains a collection of furniture, vases and jewellery boxes. Further on is the terrace leading to the tomb, with its stone elephants, horses and mandarins. The tomb itself, ritually inaccessible, is covered by dense pine forest. The tombs of Tu Duc's adopted son, Kien Phu and Queen Le Thien An lie beside the lake.

Thieu Tri's Mausoleum is located nearby. Thieu Tri, Minh Mang's son, was the third Nguyen Emperor and reigned from 1841 to 1847. His tomb

was built between 1947 and 1948 in the same elegant architectural style as his father's but on a much smaller scale.

Khai Dinh's Mausoleum is completely different from any of the other Nguyen tombs. If anything it resembles a European castle, its architecture a blend of the oriental and occidental. Made of reinforced concrete it took 11 years to complete and was finally finished in 1931. Khai Dinh, Bao Dai's adopted father, ruled for nine years during the colonial era.

A grandiose dragon staircase leads up to the first courtyard from where further stairs lead to a courtyard lined with stone statues of elephants, horses, civil and military mandarins. In the center of the courtyard stands the stele inscribed with Chinese characters composed by Bao Dai in memory of his father. The exterior lacks the tranquil charm and beauty of Minh Mang's or Tu Duc's mausoleum and the giant dragons flanking the staircase appear rather menacing. Once inside the contrast is striking. Colored tiles pave the floor, a huge "dragon in the clouds" mural, painted by artists using their feet, adorns the ceiling of the middle chamber. Jade green antechambers lead off to the left and right. Colorful frescoes composed of many thousands of inlaid ceramic and glass fragments depict various themes. Animals, trees and flowers provide a visual feast after the less inspiring blackened exterior of the mausoleum. A life size bronze statue of Khai Dinh made in France in 1922 rests on a dais on top of the tomb.

Gia Long's Mausoleum, 10 miles (16 km from Hue on the **Bach Hillside** is somewhat inaccessible by road and a more pleasant way to reach it is by boat. The tomb, began in 1814, was completed a year after his death in 1920. Unfortunately the site was in the middle of a guerilla zone during the war and the tomb has been considerably damaged by bombs. It has since become rather neglected but the wild beauty of the site itself, with its backdrop of **Mount Thien Tho** makes the effort to get there well worth while.

The **Minh Thanh Temple**, also in very bad shape, is dedicated to Gia Long's first wife, Queen Thua Thien Co. On the left is Gia Long's sepulchre where he and his first wife are buried side by side.

Further Attractions: Boats can be hired from the landing stage at the **Pavilion of Edicts** to travel up the Perfume River as far as the **Temple of Literature** (Van Mieu), dedicated to Confucius and the **Temple of Martial Arts** (Vo Mieu) which is dedicated to **Quan Cong**, the God of War and certain Vietnamese marshals.

Towards the mausoleums below the Thien Mu Pagoda is the temple known as either **Dien Hin Chen** or **Ngoc Tran Dien** where the goddess **Poh Nagar**, protector of the Champa Kingdom is worshipped. Po Nagar, greatly venerated by the Chams in the past is also to a lesser extent worshipped today by the Vietnamese who succeeded them on the narrow stretch of land which was once the Kingdom of Champa.

A festival takes place here on the 15th day of the 7th lunar month every year,

Entrance to Emperor Min Mang's mausoleum.

when worshippers march in a long procession accompanied by ceremonial music and a heavy cloud of incense.

On the West bank of the river lie the **Ho Quyen Arenas**, where in former times tigers and elephants were forced to fight against each other in bloody performances staged to amuse the king and his court. This type of arena is extremely rare in Southeast Asia.

The village of **Nguyet Bieu** nearby is known for its excellent grapefruit and longans.

Surrounded by a park of pines and conifers, the **Nam Giao Esplanade**, (Terrace of Heavenly Sacrifice) built by Emperor Gia Long in 1802, was in its day considered the most sacred and solemn place. Composed of three terraces, two square and one circular, the esplanade as a whole represents the sky and the earth. From here the emperor paid homage to heaven in his capacity as the privileged mandatory on earth. Every three years the **Nam Giao Festival** (or Festival of Sacrifice) took place at the center of the circular esplanade. A buffalo would be sacrificed to the genie of the sky who is believed to govern the destiny of the world. Unfortunately the whole area has been turned into a hideous monument to the dead.

Hue has many beautiful gardens with artificial lakes, miniature mountains and trees, roses and a great variety of flowers. The villages of **Vi Da** and **Kim Long** in the suburbs are worth visiting for their trees and gardens alone.

Not far from Hue lie the lagoons and unspoilt beaches of **Pha Tan Giang**, **Thuan An** and **Tu Hien**.

The maze of underground tunnels built on three levels in the village of **Vinh Moc** by the revolutionaries in 1965 show how highly organized the underground was.

Some 11 miles (17 km) South of Hue, National Highway 1 passes **Phu Bai Airport**, then through the village localities of **Truoi** and the picturesque fishing village of **Lang Co** with its circular white sand beach and excellent fresh sea food, particularly good atethe oysters, mussels and clams.

The busy main market in Hue.

THE THIEN MU PAGODA

At the beginning of the 17th century when Vietnam was under the nominal rule of the Le dynasty the real power was in the hands of two rival families, the Trinh and Nguyen. The Nguyen family continued the traditional march to the South in search of more land and explored the area South of the Gianh River. In 1601 Lord Nguyen Hoang visited the village of An Ninh, the present location of Hue. He was most impressed by the hill shaped like a dragon's head which emerged from the flat surrounding countryside and asked the villagers about the history of the place. They told him that the place was considered sacred and spoke of a lady dressed in a red gown and green trousers seen on the hill, who had predicted that a King would come to the place and build a pagoda which would bring all the Heavenly forces together to strengthen the Long Mach (Dragon's Veins). These, according to old geomantic principals, are the inner textures of the earth which play a vital role in the choice of a site to build a home or a burial place. A choice based on the direction of the Long Mach and their combined support to the benevolent Thang Long (Blue Dragon) in its struggle for harmony against the aggressive power of the Bach Ho (White Tiger) is believed to bring lasting prosperity and longevity.

Lord Nguyen Hoang sensed a holy presence in the place and built a pagoda on the hill. He named it Chua Thien Mu, the Heavenly Lady Pagoda. His descendants kept the pagoda in good shape, remodelling and enlarging it. In 1655 major repairs were undertaken by Lord Nguyen Phuc Tan and in 1710 Lord Nguyen Phuc Chu had a huge bell cast for the pagoda and the structure extended. He also wrote a short history of the Thien Mu's contribution to strengthening Buddhism in Vietnam. The history was engraved on a stele over eight feet (2½ meters) high, mounted on a marble tortoise. A pavil-

Thien Mu occupies a marvellous site.

ion was erected in front of the pagoda so guests from the 10 corners of the earth could stop and contemplate the meditative serenity of the Perfume River and the pagoda's surroundings.

In the ensuing decades, conflicts between rival families contending for the rule of Vietnam caused serious damage to the Thien Mu. Finally in 1802, Nguyen Anh, one of Lord Nguyen Hoang's descendants, defeated all his rivals, reunified Vietnam and proclaimed himself Emperor Gia Long. In 1815 he ordered the complete renovation and restoration of the Thien Mu. However it was Emperor Thieu Tri, (1841-1847) who put the Thien Mu on the map. He supervised the construction of a seven storey tower, each storey dedicated to the worship of one reincarnation of the Buddha, and classified the Thien Mu as the 14th on a list of the imperial capital's 20 landmarks. In 1904 the pagoda suffered storm damage, but all was repaired by 1907. In the 1930s and 1940s, the Thien Mu became something of an unspoken symbol and meeting place for

Vietnamese who realized that Buddhism could not flourish under colonialism or any other form of religious repression. It became the object of national and international attention in 1963 when the Venerable Thich Quang Duc, a 66 year old resident monk from the Thien Mu, went to Saigon to protest the repressive measures against Buddhism taken by President Ngo Dinh Diem's government. On June 11, 1963, Thich Quang Duc immolated himself on a street corner in Saigon. The flames which consumed him burnt into the consciences of the Vietnamese and American people and the international public as a photograph of the scene blazed across the world's headlines next morning. This event signalled the beginning of the end for the regime of President Ngo Dinh Diem who was murdered by his own officers following a coup d'etat on November 1, 1963.

Memorabilia of Venerable Thich Quang Duc's supreme sacrifice, including the car in which he drove to Saigon, are preserved at the Thien Mu.

The pagoda and right, one of its guardians.

CENTRAL COAST NORTH OF HUE

The rich and beautiful province of **Thanh Hoa** is the first in an almost unbroken succession of seven coastal provinces hemmed in between the South China Sea and the Indochinese Mountain Range.

Thanh Hoa, the cradle of the Dong Son culture, harbors a great many historical sites and remains and is an important settlement area for the proto-Vietnamese Muong minority. The Muong still adhere to their ancient Vietnamese language and use the bronze drums inherent to their unique culture and festivals.

At the beginning of the 20th century archaeologists discovered many relics of the Dongsonian civilization dispersed the length of the **Ma River valley**. Most were found in the village of **Dong Son** on the left bank of the Ma River. Among the finds were bronze drums, musical instruments, statues, jewellery, various tools and domestic objects.

Lord Trieu's invasion in 208 B.C. was responsible for the Viet migration towards the South and these first emigrants settled in the Phu Ly and Dong Son regions.

The first bronze drum was discovered at Phu Ly in 1902 and other similar drums were acquired from the **Long Doi Son Monastery** and the village of **Ngoc Lu** in Ha Nam Ninh Province. The figurative and stylized designs on the drums depict birds, animals and scenes from every day life. The Ngoc Lu bronze drum, 25 inches (63 cm high) and 31 inches (79 cm) in diameter, is decorated with an image of the sun. Its many rays are surrounded by 16 concentric circles of various designs depicting deer, aquatic birds, people and aspects of everyday life. The drum's surface is engraved with pairs of animals and birds heading East towards the sun. In 1924 a member of *l'Ecole Francaise d'Extreme Orient* unearthed several bronze drums and other bronze objects at Dong Son.

The **Mieu Than Dong Co**, (Temple of the Spirit of the Drum) is found in

Dan Ne Village on Mount Tam Thai. The temple contains a bronze drum, 6½ feet (2 meters) in diameter and 3 feet (1 meter) high which according to popular belief is said to have belonged to one of the Hung kings. The drum's face is decorated with nine concentric circles engraved with ancient characters.

The Muong minority village of **Lam Son** in the highlands was the native village of Vietnam's national hero, Le Loi, who became King Le Thai To. It was from here that Le Loi launched a decade–long uprising against the Ming who occupied the country at the time. The struggle waged from 1418 to 1428 in this mountainous region finally ended in complete victory for Le Loi and his troops. The temple here is dedicated to Le Loi and contains his bronze likeness which was cast in 1532. Nguyen Trai, Le Loi's advisor penned the epitaph on the large Vinh Lang stele, dedicated solely to the life and works of Le Loi, in 1433. Other memorial stelae document 12 reigns of the Le family. Remains of the Royal Palace's ancient Lam Kinh Citadel are still visible here. The **Mausoleum of Dame Trieu** at the foot of **Mount Tung Son** in Phu Dien Village, is the final resting place of the national heroine, Trieu Thi Trinh, who led an uprising against the Chinese in 247 aided by her elder brother Trieu Quoc Dat. The attempt failed and Trieu, rather than have her fate decided by the victorious Ngo rulers, committed suicide. A temple was built in her memory and a festival is celebrated here in her honor on the 24th day of the 2nd lunar month every year.

The megalithic style **Ho Citadel** in **Tay Giai Village**, Quang Hoa district, was built in 1397 under the orders of the usurper king, Ho Qui Li. He named the new citadel Tay Kinh (Capital of the West). It was more or less a replica of the citadel of Dong Kinh (Capital of the East), but unlike the other citadels of Hoa Lu and Co Loa, whose walls were built of earth, rock was used for the Ho citadel's huge wall, 16 feet (5 meters) high and 9¾ feet (3 meters) thick. Some of the huge blocks of stone used in its construction weigh an estimated 16 tons and show a high degree of quarrying and stone carving skill.

Ten miles (16 km) from the provincial capital, Thanh Hoa, the fine white sands of **Sam Son Beach** stretch for two miles (3 km) along the coast from the **Lac Hoi River** to **Mount Truong Le**. Superb scenery surrounds the clear waters of Sam Son, named after the coastal mountain of the Truong Le Range, six miles (16 km) from Thanh Hoa.

In a cave on a rocky hillside near the mouth of the **Y Bich River** is a temple dedicated to An Tiem, the man who brought water melons to Vietnam. An Tiem is said to have domesticated the wild melon seed and to have grown his first melons here on the land near the temple. A beach in Nga Son district, where his descendants still live today, is named after him.

The **Doc Cuoc Genie Temple** halfway up Mount Truong Le is dedicated to a one-legged deity who is said to have divided himself in half and is believed to have supernatural powers that protect and save swimmers and navigators in distress. It is also said to guarantee the fishermen a good catch, although the local fishermen may have a different story. At the end of the range is another temple, the **Co Tien** or Fairy Temple.

The hunting area of **Khoa Truong**, 30 miles (50 km) southeast of Thanh Hoa township is a swampy area dotted with numerous ponds covering an area of three miles (5 km). It is the habitat of many aquatic and migratory birds who become fair game during the hunting season from October to February.

Numerous Muong villages lie scattered throughout the highlands of Thanh Hoa around the ridge of the Indochinese mountain range. Although the lowland Vietnamese, the Kinh, lost their original written script after 1,000 years of Chinese domination, the Muong have retained theirs. Known as *Khoa dau van* it is similar to Thai, Lao and Indian script and has an alphabet of 30 basic consonant signs similar to Arabic.

Cinnamon trees are indigenous to this highland region. The bark, a much sought after ingredient in Sino-Viet-

Ho Chi Minh's birthplace.

namese pharmaceutical preparations, is collected in the forests by the local inhabitants.

The Ham Rong bridge which links the Ngoc and Rong mountains on either side of the Ma River was first built in 1904. It was damaged during the war of resistance against the French and rebuilt again in 1964, before 70,000 tons of rockets made their mark during the war with the U.S. The bridge was built for the third time in 1973.

Nghe Tinh Province: South of Thanh Hoa Province lies **Nghe Tinh Province**, birthplace of the revolutionaries Phan Boi Chau (1867-1940) and Nguyen Ai Quoc (Ho Chi Minh, 1890-1969) and the national poet, Nguyen Du (1765-1820), author of *Kim Van Kieu*.

The findings of archaeologists revealed the existence of both a stone age and a bronze age culture in the province.

Nghe Tinh is one of the country's largest provinces, in terms of both area and population. Mountains and midlands give way to coastal plains along a 143 mile (230 km) coastline and forests cover three quarters of the province. The notoriously harsh climate often causes rain storms and flash flooding. More than 100 rivers and streams water the province, of these the longest is the **Lam Dong River** which springs from the mountains in the West. The Lam Dong is a busy waterway plied by boats, sampans and rafts carrying bamboo and timber. Deer, raised for their antlers are a common sight grazing amongst the orange orchards. The village of **Sen**, Ho Chi Minh's native village, proudly preserves the mud and wattle palm thatched house where he is said to have spent his childhood. Nearby is Uncle Ho's memorial house where memorabilia and photographs extol the virtues of the revolutionary struggle.

Vinh, the province's main town, does not have much to offer. Twelve miles (20 km) from here lies the fishing hamlet and sea pine bordered white sand beach of **Cua Lo**. The greatest attraction here is the spectacular sight of the fishermen pulling in their nets full of long silvery fish at sunrise.

The **Cuong Temple** occupies a site

on Mo Da Mountain next to National Highway 1 in Dien Chau district. The temple is dedicated to King An Duong Vuong, who ruled as Vietnam's first king when the nation was known as Au Lac, in the third century B.C.

Travelling southwards, National Highway 1 crosses the coastal plains then climbs the transversal **Hoan Son Hills** before entering **Binh Tri Thien Province**. A detour here from Highway 1 leads to the fishing village of **Roon**, or **Mui Ron**. Vast quantities of sea slugs (*hai sam*) and abalone (*bao ngu*) are caught here. At the mouth of the Roon River is Canh Duong village, a resistance stronghold during the war against the French. Today the village is known for its silk weaving and jute tapestry. The **Mieu Ong Shrine** here is dedicated to whales, a creature this fishing community regard as friend and benefactor. During the American bombings, the shrine's whale skeleton was moved to the Canh Duong communal house.

The coastal village of **Ba Don** is well worth visiting on market day when the

place is absolutely inundated with all manner of local products, livestock and a multitude of foodstuffs more or less appreciated by the rural population.

Further South lies the **Gianh River** which once served as the demarcation line (*ranh* or *gianh*) between North and South Vietnam. Its deep and turbulent waters defy any attempt to build a bridge across it. The Gianh and the Nhat Le are the two main rivers in the province. The 158 km long Gianh takes its source in the Huong Son mountains in Nghe Tinh Province and flows through limestone mountains, forming wonderful grottoes such as Minh Can , Lac Son and Phong Na, in the process.

A visit to the beautiful **Phong Na Caves** is not to be missed when in the locality. These caves with their wonderful stalactites and stalagmites are incontestably Vietnam's second natural marvel after Halong Bay. The caves are entered via an underground river reached by following the Gianh River back up towards its source in the limestone massifs of the highlands. Below the underground river cave, another dry and airy cave extends several kilometers into the depths of the earth.

South of the Phong Nha Caves lies the provincial capital, **Dong Hoi** and the remains of the ancient **Dong Hoi Wall** at the mouth of the **Nhat Le River**. The wall served as a defense rampart against Lord Trinh from the North. It was the brainchild of the great Vietnamese statesman, Dao Duy To (1572-1634), counsellor and prime minister to Lord Sai Vuong (1562-1635). A large stone stele inscribed with Dao Duy To's biography and works stands under the Quang Binh Arch in the citadel at Dong Hoi. Dao Duy To also built another wall, the **Luy Truong Duc**. Its ruins are still visible amongst the innumerable wild strawberry trees beside **Xuan Duc** in Quanh Ninh prefecture. The locals use the fruit from the trees to make delicious wine (*ruou dau*), aromatic liqueurs with vanilla, and some aperitifs with quinine which were widely commercialized during the second world war. Towards the Nhat Le river mouth

A typical scene in the central coast region.

lies the battlefield where much bloody combat took place during the 17th and 18th centuries between the Trinh Lords of the North and the Nguyen Lords of the South. The unfathomable waters of **Lake Bau Tro** nearby are contained in the crater of an ancient volcano.

On the other side of the Nhat Le River immense sand dunes stretch all the way to the coast. The forestry service has been trying to establish plant life on these dunes since the beginning of the century but their chances of succeeding appear rather slim.

Heading South from the region of Dong Hoi, the road to the West leads in the direction of the rice growing areas of **Quang Ninh** and **Le Thuy**. Some 59 miles (95 km) North of Hue the road arrives at the **Hien Luong Bridge** spanning the **Ben Hai River**. Situated exactly on the 17th parallel, the river served as the natural demarcation line between North and South Vietnam for two decades after the frontier was set by the Geneva Agreement on 20 July 1954. More than a simple geographical fron-

tier, the river separated two ideologically opposed political currents, spanned by a bridge that could not be crossed until the fall of Saigon in April 1975 and the country's subsequent reunification.

Binh Tri Thien Province is composed of a series of small plains bordered by sand dunes in the East and forests, valleys and the green plateaus of the **Truong Son Mountain Chain** in the West. It includes the three former provinces of Quang Binh, Quang Tri and Thuan Hoa, which like many small provinces, were amalgamated into one large province after the country's unification in 1975. Its 212 mile (340 km) coastline is the longest of all the provinces.

A mountain trail built by North Vietnamese guerillas runs parallel to the national highway. Part of the Ho Chi Minh Trail, it was used by the revolutionary forces as a supply route for their troops and arms to reach the South.

A short distance off National Route 9 which leads from **Dong Ha** to **Savannakhet** in Laos, lie the remains of the **Tan So Citadel,** near **Cam Lo**.

Transporting goods and people on Highway 1 and (right) near Hue.

DANANG AND ANCIENT CHAMPA

Quang Nam Danang Province lies some 500 miles (800 km) equidistant between Hanoi and Saigon, separated from Laos by the western Truong Son Mountain Range. Forests of valuable timber – rose wood, barian king wood, iron wood and ebony cover more than 60 percent of the province.

When travelling here from Hue the climate becomes noticeably warmer and less humid once you descend the 3,961 feet (1,219 meter) summit of **Cloudy Pass** (Deo Hai Van) which adjoins another mountain called **Bach Ma** (White Horse), and descends to the scenic coastal region.

The provincial capital, **Danang,** located on the west bank of the Han River, has grown from a small fishing village into an important port and the country's fourth-largest city of 400,000 inhabitants. Known as *Tourane* under the French, Danang is perhaps best remembered abroad as the port where 3,500 American marines first set foot in South Vietnam on 8th March 1965.

In the 17th and 18th centuries the first Spanish and French landings were made here. Subsequently Danang became the scene of battles between the Vietnamese who fought first the Spanish and later the French. In the course of the 19th century it superseded Faifo (Hoi An) as the most important port and commercial center in the central region.

Vestiges of an Ancient Culture: The ancient Kingdom of Champa once stretched all the way from Hue, in central Vietnam, to **Vung Tau** (Cap St. Jacques) in the South. The kingdom incorporated the five provinces of O Ri, Amaravati, Vijaya, Kauthara, and Panduranga.

The Quang Nam Danang area was the center of the Cham civilization for many centuries. The most ancient capital, Singhapura (Lion Citadel) at **Tra Kieu** was built during the course of the fourth century. Early in the eighth century the capital was moved south to Panduranga.

In the late eighth century it was trans-ferred back to Quang Nam Danang and renamed Indrapura (City of the Genie of Thunder). Indrapura lasted until the early 11th century.

The ancient site of Singhapura at **Tra Kieu**, 25 miles (40 km) southwest of Danang, with its dozens of monuments, hundreds of statues and bas reliefs, attests to the rich culture of the kingdom which once flourished here. A stele erected by the eighth Champa king to the mem-ory of the Hindu poet Valmiki, author of the "Ramayana" still stands intact.

The sacred Buddhist-inspired site of Indrapura, now known as **Dong Duong** lies 37 miles(60km) from Danang. The site's scattered monuments, some Buddhist and others Brahman inspired, are engraved with texts about a line of nine kings and their deeds.

Archaeologists have discovered many artifacts at the site, including the 2nd century bronze Dong Duong Buddha which now resides in the National Museum in Saigon. A large Buddhist monastery and many holy shrines are also located here.

The **My Son Valley**, 43 miles (70 km) southwest of Danang, was chosen as a religious sanctuary by King Bhadra-varman I and from the 4th century onwards, many temples and towers (*kalan*) were built here. Most were dedicated to kings and Brahman divinities, including the god Shiva, who was considered the creator, founder and defender of the Champa Kingdom and the Cham royal dynasties.

Some 12th century stelae discovered here attest to a unified religious belief practised in the sanctuary's first temple which was erected for the worship of Shiva-Bhadresvara.

More than seventy architectural works of different styles and eras once stood in this ancient valley but today less than 20 remain. Tragically, My Son fell in a free-fire zone for B52 strategic bombers during the last war and was almost completely destroyed by bombs.

The Cham towers were ingeniously constructed of dried bricks stuck together with resin from the cau day tree. Once the tower was complete it was encircled

Preceding pages: Hoi An was once an important trading port. *Left*, Cham tower near Cam Ranh.

by fires which were kept well stoked for several days. The intense heat fired the whole structure, completely melding and sealing the bricks and resin together to form a structure well able to withstand the combined onslaught of time and the elements, but unfortunately not 20th century bombs.

The Chams were divided into two groups, the **Dua**, who inhabited the provinces of Amarvati and Vijaya, and the **Cau**, from the provinces of Kauthara and Pandaranga. The two clans differed in their customs and habits and contesting interests led to many clashes and even war. With a little foresight they managed to quite effectively settle their disagreements through intermarriage between the two clans.

An insight into the fascinating culture and history of the Cham people is provided the excellent **Museum of Cham Sculpture** in Danang and a booklet of the same name, printed in English, Russian and Vietnamese by the Foreign Languages Publishing House.

The museum was set up in 1936 by the *Ecole Francaise d'Extreme Orient.* Its extensive collection is displayed in rooms featuring the four different periods according to their origins, My Son, Tra Kieu, Dong Duong and Thap Mam, and the different influences which shaped the culture and history of the Cham people as revealed through their sculpture and carvings.

Five miles (8 km) South of Danang towards the coast stand five large hills known as the **Marble Mountains** or **Mountains of the Five Elements** (Ngu Hanh Son): Kim Son (metal), Thuy Son (water), Moc Son (wood), Hoa Son (fire) and Tho Son (earth).

These mountains were once a group of five offshore islets, but due to silting up over the years became part of the mainland. Mysterious caves within the mountains shelter altars dedicated to Buddha, Bodhisattvas and the different genies arising from the popular beliefs held by the area's inhabitants. The most famous of these is **Thuy Son**. Long since used by the Cham for their rituals, today these caves still serve as religious sanctuaries. Here you can visit the **Tam Thi Temple**, built in 1852, the **Linh Ung Temple** and the **Huyen Khong Grotto**.

The mountains are also a valuable source of red, white and blue-green marble. At the foot of the mountains, skilful marble carvers chisel out a great variety of *objets d'art*.

The palm-shaded peninsula of **Lang Co** rates as one of the most superb spots in the country. Located just north of Hai Van Pass, to one side lies a stunningly clear blue lagoon and on the other miles of unspoilt beach washed by the South China Sea.

Among the specialities produced in the province are cinnamon from Tra Mi, pepper from Tien Phuoc, tobacco from Cam Le, silk from Hoa Vang, saffron from Tam Ky and sea swallows nests from the islands off the coast.

The *nuoc mam* produced in the fishing village of **Nam O**, 9½ miles (15 km) from the city towards Hai Van Vass is reputedly the best in Vietnam.

Cham, Mnong, Hoa, Ka Tu, Sedang and Co are among the many minorities found in the province.

Cham sculpture in the Danang Museum.

HOI AN

About 15 miles (25 km) southeast of Danang, the ancient town of **Hoi An** nestles on the banks of the **Thu Bon River** 3 miles (5 km) inland from the coast. This charming old town was once a flourishing port and meeting place of eastern and western cultures in central Dai Viet under the Nguyen lords. It appeared in western travelogues in the 17th and 18th centuries as **Faifo** or Hai Po.

Originally a sea port in the Champa Kingdom known as Dai Chien, by the 15th century it had become a coastal Vietnamese town under the Tran Dynasty. In the beginning of the 16th century the Portuguese came to explore the coast of Hoi An. They were followed by the first western traders in the area. Then came the Chinese, the Japanese, the Dutch, the British and the French. With them came the first missionaries, Italian, Portuguese, French, Spanish and among them Alexander of Rhodes.

For several centuries Hoi An was one of the most important trading ports in Southeast Asia and an important center of cultural exchange between East and West. By the end of the 18th and the beginning of the 19th centuries, Hoi An's social and physical environment had changed drastically. The conflict between the Trinh and Nguyen Lords and the Tay Son caused Hoi An considerable damage. Rivers changed course as the mouth of the Thy Bon River silted up and prevented the flow of sea traffic. Another port was built at the mouth of the Han River and Danang succeeded Hoi An.

In the early 1980s UNESCO and the Polish Government took the initiative and funded a restoration programme to classify and safeguard Hoi An's ancient quarters and historic monuments.

The old town area borders the Thu Bon River in the South of the town. Le Loi Street was the first street to be built four centuries ago. The Japanese quarter with its covered bridge, Japanese-style shops and houses followed half a

A Chinese temple in Hoi An.

century later, followed by the Cantonese quarter 50 years later.

Hoi An's ancient past is superbly preserved in its architecture. The old quarter is a fascinating blend of temples, pagodas, community houses, shrines, clan houses, shop houses and homes.

One of the most remarkable historical architectural examples is the covered Japanese Bridge. Built by the Japanese community in the 17th century, it links the districts of Cam Pho and Minh Huong. The bridge's curved shape, and undulating green and yellow tiled roof, give the impression of moving water. In the middle of the bridge is a square pagoda dedicated to Dac De and Tran Vu, two legendary figures.

Some pagodas and 20 clan houses stand in the center of the ancient town. The **Chua Phuc Kien**, on Tran Phu Street, built in 1792, has been the meeting place of many generations of the same clan who arrived from Fukien. Here they remember their origins and worship their ancestors. The temple is dedicated to the cult of Lady Thien Hau

and contains many exquisite woodcarvings. Most of these temples and houses were built by the Chinese migrant community over a span of 40 years between 1845 and 1885.

Also on Tran Phu Street the **Mieu Quan Cong**, built in 1904, is dedicated to Quang Cong, a talented general of the Three Kingdoms period in Chinese history. Many of the temples venerate Buddha along with confucianism, Taoism a diversity of other gods, goddesses, and genies. The 15th century **Phuc Thanh Pagoda** on the outskirts of Hanoi contains many beautiful statues and is one of the oldest in the region.

Although many of the old homes and monuments have been restored over the years, they retain their original wooden framework, carved doors and windows and sculpted stuccos as well as very rare and ancient furniture from Vietnam, China, Japan and the West.

The most characteristic examples of Hoi An's architecture are the old houses along Nguyen Thai Hoc Street, particularly at Number 1001. These elongated houses front onto one street and back on to the street behind, linking the two streets. All the houses are built of precious wood in a very refined double-storey style. The front facade serves as a boutique and the area behind is generally used as storage space. The interior is terraced for living and an inner a courtyard is open to the sky with a verandah linking several living quarters. One of the most remarkable features of these old homes is the diversity in their architectural structure. This varies greatly from one house to another in terms of space distribution, sculptural art, decoration and inner courtyard gardens. Space is utilized to the utmost. The unique crab shell roof style extensively used is typical of Hoi An. Walking in the streets of this beautiful and charming ancient town, a living vestige of the past, one can observe the influence of the architecture, sculpture and decorative styles of China and Japan and the skill of the Vietnamese architects who have absorbed their influences and created something similar yet somehow uniquely different.

Catching up on the latest news. Right, lacquered smile.

CENTRAL HIGHLANDS AND DALAT

A part of the country that does not as yet feature on any of the regular programmes run by the tourist authorities is the Central Highlands region ranging across the two provinces of **Gia Lai Kon Tum** and **Dac Lac**. This relatively untamed corner of Vietnam is home to many ethnic minorities, hardy people who have resisted any attempts, colonial or communist, to modify their traditional way of life.

This region with its beautiful mountain scenery, mist-shrouded valleys and plateaus, waterfalls, lakes and rivers and cool climate is unfortunately still a sensitive area and largely inaccessible to tourists.

Gia Lai Kontum: The two large plateaus of Gia Lai and Kon Tum make up this province which covers an area of 9,576 square miles (25,536 square km) and shares a border with both Laos and Cambodia in the West. Some 27 ethnic minorities, including Jarai, Bahnar, Ra De, Sedang, Nhang Thai, Kohor and Mnong are found here.

With an average annual temperature of 23.9°C, the region experiences two distinct seasons, the rainy season from May to November and the dry season from December to April.

Forests rich in timber, medicinal plants, birds and animals cover half the province's land area. Coffee, rubber, tea, groundnuts and soya beans are grown on the plateaus, while cotton and rice are cultivated in the fertile valleys. Lush pastures support thousands of head of livestock. The land is also rich in titanium, tin, gold, copper, chromite, bauxite and other minerals.

The provincial capital, **Plei Ku** perches at an altitude of 2,487 feet (785 meters) on a vast plateau, populated by Jarai and Ra De minorities. Six miles (10 km) from here T'nung Lake, a natural lake created by an ancient volcano, mirrors the surrounding forests.

Kon Tum, the other sizeable town in

Preceding pages: Tea plantations in the central highlands. *Left*, war memorial in Buon Me Thuot.

the province, is located on a marshy lakeside plain at an altitude of 1,722 feet (525 meters). This large market town with its population of 35,000 is peopled by ethnic minorities, mainly Bahnar, Sedang and Jarai. Some Cham remains, including a 13th century tower at Ya Liao, can also be seen in the area. Hot springs can be found at Dac To, Cong Ray, Dac Ro, Cong Phu and Rang Ria. Boating and hunting trips can be arranged. Although permission to visit ethnic minority villages is still difficult to acquire, it is well worth trying for.

Dac Lac Province to the South, covers an area of 7,425 square miles (19,800 km) and shares a 125 mile (200 km) western border with Cambodia. The population consists mainly of Ra De, Kinh and Mnong. Many rivers, streams and waterfalls grace the richly-forested landscape of this province where Ra De longhouses loom shadowy in the misty mountain passes.

The moderate climate is slightly cooler than that of Gia Lai Kontum and here the rainy season lasts from April to October, followed by a dry season from November to March.

The provincial capital, **Buon Me Thuot** with its population of 65,000, constitutes the most densely populated area in the Central Highlands. It is served by an airport linking it with Hanoi and Saigon and can be reached via Highway 21 from Ninh Hoa, just North of Nha Trang.

As far as war memorials go, the incongruous Russian tank set on a slanting pedestal in Buon Me Thuot's town center has to be one of the most original.

The museum, across the road from the Thang Loi Hotel, provides an insight into the lives of the region's ethnic minorities. Among the items on display are musical instruments, traditional costumes, fishing and hunting gear and weaving looms. Special permission must be obtained from the authorities well in advance if you wish to visit any of the minority villages and should you be successful be sure to take gifts of salt, sweets and cigarettes as these are much appreciated by the villagers.

Elephant races are a popular attraction.

The Ra De village of **Buon Tu** some eight miles (13 km) East of the town comprises extended family groups living in wonderful stilt longhouses. Home brewed rice wine and local dances accompanied by gongs are turned on for visitors here. On the way to the village you can visit the Dray Sap waterfall or stop to go fishing and enjoy a meal on a fishing boat.

About 12 miles (20 km) South of here, Emperor Bao Dai's summer house nestles on a hillside beside **Dac Lac Lake**. Mountains, hills, and marshes surround this lake where great numbers of storks and cranes turn the area white during their migratory visits. The lake becomes a scene of noisy animation during the boat and elephant races that take place here every spring.

Buon Don, a village 28 miles (45 km) northeast of Buon Me Thuot in E Sap district, is home to various minorities, but chiefly Mnong. The Mnong are wild elephant hunters and for several hundred years Buon Don, like other villages in Dac Lac, has been famous for its el-ephant hunters and tamers and their trade between Vietnam, Burma and India. The villagers grow vast amounts of sugar cane and grass to feed the enormous appetites of their 50 odd domestic elephants which are indispensable to the hunt. Some men living in the village claim to have captured as many as 300 elephants. It takes between two to three years to tame an elephant and there are always about 50 or 60 in the village. The best time to visit is during the spectacular elephant races. Visitors to the village are usually invited by the chief and village elders to join them in a circle around a large ceramic jar and partake of some home brewed rice wine through long bamboo straws. If you are very lucky you may be treated to a traditional musical performance accompanied by dancing.

To reach any of these villages you will need a guide and the patience of a saint to deal with the brick wall of bureaucracy that greets requests to visit these wonderfully warm-hearted and hospitable minorities.

Dalat's cool climate is ideal for market gardening.

Lam Dong Province: Geographically part of the Tay Nguyen Highlands, **Lam Dong Province**, bordering Dac Lac Province in the West and Thuan Hai Province in the East, lies across the Lam Vien, Don Duong – Lien Khuong and Bao Loc – Di Linh plateaus. The population comprises of more than 20 ethnic groups, including Kohor, Lat, Ma and Si La. Forests cover 68 percent of this often mist-shrouded region. Lam Dong boasts Vietnam's most popular mountain resort, **Dalat**.

The City of Eternal Spring: Dalat nestles amongst mountains, pine-clad hillsides, lakes and forests on the Lam Vien plateau beside the **Cam Ly River**. The city has a population of 125,000 with an economy based mainly on horticulture and tourism. The average annual temperature of 17°C, fresh mountain air and tranquil beauty attracted the French who developed the resort and built their holiday villas on the hillsides. Dalat has long been a favorite destination for lovers and honeymooners. Its temperate calm and beauty provide a welcome retreat from the heat, noise and bustle of Saigon and the heat of the coastal plains. Many natural beauty spots await the visitor in and around this charming old town which retains something of a colonial air thanks to its many colonial villas with their attractive gardens where roses, poppies, geraniums, hibiscus, sunflowers, gladioli and other European flowers bloom alongside the beautiful native orchids.

Its name derives from two words, Da meaning river or source – in reference to the Cam Ly River, and Lat the name of an ethnic minority living there.

Dalat was at one time projected to become the eventual capital of the Indochinese State Federation under the French. In the late 19th century the French Governor of Cochinchina sent a delegation headed by Dr. Alexandre Yersin, to explore the Dalat region. On the strength of their findings, Governor Paul Doumer established a meteorological and agricultural research center here.

Although accessible by several in-

Waiting for customers. Right, differing modes of transport.

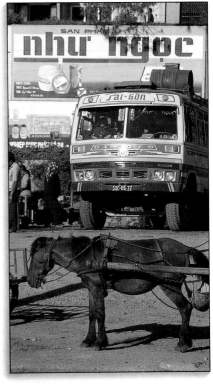

land routes from the coastal provinces of Phu Khanh and Thuan Hai, the most used is the 180 mile (300km) route via Bien Hoa Province from Ho Chi Minh City. Another route, from Nha Trang on Highway 11 passes through areas rich in Cham relics.

The old French quarter near the bridge spanning the Cam Ly River has lost none of its charm or character. Here you'll find the **Dalat Catholic Cathedral**, Nha Tho Con Ga, which was built in 1931. Its stained glass windows were made by Louis Balmet in Grenoble. Mass is held twice daily at 5.30 a.m. and 5.15 p.m. on week days and at 5.30 a.m., 7 a.m. and 4 p.m. on Sundays.

Another Catholic church, the Du Sinh, rests on a hilltop up Huyen Tran Cong Chua Street where it commands a superb view of the surrounding area. It was built in 1955 by northern Catholic refugees.

The Summer residence of Vietnam's last Nguyen emperor, Bao Dai stands in a well maintained park further on from the cathedral. It was begun in 1933 and finished five years later. Although the building's exterior may appear nothing special, the interior is worth visiting. Not too far from here, at 2 Thien My Street is the **Lam Ty Ni Pagoda** which was founded in 1961. The pagoda's attractive flower beds and gardens and much of its wooden furniture are the handiwork of the pagoda's sole monk, the venerable Vien Thuc.

The pink Evangelical Church at 72 Nguyen Van Troi Street was built in 1940. Since 1975, Vietnam's Protestants have suffered persecution and even today the government restricts the activities of this church whose congregation is composed mostly of hilltribe people. A Bible study from 7.00 to 8.00 a.m. preceeds the worship service from 8 to 10 a.m. and the youth service held from 1.30 to 3.30 p.m. Also pink, the Domaine de Marie Convent, built between 1940 and 1942, perches on a hilltop at 6 Ngo Quyen Street. Mass is held in the chapel daily at 5.30 a.m. and also at 4.15 p.m. on Sundays.

The morning market in the heart of

Left, preparing to pay their respects. Below, city of eternal Spring.

Dalat is a an ideal place to encounter some of the ethnic minorities, distinctive in their traditional dress, who come from the surrounding villages to sell their produce. Here you will also discover the great diversity of fruit, flowers and vegetables produced in this region. Dalat's strawberries and delicious strawberry jam are famous throughout the country. Avocados, artichokes, mushrooms, tomatoes, in fact all the fruit, flowers and vegetables found in Europe can be grown in the region. Flowers from Dalat are sent to all parts of Vietnam and even further afield. A wide range of handicraft items find their way to the market from various parts of the country. These include bamboo handbags, rattan boxes, pressed flowers, fur hats and clothing.

Dalat's **Ethnic Minority Museum** is a must for anyone visiting Lam Dong province. Exhibits include traditional costumes, ornaments, jewellery, basketware, hunting implements and interesting musical instruments. The museum's archaeological display features a statue of the Hindu goddess, Uma, 12th and 14th century Cham pottery vases, rice wine jars over 200 years old, an unusual stone xylophone and tools used in the province over 1,500 years ago. The curator of the museum is a wealth of information on the minorities.

Visits can be arranged to hillside minority villages and hamlets where villagers make a meager living from the rice, corn, pumpkins, squash, tobacco and sometimes cotton they grow on the hillsides. They also work in the tea and coffee plantations. The Ma minority women are excellent weavers and dye their cloth using natural bark extracts. Their menfolk use simple traps and spears to hunt and fish. A toxic substance extracted from leaves is sometimes used in fishing. This paralyses the fish but is apparently harmless to humans.

Horse and carts are still a common sight and means of transport in and around Dalat; you can also opt to explore some of the scenic spots in and around the township on horseback.

Lake Xuan Hoang, formerly part of

Taxi rank features a fleet of Peugots, of course.

the town's golf course during the colonial era, lies in the heart of the town. The surrounding low hills, villas and pine forests are mirrored in its still waters.

In front of the lake are the Orchid Gardens which were established in 1966.

The **Linh Son Pagoda** at 120 Nguyen Van Troi Street in the North of the city roughly ½ mile (1 km) from the center, was established in 1938.

Three miles (5 km) from town, in **the Valley of Love**, (Thung Lung Tinh Yeu), you can wander in the forest where Emperor Bao Dai used to hunt. Colorful sail boats can be rented on the artificial lake which was formed during flooding in 1972.

The **Lake of Sorrows** or Ho Than Tho lies 3 miles (5 km) northeast of Dalat. It derives its name from the patriotism of a young couple, Hang Tung and Mai Nuong. As the story goes, when Hang joined Quang Trung's resistance forces against the Tsin invaders, Mai, believing that Hang would be better able to serve his country unencumbered drowned herself in the lake. Since then the lake has been known by its present name.

It would be impossible to visit Dalat and Lam Dong Province without visiting at least one of the innumerable waterfalls liberally sprinkling the landscape. In a park about two miles from Dalat you can visit the **Cam Ly Falls** and about three miles (km) further South the **Da Tanla Falls** cascade into a pool enclosed by high rock walls surrounded by luxuriant forest.

Enclosed within the **Thousand Flowers Valley** and pine-clad hills, the **Prenn Falls**, also known as Thien Sa, eight miles (13 km) south of Dalat, descend 50 feet (15 meters) across the mouth of a cave which you can enter from behind the falls via a small bridge.

Water from the Ankroet or **Golden Stream Falls**, seven miles (12 km) from Dalat falls from a height of 50 feet (15 meters).

Some 18 miles (30 km) from town are the **Lien Khuong Falls** and 5 miles (8 km) further on the silvery waters of the **Gougah** or Pot Hole Falls drop from a height of 66 feet (20 meters), creating a rainbow-like effect on sunny days. The **Pongour Falls**, 30 miles (50 km) from Dalat lie deep within thick primeval forest. The sound of the waters falling from a height of 98 feet (30 meters) can be heard two miles away during the rainy season.

The Lang Biang Mountains, which flank the town to the north and northeast comprise of five volcanic peaks which range in height between 2,100 and 2,400 meters. A three-to-four-hours' hike up to the top will reward you with a splendid view. Another good place for trekking is **Mount Nui Ba**. The holy waters in the area are said to cure many ailments.

The road heading South from Dalat passes through pine forests and into the Di Linh district where pineapple plantations and tall elephant grass line the roadside. Here and also in Bao Lac district it is not uncommon to see members of the Ma minority walking along the road carrying large stick baskets supported by head straps.

The **Bao Lac Mulberry** and **Silkworm Farm**, one of the largest in the world, is well worth a visit, but here again special permission must be obtained from the authorities before a visit can be arranged. Here new silkworm hybrids, bred to survive the cooler highland climate are raised all year round. The silkworms dine on mulberry leaves from the farm's 10,000 odd hectares of mulberry plants and spin silk cocoons which produce 37 tons of silk per year.

The climate here is also ideal for tea growing and visits can be arranged to one of Ba Lac's tea plantation and processing factories.

The **Krayo Temple**, 44 miles (71 km) from Dalat beside Highway 20, contains some personal belongings of the Cham kings, among which are costumes and valuable jewellery.

Lam Dong is by far the most accessible and developed of the Central Highland provinces and provides an opportunity to catch a glimpse of the diverse highland ethnic minorities without the often insurmountable bureaucratic wall that accompanies requests to enter Gia Lai Kon Tum and Dac Lac provinces.

Dalat's charming cathedral.

THE SOUTH CENTRAL COAST

Nha Trang: Vietnam's most picturesque coastal town and beach resort is the ideal place to break a journey, relax and soak up the sun. Established on the orders of a Nguyen king in 1924, Nha Trang with its population of 200,000 is now the provincial capital of **Phu Khanh Province** which incorporates the former provinces of Phu Yen and Khanh Hoa and lies to the East of the Central Highlands. According to popular belief, the town derives its name from the Cham word, *Yakram* meaning bamboo river.

At the town's northern entrance stand the majestic towers of the famous Brahman sanctuary and temple, **Po Nagar**. The main tower is dedicated to the Cham goddess, Po Ino Nagar, the Lady Mother of the Kingdom, reputedly Siva's female form. Today she is still worshipped, adopted by Vietnamese Buddhists who refer to her as Thien Y A Na. Her statue resides in the main

temple. It was decapitated during French rule and the original head now resides in the Guimet Museum in Paris. Only four of the sanctuary's original eight temples, all of which face East, remain standing. These date from between the 6th and 11th centuries. From the top of San Hill behind the ancient Cham Towers, a superb panoramic view looks out over Nha Trang.

Palm trees line the dazzling fine white sands and clear waters of Nha Trang's gently curving bay. Idyllic islands, easily accessible by boat, lie just off the coast. Boat excursions can be arranged to visit the islands and coral reefs, the snorkelling is excellent or you may prefer to try your hand at deep sea fishing. The islands, particularly **Hon Yen** (Salagande Island) are home to sea swallows whose famous nests, gathered in vast quantities, constitute a valuable source of both nutrition and income.

The nests are collected twice a year here, in Spring and Autumn. They vary in color from grey and white to the greatly appreciated and much rarer or-

Preceding pages: Nha Trang harbor. Below, resort appeal.

ange and red nests. These are naturally a lot more valuable and are believed to have certain therapeutic properties which no doubt add to the price.

A huge white Buddha statue commands an excellent view from his seat at the top the hill behind the Long Son Pagoda. The pagoda was established in the latter part of the 19th century and has been reconstructed several times since. Glass and ceramic mosaics depicting dragons adorn the main entrance and roofs, and colorful dragons are entwined around the pillars of the main hall.

The **Pasteur Institute** on the sea front was founded in 1895 by Dr. Alexandre Yersin, a French microbiologist and military doctor who had worked as an assistant to Dr. Pasteur in Paris. He arrived in Vietnam in 1891 and was among those who discovered Dalat. Dr Yersin was also responsible for introducing and establishing Brazilian rubber trees and quinquina plantations – quinine producing trees – in the region of **Suoi Dau** southwest of Nha Trang. He is buried here among his rubber trees according to the wishes of his will.

Dr. Yersin's library and office have been converted into a museum. On display here, are some of his personal effects and laboratory equipment. Many of his books are kept in the library opposite the museum.

Today the institute still produces vaccines and carries out research with a very limited budget and equipment that looks as if it should join the exhibits in the museum.

While at Suoi Dau you may like to visit Hon Ba Hill and a lagoon known as **Ho Tien**, the Lagoon of the Immortals. The lagoon is formed by a stream which tumbles down the Hon Ba hillside. According to legend the flat rocks that jut above the surface of the lagoon were once a meeting place for immortals who gathered there to play chess and inscribe their wins and losses on the rocks.

The **Oceanographic Institute** is located two miles (6 km) South of the town in the fishing village of Cau Da. The Institute was founded in 1927 on the initiative of a biologist, Armand Krempf. Today it houses a comprehen-

sive collection of aquatic flora and fauna. Its aquariums are greatly admired and no small wonder. A fascinating variety of the most strange and incredibly beautiful fish swim around in an almost natural environment. The Institute's most important section contains a complete collection of the rarest species found in the Pacific Ocean. Behind the main building a large hall is packed with thousands of stuffed birds and fish, coral and specimens preserved in jars.

Cau Da does a brisk business in shells, coral and tortoiseshell items at reasonable prices. The ever-present Vietnamese condiment, *nuoc mam*, is produced here in large quantities. Five tons of a sardine-like fish, *ca nuc*, left to break down in two tons of salt will yield 70,000 litres of *nuoc mam* and the most overpowering odour in the process. The seafood, particularly fresh lobster, is worth stopping for. Another good eating place is the floating sea food restaurant on the artificial lake at the Tri Nguyen fish breeding farm near Cau Da.

Just North of Cau Da, Emperor Bao

Dai's five villas are set amongst well established trees and shrubs on three hills. The villas were built in the 1920s, their location was obviously carefully chosen for the superb views over the sea, the bay and the port. From the mid-1950s until 1975 the high ranking officialdom of the South Vietnamese government enjoyed the views, but everything changed in 1975 when they were requisitioned by their high-ranking communist counterparts. Today, you too can enjoy the accommodation and view enjoyed by the country's elite for a modest US$35 a night.

During the day you can catch the interesting sights and smells of Nha Trang's bustling main market, Cho Dam, which was built in 1972. Goods include everything from fruit and vegetables to items ingeniously made from old aircraft parts.

A sight well worth making the effort to be around for is the local fishing fleet returning in the evening with the setting sun – quite spectacular – best seen from the Xom Bong bridge across the **Cai River**. The Cai, which joins several waterways from the western forests, flows to the Nha Trang river mouth. The province's largest river, the 180 mile (300 km) long **Da Rang River** is the longest in Central Vietnam, from it hundreds of kilometers of canals branch off carrying water to the vast fields of rice, maize, beans and tobacco.

The three hills at Nha Trang's western exit each sport a pagoda. The most important of these is the **Hai Duc**, a religious center led by the head of the South Vietnamese Buddhist Church, Thich Tri Thu.

Six miles (10 km) further west lie the remains of the old vauban-style **Dien Khanh Citadel**, built in 1793 by French engineers employed by Lord Nguyen Anh, who became Emperor Gia Long in 1802. Little is left of it today apart from a few straggling sections of the walls and gates.

Not far from the town the **Hon Chong Rocks** jut out into the clear aquamarine waters of the South China Sea. Northeast of here is **Mount Tien Co**, Fairy

Coconut palms add to the tropical ambiance.

Mountain, so named because its three summits are thought to resemble a fairy lying on her back.

To the north, National Highway 1 traverses the **Minh Hoa Plain**, crosses the Ro Tuong and Ru Ri Passes, before climbing the sinuous 7 mile (12 km) **Deo Ca Pass** over **Mount Dai Lan**. Here, in 1470, King Le Thanh Tong and his troops stopped and erected a stele to mark the boundary between Dai Viet and the Kingdom of Champa. Later on in history the same spot marked the boundary between the former provinces of Phu Yen and Khanh Hoa which was once the fourth region of the ancient Kingdom of Champa. The Deo Ca stretches all the way down to the coast, causing the railway to pass through seven tunnels.

To the East lies **Cap Varella** and in the West the famous **Mother and Child Mountain** reaches a height of 6,632 feet (2,022 meters). The mountain can be seen on a clear day by fishermen far out at sea and was so named because from a distance its silhouette resembles a women carrying a child.

From Cap Varella the road descends sharply towards the market town of **Tu Bong** and from there to **Van Gia**.

The **Long Son Pagoda** at **Van Gia** made the headlines after one of its officiating bonzes, the Buddhist martyr, Thich Quang Duc, immolated himself in the center of Saigon in 1963. The pagoda's enormous white Buddha, erected in 1963, commemorates the Buddhist struggle against the repressive Diem regime. Images of the Buddhist nuns and monks who laid down their lives as a final protest lie beneath the foot of the statue.

As well as beautiful unspoilt beaches, Phu Khanh Province is generously endowed with thermal springs. Take your pick from those at Phu Sen, Triem Duc, Truong Son, Phuoc Long, Cay Vung, Ninh Hoa, Duc Mai or Tu Buong.

The scenery throughout the province is varied and quite magnificent. Forests in the North produce many precious essences and wood, including sandalwood, aloe wood, eaglewood, barian

The beach is "flipping" wonderful.

kingwood, rosewood and ebony.

An abundance of high quality sea salt is produced at **Hon Khoi**, the Smoking Mountain. The area of Cam Ranh alone has more than 300 hectares of salt marsh which yield around half a million tons of salt per year. Immense sugar cane plantations cover certain areas of the province. Molasses produced from the sugar residue is combined with sand and lime to produce an inexpensive and excellent mortar substance used in construction.

Leaving Nha Trang via the South, the coastal road passes **Cam Ranh Bay**, the deep water bay used as a naval base, first by the Americans and later by the Russians. The base remains a sensitive military area and no photography is permitted. The sand from the bay is of a quality much sought after for manufacturing lenses and high quality crystal. Before the war enormous quantities of it were exported to Japan, Europe and the United States.

Not far South of Cam Ranh the road enters **Thuan Hai Province**. Lying in the southernmost stretch of Central Vietnam, Thuan Hai incorporates the three former provinces of Ninh Thuan, Binh Thuan and Binh Thy. Mountains and forest cover two-thirds of Thuan Hai, however, it remains one of the country's poorest areas due to its lack of agricultural resources – only 10 percent of the province is suitable for farming. The coastal road southwards passes through a rather monotonous, infertile, sand covered landscape.

The town of **Phan Rang**, an ancient Cham principality on the **Chai River**, lies in an extremely arid landscape dotted with mean looking cacti and poinciana trees. From here a scenic inland road leads to Dalat. Some four miles (7 km) down this road , four 13th century Cham towers known as **Po Klong Garai** stand on an arid hill. These brick towers were built under the reign of the Cham King Jaya Simhavarman III. The entrance to the largest tower is graced with a dancing six-armed Shiva and inside a statue of a bull known as *Nandin* is the recipient of offerings brought by farmers to

Ambling along the highway near Nha Trang.

ensure a good harvest. Under a wooden pyramid is a *linga* painted with a human face. A rock on a nearby hill bears inscriptions commemorating a linga's erection by a Cham Prince in 1050. Further down the road, 25 miles (41 km) from Dalat, is **Krong Pha**, the crumbling remains of two old Cham towers.

More interesting still are the colorful, traditionally clad Cham people who live in the foothills around this extremely poor area. However, before you can visit their traditional homes permission must be obtained from the authorities. This region is renowned for its grape production.

About 10 miles (15 km) south of Phan Rang is the Cham tower of **Po Ro** which is named after the last King of Champa, Po Ro Me who ruled from 1629 to 1651 and died a prisoner of the Vietnamese.

The lovely white sand beaches and turquoise waters of **Ca Na Beach** roughly 20 miles (30 km) south of Phan Rang is an excellent place to break your journey.

The provincial capital **Phan Thiet**

Lots of sun, sea, sand - and no people!

has a population of 76,000. Fishing is the mainstay of Phan Thiet and the province as a whole. A great many different varieties of fish are caught in the region. Visit the fishing harbor early in the morning when the fishermen are unloading their catch and you'll be treated to an unusual and quite spectacular sight.

The unpleasant odour of *nuoc mam* intermittently hovers over the town, dissuasion enough for anyone who previously entertained notions of visiting one of the factories. Among the other products of the region are mineral water from Vinh Hao Spring, cashew nuts, grapes and cuttlefish.

The impressive stark beauty and graceful sculptured forms of the **Mui Le sand dunes** is a must for photographers. The dunes and a beach of the same name are located 12 miles (22 km) East of Phan Thiet. Other scenic points of interest in the province are the **Belle Vue Pass** and the hot springs at Tan My, Vinh Hao, La Nga, Dong Ko, Phong Dien and Ta Ku.

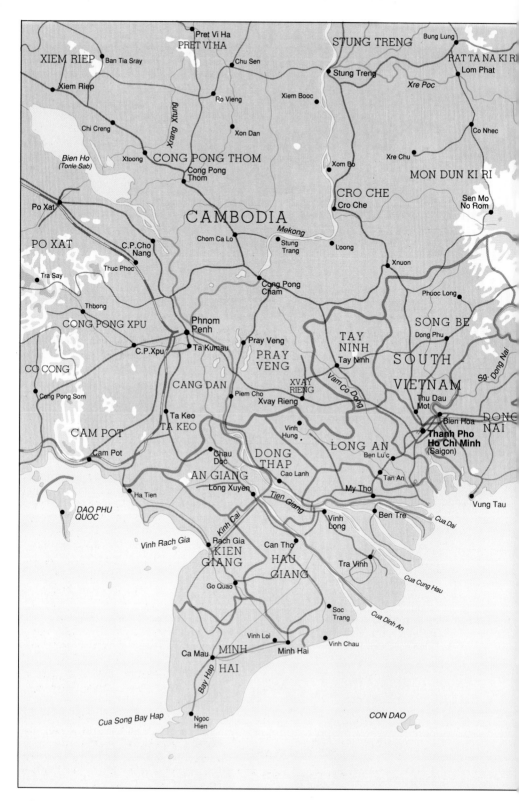

GIA LAI KON TUM
Chu Tê

Quy Nhon

A Yun Pa

Dong Xuan

Ea H'Leo

Son Hoa   Tuy Hoa

Ea Sup   VIETNAM
Krong Buk

Song Hinh

DAC LAC

Buon Me Thuot

PHU
KHANH

Ninh
Hoa

Lak

Nha Trang
Dien Khanh

Lac Duong

Nong   Dalat

Cam Ranh

LAM DONG

Vinh Cam Ranh

Di Linh

Bao Loc
uoai

Phan Rang

THUAN HAI

Tuy Phong

am Tan

Phan Thiet

PHU QUY

South China Sea

Ayun

Krong

South Vietnam
80 km/ 50 miles

THE SOUTH

The Cosmopolitan South: Far removed from the more traditional North and Center, South Vietnam has a character all of its own. Saigon, the former capital of South Vietnam until 1975, when it collapsed along with the anti-communist resistance struggle, now bears the name of Ho Chi Minh City, a name that many of its residents still resist. This bustling commercial city is definitely a city on the move, with its throngs of Honda motorcycles and ever increasing numbers of cars. Here, like everywhere else in the country, bicycles and pedicabs, are an ever-present feature of daily life.

People from all over the country flock to this busy metropolis, eager to make their fortunes or a least a decent living. Many have become disillusioned, but this has done little to deter the flow of hopefuls, young and old alike.

Bold and enterprising. Cholon, the long established and thriving chinatown in Saigon's 5th District never seems to sleep.

Some 73 miles (125 km) east of Saigon in Dong Nai Province lies the Special Zone of Vung Tau – Con Dao, the center of Vietnam's growing oil industry and one of the country's eight major ports. The region's mild climate and proximity to Saigon make it a popular weekend seaside resort.

South of Saigon, the vast Mekong Delta stretches from the eastern coast to the western border with Cambodia and culminates at Cau Mau Point, the southernmost tip of the country.

An extensive network of waterways, irrigation canals and rivers, crisscrosses the delta region plied by ferries and every type of sailing vessel imaginable, linking the various towns and provinces to Saigon.

Vast rice fields stretch as far as the eye can see creating a many hued and textured a patchwork pattern, the rural landscape and life style a far cry from Ho Chi Minh City where our journey through the South begins.

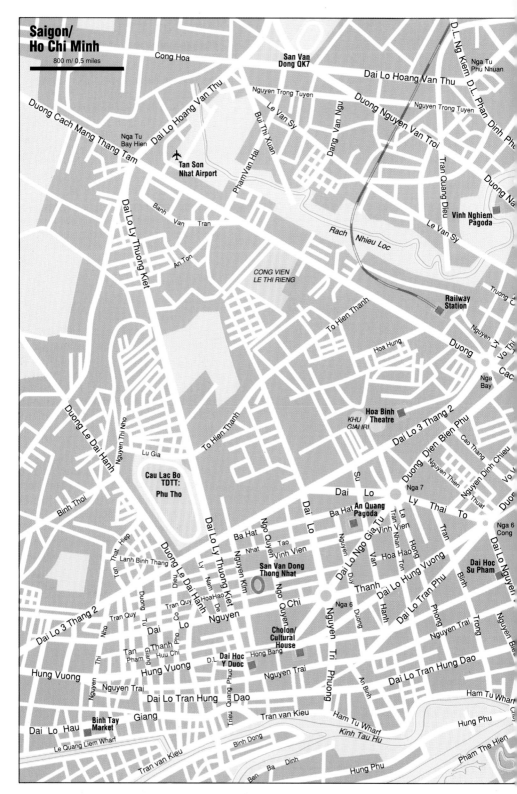

Saigon/
Ho Chi Minh

800 m/ 0.5 miles

Cong Hoa

San Van Dong QK7

Dai Lo Hoang Van Thu

Nga Tu Phu Nhuan

Nguyen Trong Tuyen

D.L. Ng Kiem D.L. Phan Dinh Ph

Le Van Sy

Duong Cach Mang Thang Tam

Dai Lo Hoang Van Thu

Nguyen Trong Tuyen

Duong Nguyen Van Troi

Nga Tu Bay Hien

Bui Thi Xuan

Dang Van Ngu

Tran Quang Dieu

Duong Na

Tan Son Nhat Airport

Pham Van Hai

Le Van Sy

Vinh Nghiem Pagoda

Duong Cach Mang Thang Tam

Dai Lo Ly Thuong Kiet

Banh Van Tran

Rach Nhieu Loc

An Ton

CONG VIEN LE THI RIENG

Truong C

Nguyen Thi Nho

Duong Le Dai Hanh

To Hien Thanh

Hoa Hung

Duong

Railway Station

Nga Bay

Nguyen Z Vo Thi

Duong Cac

To Hien Thanh

Hoa Binh Theatre

Dai Lo 3 Thang 2

Cao Thang

Binh Thoi

Lu Gia

KHU GIAI IRI

Duong Dien Bien Phu

Nguyen Dinh Chieu

Vo L

Cau Lac Bo TDTT: Phu Tho

Duong Le Dai Hanh

To Hien Thanh

Nga 7

Duong Nguyen Thien Thuat

Duon

Binh Thiep

Ton That Hiep

Lanh Binh Thang

Ba Hat

Ngo Nguyen

Tao Nhat

Dai Lo

Ba Hat

An Quang Pagoda

Su

Dai Lo

Ly Thai To

Nga 6 Cong

Duong Na

 Lu

Nguyen Kim

Vinh Vien

Nguyen Duy

Le Tran Nhan Ton

Vinh Vien

Hoa Hao

Hong

Dai Lo Hung Vuong

Binh

Dai Hoc Su Pham

Nguyen Trai

Trong

Nguyen Bie

Dai Lo 3 Thang 2

Tran Quy

Nho

Dai Lo

San Van Dong Thong Nhat

Ngo Quyen

Thanh

Dai Lo Tran Phu

Phong

Nguyen Trai

Duong Tu

Tan Thanh

Pham Giang

Huu Chi

Hong Bang

Ngo Quyen Chi

Cholon/ Cultural House

Nga 6 Duong

Hanh

An Binh

Dai Lo Tran Hung Dao

Hung Vuong

Thi

Nguyen

Hung Vuong

D.L. Dai Hoc Y Duoc

Nguyen Tri

Ham Tu Wharf

Hung Phu

Dai Lo Hau

Nguyen Trai

Dai Lo Tran Hung Dao

Triu Quang Phuc

Tran van Kieu

Phuong

Dai Lo Tran Hung Dao

Binh Tay Market

Giang

Tran van Kieu

Binh Dong

Ham Tu Wharf

Kinh Tau Hu

Hung Phu

Pham The Hien

Le Quang Liem Wharf

Tran van Kieu

Ben Ba Dinh

Hung Phu

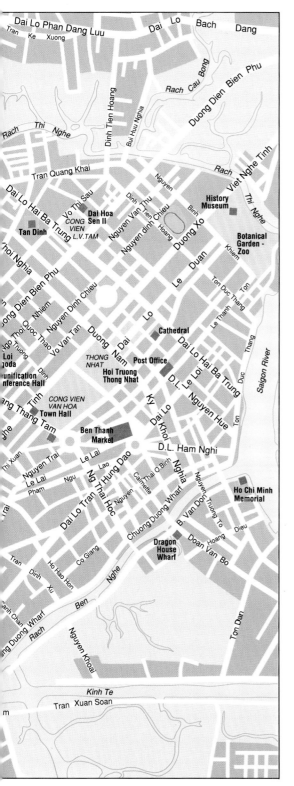

HO CHI MINH CITY (SAIGON) AND THE SOUTH

Built on the site of an ancient Khmer city, Ho Chi Minh City was a thinly populated area of forests, swamps and lakes until the 17th century. By the end of the 18th century, *Ben Nghe*, as the area was known, had become an important trading center within the region.

Different theories expound on the origins of the name Saigon. Some say it derives from the former name *Sai Con*, a transcription of the Khmer words, *Prei Kor*, the Kapok Tree Forest or *Prei Nokor*, the Forest of the Kingdom, in reference to the Cambodian Vice Roi's residence which was located in the region of present-day Cholon.

In the 19th century, South Vietnam and particularly Saigon, continued to prosper despite the almost incessant fighting between the Vietnamese and Cambodians and between the Vietnamese themselves, who were divided in their support of either the Nguyen Lords from Hue or the Tay Son Insurgents from Binh Dinh.

In 1859 French and Spanish ships penetrated Saigon. The French unloaded troops and weapons and embarked upon their conquest of the country. Saigon was captured later the same year and became the capital of the French colony of Cochinchina a few years later. Ironically, modernization accompanied colonization. The French filled in the ancient canals, drained marshland, built roads, laid out streets and quarters and planted many trees. The city developed rapidly, acquiring something of the character of a French provincial town in the process and was served by two steam tramways.

After the division of the country in 1954, Saigon became the capital of the Republic of South Vietnam until it fell to the communists in May 1975. The revolutionary authorities renamed it Ho Chi Minh City, yet to most of its 4½ million inhabitants, the city remains Saigon.

Today, 50 miles (80 km) inland from

the coast as the crow flies, Saigon, Vietnam's largest city and river port, sprawls across an area of 761 square miles (2,030 square km) on the right bank of the Saigon River. The city is divided into 12 urban and six rural districts. Here, the dry season lasts from November to April and the rainy season endures for the rest of the year.

An endless stream of humanity astride bicycles and Japanese motor scooters, *cyclos* – the pedal powered Vietnamese "taxi" and an array of ancient and modern cars join the fray on the streets of Saigon. Incessantly blaring horns add to the din of two stroke engines. Crossing the street you take your life into your own hands, its entirely up to the pedestrian to avoid the traffic, not the other way round. Saigon appears a city on the move, all be it in a somewhat uncertain direction. You cannot go far without seeing enterprising individuals squatting by the roadside running their small businesses, particularly prevalent are those providing bicycle repair services or selling petrol in small quantities.

In a sense the French presence remains, lingering not only in the minds of the older generation but physically in the legacy of colonial architecture, long treelined avenues, streets and highways they left behind.

As fast as the French and later the Americans were establishing their Western culture and architecture in Saigon, the Vietnamese were retaliating with the many pagodas, shrines and temples that sprung up all over the city. Countless religious buildings are scattered all over the city and in addition to the Buddhist temples are a small number of Indian Temples and Muslim Mosques. Many of the Vietnamese and Chinese Temples are not actually Buddhist, but instead are dedicated to the worship of certain legendary or historical heroes.

The **Gia Lam Pagoda** at 118 Lac Long Quan in Tan Binh district, thought to be the oldest in the city, dates from the end of the 17th century. Reconstruction work was last carried out on it in 1900. Carved wooden pillars within the main building bear gilded inscriptions in old Vietnam-

Preceding pages: Saigon - heart of the cosmoplitan South; getting hitched in style. <u>Below</u>, early view of Chinatown.

ese nom characters which have also been used on the red tablets recording the biographies of the monks of previous generations whose portraits adorn the left wall. The pagoda houses many beautifully carved jack wood statues. Buddha, reincarnations of Buddha, judges and guardians of hell and the goddess of mercy, are all present here.

The more recent Buddhist **Vinh Nghiem Pagoda** at 339 Nam Ky Khoi Nghia in district 3, is the newest and largest of the pagodas in the city. Built with aid from the Japanese Friendship Association, this Japanese-style pagoda was begun in 1964 and finished in 1973. Each stage of its seven-storey tower contains a statue of Buddha. In the huge main hall stands a large statue of Buddha surrounded by his disciples. Behind are the altars consecrated to the dead where tablets and photographs of the deceased are placed for the first one hundred days after their death.

The temple's screen and large bell were made in Japan. The bell, a gift from Japanese Buddhists, was presented during the Vietnam war as the embodiment of a prayer for an early end to the conflict. The large three-storey funeral tower behind the main temple holds ceramic burial urns containing the ashes of the dead. The pagoda becomes the scene of great animation and color during the Ram Thang Gieng Buddhist festival which takes place on the 15th day of the first lunar month.

The small Sino-Vietnamese **Ngoc Hoa Pagoda** (Emperor of Jade Pagoda) at 73 Mai Thi Luu dates from around 1892. It was built by Cantonese Buddhists and is one of the cities most colorful pagodas. A haze of heady incense and candle smoke envelops a fascinating array of weird and wonderful naive style wooden statues, some Buddhist and others Taoist inspired. The elaborately-robed Taoist Jade Emperor surveys the main sanctuary.

Just to his right, the triple-headed, 18-armed statue of Phat Mau Chau De, mother of the Buddhas of the Middle, North, East, West and South looks out in three directions from her encasement.

Dockside seat by the Saigon River.

A door off to the left of the Jade Emperor's chamber leads to the Hall of Ten Hells where carved wooden panels portray in no uncertain detail the fate that awaits those sentenced to the diverse torments found in the ten regions of hell. Despite the hellish scenes and prolific number of strange deities, an atmosphere of calm pervades the temple and its surrounding garden.

Two interesting temples can be visited on Nguyen Trai Street. At number 710 is the richly decorated **Thien Hau Temple** (Heavenly Lady). This Chinese Temple, dedicated to the Goddess Protector of Sailors, was built by Cantonese Buddhists at the end of the 18th century. The temple is frequented mainly by women who bring their offerings to the altar of the Heavenly Lady with its 3 statues of Thien Hau located at the back of the temple. Votif paper offerings are also burnt in the big furnace to the right of the altar.

Among the other altars is one dedicated to the protection of women and newborn babies and yet another to ster-ile women or mothers who have no sons. Ceramic figurines, richly attired statues, and a model boat commemorating the arrival of the first Chinese from Canton are among the items of interest here. The pagoda's bronze bell was cast in 1830.

The smaller **Ha Chuong Pagoda** at number 802 contains wooden sculptures and statues, including a statue of the god of happiness and an altar for sterile women.

The Buddhist **Giac Vien Pagoda** on Lac Long Quan Road was built in 1803. It was formerly known as Chau Ho Dat (Earth pit Pagoda) due to the vast amounts of earth required to fill in the site before its construction. Some 153 beautifully carved statues and statuettes are housed within the pagoda. One of the most valuable items in the pagoda is a richly decorated palanquin which was presented to the pagoda's founder, Bonze Superior Hai Tinh Giac Vien, by the Nguyen Court. His statue stands near the rear of the temple's second chamber.

Mausoleums of the generals who fought

Saigon's National Museum.

for Emperor Gia Long of the Nguyen Dynasty during the 19th century can also be found in the city.

A large and elegant Mosque at 66 Dong Du Street serves Saigon's Islamic community. It was built on the site of an older mosque by Southern Indian Muslims in 1935. Only a handful of Indian Muslims remain, since most fled the country after 1975.

The **Mariamman Hindu Temple**, three blocks from Ben Thanh market at 45 Truong Dinh Street was built at the end of the 19th century and caters to Saigon's small population of 70-odd Hindu Tamils.

The **Botanical and Zoological Gardens**, (Thao Cam Vien) in the East of the city, provide a welcome alternative to the noisy chaos of the streets and must constitute the calmest and most peaceful 82 acres (33 hectares) in Saigon. The attractive gardens were established by two Frenchmen, one a botanist, the other a veterinarian, in 1864, as one of the first projects the French embarked upon after they established their new colony. The zoological section, although somewhat rundown and under repair, houses rather dejected looking birds, tigers, elephants, crocodiles and other indigenous species in cages built during the colonial era.

The **National History Museum (Vien Bao Tang Lich Su)**, located just within the entrance of the Botanical Gardens, was built by the French in 1927. It documents the evolution of Vietnam's various cultures from the Dong Son Bronze Age civilization through to the Funan civilization, the Chams and the Khmers. Among its exhibits are many stone and bronze relics, stelae, bronze drums, Cham art, ceramics and a display of the traditional costumes of some ethnic minorities. Behind the building on the third floor is a research library which houses an interesting and quite extensive collection of books from the French era. Shut on Mondays and public holidays, the museum is open between 8-11.30 a.m. and 1-4 p.m.

Just opposite the Museum is the **Den Hung**, a temple dedicated to the ancestors of Hung Vuong, the founding king of Vietnam.

Continuing down Le Duan Boulevard from the gardens you will come across the **Cathedral of Our Lady** standing in the square across from the Post Office. This neo-Roman style cathedral with its two bell towers was begun in 1877 and consecrated in 1880. A statue of the Virgin Mary stands on a pillar in front of the cathedral looking down Dong Koi Street (formerly rue Catinat).

From the Cathedral, Nguyen Du Street leads to the **Reunification or Thong Nhat Conference Hall**. Surrounded by large gardens, this large modern edifice, a symbol of the old regime, rests on the site of the former French Governor's residence, the Norodom Palace which dates back to 1868.

After the Geneva Agreement put an end to French occupation, the new president of South Vietnam, Ngo Dinh Diem, installed himself in the palace. In 1963 the palace was bombed by a South Vietnamese airforce officer and a new building known as the Independence

French dressing on the Town Hall.

Palace was erected to replace the damaged structure. The present 1960s style structure was designed by Ngo Viet Thu, a Paris-trained Vietnamese architect, and completed in 1966. The left wing was damaged by another renegade pilot in early April 1975, but before the month was out, on April 30, tanks from the revolutionary forces crashed through the front wrought iron gates and overthrew the South Vietnamese government. General Minh had become head of state only 43 hours before this decisive historical event.

Today the former palace is visited like a museum, with everything left much as it was on April 30, 1975. The ground floor comprises of: the Banquet room, where a large oil painting given to President Thieu by the architect on the palace's inauguration day in 1967 takes precedence; the State Chamber, from where the South Vietnamese government abdicated and the Cabinet room which was used for the daily military briefings during the period leading up to the overthrow of the South Vietnamese government.

On the first floor is President Tran Van Huong's reception room and President Thieu's reception and residential domain, complete with a chapel, dining room and bedroom. The second floor hosts the reception rooms of the president's wife. A private theater and a helipad are found on the third floor which commands an excellent view over Le Duan Boulevard. The hall is open to visitors from 8 to 10 a.m. and 1 to 5 p.m. daily, except on Sunday afternoons and when in use for official functions.

Looking a little incongruous on Nguyen Hue Boulevard, the colonial era's rather lavish **City Hall**, decorated by Ruffier, stands proud behind its surprisingly well manicured garden. Finished in 1908 after almost sixteen years of ferment over its style and situation. its ornate façade and equally ornate interior, complete with crystal chandeliers, is now the headquarters of the Ho Chi Minh City People's Committee.

The **War Museum** occupies the former US Information Service Build-

Electronics market on Yersin Street.

ing on Vo Van Tan Street. Among the grisly items on display here are American tanks, infantry weapons, photographs of war atrocities committed by the Americans and Chinese and the original French guillotine brought to Vietnam in the 20th century, which saw a lot of use between late 1959 and 1960. A visit here is likely to jolt the senses, as many pictures depict shocking atrocities committed during the war.

The Museum of the Revolution (Vien Bao Tang Cach Mang), one block from the Museum on Ly Tu Trong Street, is found in a white neo-classical structure once known as Gia Long Palace. The walls of the former ballrooms of this colonial edifice built in 1866, are now hung with pictures of the anti-colonial executed.

A network of reinforced concrete bunkers which stretches all the way to the Reunification Hall lies beneath the building. Within this underground network were living areas and a meeting hall. It was here that President Diem and his brother hid just before they fled to

the church in Cholon where they were captured and subsequently shot.

The **Municipal Theater** (Nha Hat Thanh Pho) which stands on Dong Khoi Street between the Caravelle and the Continental hotels, was originally built in 1899 as a theater, but ended up later as the fortress headquarters of the South Vietnamese National Assembly. These days it serves more its original purpose and every week a different programme is on show – anything from traditional Vietnamese theater to acrobatics, gymnastics and disco music.

At the junction of Ham Nghi, Le Loi and Tran Hung Dao Boulevards in the center of town, is Saigon's busy **Ben Thanh Market**. The market covers over 118,400 square feet (11,000 square meters) and was inaugurated in 1914. Here you'll discover an amazing array of produce, foodstuffs and imported goods–transistor radios, cassette players, walkmen, televisions, cameras, calculators, refrigerators, fans–coming from Taiwan, Italy, France, West Germany, Singapore and the United States! The smell of spices and dried sea food assails the nostrils and the color of the many varieties of fresh fruit and vegetables provides a veritable feast for the eyes. At the back of the market small food stalls serve a wide variety of local dishes. Stalls spill out onto the pavements outside the market and into the surrounding streets, selling all manner of stuff including food, drink, cigarettes and imported goods.

Saigon's "Thieves Market", found on Huynh Thuc Kang and Ton That Dan Streets, earned its name during the last war when new goods diverted from American military supply shops were resold here. Today the items sold are mainly imported goods brought back by Vietnamese sailors or sent by overseas Vietnamese to their families back home.

The **Nha Rong** (Dragon House), on Nguyen Tat Thanh Road, has been kept as a memorial to Ho Chi Minh since 1979. Documents and pictures relating to Ho's life and revolutionary activities are displayed here. The house was built in 1862 and was originally used as the head office of a French Shipping company. It was from this place that Ho Chi Minh, then going under his given name of Nguyen Tat Thanh, left Vietnam on June 5, 1911 as a cook on a French merchant ship.

Cholon (Big Market), Saigon's Chinatown, was formerly a separate sister city, but today is found in the city's 5th district, thanks to the outward growth of the suburbs. As the name indicates, Cholon remains a thriving commercial center in its own right.

With a population composed of around half a million *Hoas*, Vietnamese of Chinese origin, Cholon has come a long way since 1864 when its inhabitants comprised of some 6,000 Chinese, mostly shopkeepers or traders, 200 Indians and 40,000 Vietnamese.

Today, countless small-scale family businesses operate in this bustling Vietnamese Chinatown. Day and night Cholon's streets, markets and restaurants are scenes of noisy animation and much activity. The many richly decorated Chinese temples and pagodas found here are distinctly different from

their Vietnamese counterparts and are best visited in the morning if you wish to see the faithful at their prayers. The Cholon Mosque at 641 Nguyen Trai Street was built by Tamil Muslims in 1932.

One of the largest churches in the city is the Cho Quan Church at 133 Tran Binh Trong Street, Built in the late 1800s by the French, it has a belfry with an excellent view. The neon halo which glows around the head of the statue of Christ is glaringly late 20th century.

At the end of Tran Hung Dao Boulevard is **Cha Tam Church** where President Ngo Dinh Diem was captured and shortly after assassinated along with his brother in November 1963. The church was built around the turn of the century. Not far West of here on Hau Giang Boulevard is the large **Binh Tay Market**, Cholon's main marketplace.

A birds-eye view of Saigon reveals the network of tidal waterways of the Saigon, Nha Be and Long Tau rivers which cut into the city.

Beyond Saigon: To see Saigon and its suburbs from a different perspective take a boat trip on the Saigon River. The picturesque village of **Thanh Da**, 3 miles (5 km) in the countryside North of Saigon is a pleasant destination and an ideal picnic spot.

Venturing further afield, 22 miles (35 km) northwest of Saigon lies **Cu Chi** district, an area which played an important role in the wars against both the French and the Americans. Cu Chi is famous for its 124 mile (200 km) network of underground tunnels used by the communist guerillas.

These tunnels constitute a subterranean village comprising many networks of underground shelters connected together on several levels. Their main axis is only between 21 to 27 inches (60 - 70 cm) wide and (1.5 meters) high. The 9.8 to 13 foot (3 to 4 meters) thick roof of the tunnel could withstand the weight of a 60 ton tank or howitzer of any size and the impact of bombs weighing up to 220 lb (100 kg).

The Viet Cong managed to dig down 4 feet (12 meters) in Cu Chi's rock-like soil using only the most rudimentary

Roof garden of the Caravelle Hotel affords a good view of the city.

tools. The thousands of tons of soil resulting from this massive burrowing operation were scattered far and wide and the entrance to the tunnels could not be found. These days the entrance is well marked and for those who want to brave it, a tour guide awaits to lead you underground.

West of the Southern Capital: Northwest of Saigon, **Tay Ninh Province** shares a 138-mile (232-km) border with Cambodia. The province's main river, the Vam Co Dong, separates Vietnam from Cambodia. From the 7th to the 14th centuries, Tay Ninh belonged to the powerful Funan Empire. Later it became part of the Chen La Kingdom, the forerunner of the Champa Kingdom.

In the early 18th century, the Nguyen Lords defeated the last remnants of Champa and established the province of Gia Dinh which integrated and administered Tay Ninh.

During the war against the French, Tay Ninh became a hot bed of anti-colonial resistance, and in the 1950s, bearing the standard of the Cao Dai religious sect, a hero of the armed resistance forces conducted his efforts against the Central Government in the Nui Ba Den (Black Lady Mountain) area.

Tay Ninh's greatest attraction is found approximately 54 miles (90 km) northwest of Saigon in the township of Tay Ninh itself. Here, resplendent in all its glory stands, the Holy See of the Cao Dai religious sect. This surreal temple has to be seen to be believed. The best time to arrive is before the daily ceremony at noon. The interior is like something out of fantasy land and the followers in their colorful ceremonial gowns of azure, yellow and white cut striking figures in their procession towards the altar.

Permission to attend the ceremony is not a mere formality and may not be given. Special permission must be granted if you wish to photograph the interior, but the use of a flash is strictly forbidden.

The most outstanding natural feature in the province, **Mount Ba Den**, the Black Lady Mountain, overshadows the

Restaurant ad reflects Saigon's cosmopolitan character. Right, baguettes for sale.

village. The mountain is dotted with many temples and pagodas and shelters a black stone statue of a Brahman goddess, the Bhagavati protectress of the region. More than 1,500 steps, a 1,000-foot (300-meter) climb, lead up to the Linh Son Pagoda at mountain's summit from where a splendid view takes in the region and the Mekong delta beyond. The Nui Ba Den or Black Lady Mountain Festival takes place here during the Spring months from February to May. Within the mountain is a beautiful grotto which is the source of pure, crystal-clear water. At the foot of the mountain is a monument to the soldiers killed in the fierce fighting that occurred in the province during the war.

Among the province's population are Khmer-krom and Cham descendants.

Leaving Saigon via the east-northeast exit, the road passes through **Ba Chieu**. Located here is a temple dedicated to Le Van Duyet, the ancient viceroy of Cochinchina under Emperor Gia Long's reign. Quite a story surrounds this historical figure who loomed even larger than life after his death. According to numerous records this respected personage is said to have manifested his presence throughout the Mekong Delta area after his death and performed miracles.

This phenomena caused quite a stir, not only among the Vietnamese but also among the equally superstitious Chinese community, particularly those in Cholon. Anyone who perjured an oath taken before the tomb of this revered individual could expect to be punished by death within 24 hours.

Nobody was in any doubt as to the occult powers the great man possessed. In serious cases when mortal judges were unable to decide a person's guilt or innocence the course of justice would move to the temple. Here the course of justice would be pursued in the ritual manner which involved the two contesting parties having to slit the throat of a hen and drink its blood. In doing so they were obliged to repeat the ritual formula, "If I lie I will die like this innocent hen whose blood I have drunk."

Saigon's most exclusive hotel.

The temple, built within the enclosure of the tomb itself, is set in a park shaded by old trees. Emperor Ming Mang destroyed the tomb, after Le Van Duyet was posthumously tried and found guilty of treason. Later, Emperor Tu Duc repaired the injustice and restored the marshall's tomb and standing through a royal decree made in 1848.

The **Ba Chieu Temple**, better known as the *Lang Ong*, is easily recognized from a distance by its large triple entrance gate. Inside the temple are several altars dedicated to various cults. A portrait of Le Van Duyet in full court cos-tume hangs over the central altar. During the Tet festivities thousands of Vietnamese and Chinese pilgrims visit the temple and have their horoscopes read.

From Ba Chieu the road continues to the market town of **Thu Duc**, 12 miles (19 km) northeast of Saigon.

Further along the road, a village path leads off to the right to several ancient tombs belonging to the Ho family, the family of Emperor Minh Mang's wife, Queen Ho Thi Hoa. Her name became taboo and a lot of name changing went on in South Vietnam out of respect for this queen.

Travelling North from Thu Duc the road crosses into **Song Be Province**, renowned for its orchards of **Lai Thieu** and **Thu Dau Mot.** These orchards are an absolute haven for tropical fruit lovers from May to July. Here you can feast on the diverse textures and succulent flavors of a huge variety of freshly picked fruit.

The pottery kilns surrounding the church at Lai Thieu were built by Chinese immigrants who put the region's clay reserves to good use.

The **Cat Tien Reserve** lies in an area adjacent to the three provinces of Dong Nai, Song Be and Lam Dong. This primeval forest covering an area of roughly 25,000 acres (10,000 hectares) is the natural habitat of some rare and unusual creatures, among them, various species of pythons, crocodiles and animals such as flying squirrels and the nearly extinct Asian rhinoceros.

Tai chi is a popular pursuit.

THE REUNIFICATION EXPRESS

The Thong Nhat or Reunification Express, a somewhat misleading title in every sense, refers to the train that crawls along at an average speed of about 19 miles (30 km) per hour, making the journey between Hanoi and Saigon in anything between 48 and 58 hours, depending on which "express" you travel on. In the early days of train travel in the 1930s, this same journey could be made in about 40 hours 20 minutes. Back then the trains averaged 27 miles (43 km) per hour! A curious example of progress in reverse.

to pass and if, as is often the case, one train is running late, then the other and any subsequent trains will follow suit! Considering derailments, buffalos and stalled vehicles on the tracks, floods and typhoons, it is an engineering miracle that the trains run at all!

The Reunification Express trains first rattled down the re-repaired tracks between Hanoi and Saigon, on December 31, 1976. The massive reconstruction campaign carried out to make this possible, one of the government's first rehabilitation programs

Today's slowest trains may average as little as 9 miles (15 km) per hour; however, the trains themselves are not solely to blame for the lack of progress. This can be put down primarily to the fact that only one track runs between Saigon and Hanoi and apart from a 186 mile (300 km) stretch in the north, the whole track system is meter gauged and in very poor condition, despite the reconstruction efforts which addressed the results of the American bombing in the North and the Viet Cong sabotage efforts in the South. Trains may only pass each other at the few points where a siding provides for this, thus one train has to wait on the sidetrack for the other

after the 1975 reunification, included the repairing of some 1,334 bridges, 158 stations, 1,370 shunts and 27 tunnels.

Vietnam must be one of the few countries where you can still experience the heady sensation of being transported by steam. Over a hundred steam engines are still in service; some date from the colonial period, one was even built in Vietnam in 1962; and others were purchased from Poland. Among the slightly larger number of diesel engines are an assortment of French and Belgian-built ones and American military engines. Of the 4,000 wagons still in use, 600 carriages date from the French colonial era.

For all the speed and efficiency of modern day bullet trains and the like, they lack the atmosphere and sense of the unexpected that accompanies a journey on one of these old mavericks which ply the rails of Vietnam. What Vietnam rail travel lacks in comfort and speed, it certainly makes up for in local color and a certain unique "charm" reminiscent of train journeys of a bygone era. Be prepared for frequent unscheduled stops, flickering lighting and a tannoy system that crackles forth Vietnamese songs interspersed with announcements.

To take in the sights, sounds and smells of a fascinating country at a leisurely pace amidst an equally fascinating array of travelling companions is an experience that will

sleeper, forget about class. Arm yourself for the adventure with a torch, toilet paper, drinking water and plenty of small denomination *dong* and cigarettes (for sharing out).

The journey for some is inspiring – Noel Coward's famous line, "Only mad dogs and Englishmen go out in the midday sun" was penned on board in 1936.

If your time is limited you may feel tempted to give the train journey a miss, but think again, you may be forgoing one of the experiences of a lifetime as this rather antiquated rail system may soon be replaced by something of a more recent vintage.

The weekend journey begins from Saigon station on a Saturday at 9 a.m. or from Hanoi

provide those game enough to do so with a wealth of images, memories and stories to recount back home for years to come. The crew are enchanted to find the increasingly familiar foreign face and this voyage certainly forges friendships out of fellow travellers, particularly if you decide to brave second or third class.

The seats are very hard and really the bottom line is either very hard seat or hard

Left, all smiles aboard the Reunification Express.
Above, the scenery alone makes the trip worthwhile.

the same day at 9.30 a.m. As the train heaves out of the station, its cargo an unlikely hodgepodge of humanity, livestock and goods, you are about to embark on a journey of 1,250 miles (2,012 km), one of the most beautiful journeys in the world.

The scene in the carriages at the beginning of the journey is enough to defy the imagination. Compartments designed for four to six passengers are crammed with food vendors squatting in the isles, men, women and children slung in hammocks or curled up in whatever space is left. Bulky packages and bags, jutting limbs and bales of clothes clog any available space between the seats, spill over from luggage racks, hang suspended from the ceiling and turn the cigarette-strewn aisles into a veritable obstacle course. A somewhat daunting lot to negotiate should you pluck up the courage to brave a sortie to the washroom or the restaurant car. Added to this chaotic assortment, in the vestibules and corridors are the ubiquitous Hondas and a hoard of temporary passengers, vendors dispensing *pho*, food, hot water, *bongs* (pipes) of tobacco, or knick-knacks to their captive clientele. The scene is one of noisy animation which stamina and an unflagging sense of humor will see you through.

The on-board vendors are a mafia unto themselves, descending on the train as it

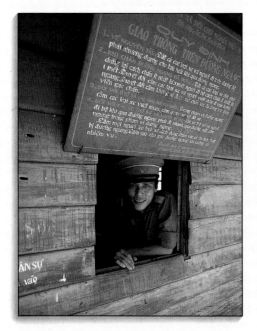

slows from its average 19 miles (30 km) per hour speed and grinds to a halt, scheduled or otherwise, at strategic wayside villages or in the middle of nowhere. With an uncanny sense of timing, they materialize out of bush, rubber plantations and paddy field to swarm aboard and profer their welcome glasses of green tea or freshly cut sugarcane chunks.

As on all long-haul trains in the Orient, the tidbits on offer vary from one region to the next as the train progresses. Each province, town or village peddles its own particular local speciality. The smart traveler stocks up on finger bananas in Xuan Loc, dried squid in Nha Trang, prawn fritters at Dieu Tri and

soft-shelled crabs and conical hats in Hue.

Woman attendants in dark blue tunics and trousers take orders for lunch. Rice with meat or *pho*, the delicious beef noodle soup, is cooked over open braziers and served at 11.30 a.m. and 5.00 p.m.

As the passing landscape becomes drier, cacti and giant anthills thrust their way up from a desert-like landscape. The sun, a glowing fireball ready to roll behind the mountain range casts its lasts ray on the massive limestone outcrops which herald a glimpse of the ancient Cham towers. At 7 p.m. a half hour stop at Nha Trang provides a welcome opportunity to stretch your legs in the shabby *ga* (station).

Back on the train, bunking down for the night means securing window shutters, a guillotine for the unwary; and doors, to discourage unwelcome rocks and riders. The 38 strong crew dispense a blanket, sheet and pillow to each berth, but even the blanket provided is apt to disappear during station stops. Petty theft is a bit of a problem so don't let your belongings out of your sight

The unceremoniously dumped bucket of water is for the purpose of night and morning ablutions. However, the majority clean their teeth in the corridor, spitting into the wind, anything to avoid extra time in the fetid washroom which demands the nigh on impossible of one's sense of balance when squatting over a hole as the train lurches and jolts through intersections.

A cup of strong *cafe den* (black coffee) will assist recovery as the new day dawns over lush rice fields where the conical hats of the villagers form intricate geometric patterns as they labor in the patchwork paddy fields; and fisherman cast their nets in the rivers amidst buffalo wallowing in the mud.

A half-hour stop at Danang begins at around 10 a.m., vendors jostle for custom, displaying their goods – boiled eggs, tropical fruits, sweetcorn and spiced pork *pate* wrapped in banana leaf (*do lua*) – delicious with the local French-style bread. The train backs down towards the coastal track which snakes around mountains rising 6,000 feet (1,830 meters) with a sheer drop to the sparkling turquoise sea and white sand beaches below. The snail's pace progress on this leg of the journey allows for breathtaking views of the Vinh Da Nang estuary, a scene teeming with boat life. The train crawls into Hue at about 1 p.m., time enough to make a few purchases and catch a glimpse of this former imperial city hugging the banks of the Perfume River. Some 31 miles (50 km) to the north, massive bomb craters scar the countryside – a legacy of the Vietnam war and the B-52 carpet bombings – these craters now serve as artificial watering holes for buffalo.

Dawn breaks over the lush emerald paddy fields of the northern Red River delta and you arrive in Hanoi with the early morning sun. Thus ends the journey of over a thousand miles.

The three categories of "express" running between Saigon and Hanoi are classified by journey time rather than comfort – the first

Trang and or Hue, it is not possible to make the reservations for the onward journey from Saigon or Hanoi as all onward reservations must be made from your point of embarkation. So the best idea is to get this sorted out as soon as you arrive if possible.

The local trains that crawl between the coastal cities offer an excruciatingly slow ride, stopping at every local station on route. The very hard seat category is the only option and as the "express" trains are given priority you can be stuck in a siding with the seat getting harder as time ticks slowly by.

The cost of a ticket in a first-class sleeper between Hanoi and Saigon is US$116 for foreigners and about US$20 for the locals.

category takes 48 hours, the second 52 hours and the third 58 hours – take your pick, but bear in mind that, like most transport services in Vietnam, demand is greater than supply and reservations, even for short trips, should be made as much in advance as possible. Failing this, station staff may be able to sort something out for you if you show up at the station within half an hour of departure time, but don't count on it.

If you wish to break your journey at Nha

Far left, railway guard at Hai Van Pass. **Above**, a tempting array of goods is available at every stop.

Officially foreigners and Viet Kieu (Overseas Vietnamese) are required to pay a hefty surcharge.

Local trains also run between Hanoi and Pho Lu in the northwest and in the northeast Lang Son and Dong Dang, the end of the line. The daily steam train from Lang Son to Hanoi is packed with traders laden with Chinese goods – thermos flasks, and tea sets are the hot items. In Hanoi they transfer to a southbound train and head for one of their pre-arranged drop off points. The merchandise going south will pass another train of Thai, Japanese or Malay goods heading north.

EAST OF SAIGON

Lying a little east of Saigon, **Dong Nai Province**, the eastern gateway to Saigon, incorporates the former provinces of **Ba Ria**, **Long Khanh** and **Bien Hoa**. Dong Nai is the name of a large river originating in the Central Highlands, which flows through the province for a distance of some 120 miles (290 km).

The province's fertile red soils produce an abundance of sugar cane, hevea (rubber trees), maize, tobacco, coconut and peanuts. The fields of such diverse vegetation contribute to the greatly varied texture and color of the scenery.

Mountains and forests, rivers, lakes, waterfalls and jungle give way to long stretches of white sandy beaches along the province's 60 mile (100 km) coastline.

Raffia plantations produce the brilliant yellow strands which lie drying by the roadside. These are later woven into hats, baskets, mats and used also as a roofing material. The rubber plantations here were originally established by the French.

The **Binh Chau Hot Springs** are located in the cajeput forest of Xuyen Moc district. The waters flow at a temperature of up to 80 °C and are believed to possess curative properties.

The attractive town of **Bien Hoa** is an important industrial center lying 20 miles (32 km) from Saigon on the banks of the **Dong Nai River**. In the 15th and 17th centuries, Bien Hoa was a focal point for Chinese emigration. One of their leaders, Tran Thuong Xuyen, built a colonial fort on **Cu Lao Pho Island** in the Dong Nai River.

The tomb of Trinh Hoai Duc, the minister Emperor Gia Long sent to China to negotiate the country's change of name to Viet Nam, is found on the island.

Towards the wharf on the left bank of the river stands a large temple dedicated to Generalissimo Nguyen Huu Canh (1650-1700). In true Vietnamese fashion, this national hero, better known in

Preceding pages: Vung Tau's unpretentious beachfront. **Left**, the former Cap Saint Jacques.

South Vietnam as Chuong Binh Le, has acquired the status of a saint and is venerated by the population as their protector. Several times a year, notably on the Generalissimo's birthday and during Spring and Autumn, festivities are held at the temple.

Classical theater performances are a major form of entertainment during the festivities classical theater performances. The temple rests in the shade of two huge trees, many centuries old, their heavy tops seem to bow before their genie protector.

The town's **Buu Son Temple** shelters a 15th century Cham statue. A school attached to the temple teaches pottery and bronzework.

From Bien Hoa the road heads southeast towards the coast and the **Vung Tau Peninsula**. Some 44 miles (70 km) further on the road passes through **Long Hai,** a coastal district with beautiful scenery and a beach stretching for a distance of several kilometers. Some ancient pagodas stand near Mount Minh Dam, not far from the beach. The **Dinh Co,** near the beach, is dedicated to a young lady, who, as the story goes, was carrying a letter to Emperor Quang Trung when huge waves sank the boat she was travelling in. The local people reputedly built the temple in memory of this patriotic girl.

Vung Tau, the Bay of Boats, is located on a peninsula approximately two hours by road, 78 miles (125 km) southeast of Saigon. In the 15th century, after Le Thanh Tong had conquered the Kingdom of Champa, Portuguese merchant ships were already anchoring in the bay of Vung Tau.

Known as Cap Saint Jacques under the French, this popular seaside resort is bathed in sunshine all year round. Referred to by the present government as Vung Tau Con Dau Special Zone, this important seaport and economic center has a growing oil and gas industry. However, all this industry does not detract from the area's natural beauty.

Restaurants, colonial villas and cafes line the resort's largest beach, **Thuy Van**, which stretches for 4 miles (7 km)

The one that didn't get away.

along the eastern coast. Here, for a small fee, you can relax on deckchairs under gaily colored umbrellas. Thuy Van is very popular with the locals and becomes quite crowded at weekends. For those who prefer a little more privacy and natural shade, head for the quieter tree-lined beaches or the small **Tam Duong Cove** on the west coast.

The beach opposite the main hotel area is very silty due to its proximity to the mouth of the river and is not really suitable for swimming. Aside from the beaches, Vung Tau has over one hundred Buddhist pagodas and temples.

A visit to the **Lang Ca Ong**, Whale Temple, on Hoang Hoa Tham Avenue is a must. Built in 1911, the temple is consecrated to the whale cult. Its most frequent visitors are fishermen who revere the whale as man's saviour from the perils of the high seas. Skeletons of whales that have been beached on the shores in the region are kept in huge cases, some 13 feet (4 meters) long. Some of the skeletons date from as far back as 1868. The Vietnamese adopted

the whale cult from the people of Champa who worshipped the Whale Genie. Every year, on the sixteenth day of the eighth lunar month, fishermen gather at the temple to make offerings to the whales.

During their long march towards the south, the Vietnamese adopted a number of the beliefs they encountered among the people of Champa and Chen La. Thousands of detailed anecdotes occur in Vietnamese folklore supporting the popular belief of the whales as saviours.

In the northeast of the peninsula a winding track leads inland across Mount Nui Lon to the **Cakya Mouni Pagoda**, the Pagoda of the Buddha. The pagoda was built in 1957 and was later enlarged in 1963. An enormous white statue of the Grand Buddha sitting on a pedestal looms in the distance.

The **Bao Thap Tower** has four urns placed at its four corners. These are said to contain lumps of earth taken from the four places in India relating to Buddhism – Buddha's birthplace, his place of enlightenment, where he preached

Vung Tau is known as the Bay of Boats.

274

and where he attained Nirvana.

Set in lovely grounds of frangipani, bougainvillea and rare trees on the Nui Lon hillside, the **Villa Blanche** commands a superb view over Vung Tau. It was built by the French administration, who referred to it as the Governor general's palace.

King Thanh Thai resided here between 1907 and 1916, until he was packed off, exiled with his son, King Duy Tan, to Reunion Island. Later the villa became the seaside residence of South Vietnam's presidents Diem and Thieu.

The Lam Son cafe next door provides a panoramic view of the sea along with refreshments.

The scenic coastal road in the south west of the peninsula, the former *Route de la petite Corniche,* follows the contours of **Mount Nui Lon**.

As if giving a sermon on the mount, a 98 foot (30 meter) statue of Jesus Christ looks out across the Pacific Ocean at the peninsula's southern point. The statue was erected by the Americans in 1971.

A small inland road leads along Mount Lui Non's eastern flank to Vung Tau's oldest pagoda, the **Linh Son Tu**, Pagoda of the Sacred Mountain, which dates from 1911.

Inland from Bai Dua Beach, is the most celebrated of Vung Tau's pagoda's, the **Niet Ban Tinh Xa**. Niet Ban, Vietnamese for Nirvana, is symbolized in the pagoda's long reclining Buddha, who having attained Niet ban can lie back and enjoy it. The statue is made of concrete overlaid with marble. Each of the Buddha's 12 meters represents one of the twelve stages of reincarnation, all of which are engraved on the Buddha's feet. The goddess Quan Am is also represented here.

The statues standing at the entrance gate are those of Than Thien, the good genie and Than Ac, the evil genie, who are believed to guard the entrance to Nirvana.

The **Thang Tam Communal House** one of Vung Tau's oldest monuments ,is located on Hoang Hoa Tham Street. It contains an ancient khmer statue of the

meditating Buddha dating from pre-Angkorian times. This grey stone Buddha was discovered at the summit of Mount Nui Lon.

From Vung Tau, a 13 hour boat trip or 50 minute plane trip links the mainland with the **Con Doa Archipelago**.

The archipelago comprises 14 islands, which boast unspoilt beautiful beaches, coconut groves, corals and clear waters. Sea turtles laboriously make their way onto the beaches here to lay their eggs. Between the months of February and July they are captured and relieved of their shells.

Dense virgin forest, rich in precious woods, covers the island's interior.

Today's image of unspoilt natural beauty is a far cry from that of the dreaded penitentiary of Poulo Condore (Devil's Island) run by the French on the main island for almost a century. Reminders of the island's less attractive past are present in the remains of the penal colony, a museum and the Hang Duong cemetery. Only the main island has any hotel accommodation.

The conflicting symbols of colonialism.

THE MEKONG DELTA

This vast delta is formed by the alluvium deposited by the multiple arms and tributaries of the Mekong River which descends from it source high in the Tibetan plateau to follow its 2,812 mile (4,500 km) course flows through China, Burma (Myanmar), Laos, Cambodia and South Vietnam before flowing out into the South China sea.

The Mekong's Vietnamese name, Cuu Long, means Nine Dragons, which by mere coincidence is the number of mouths which terminate the flow of this great river as it is swallowed up by the sea.

This ancient Khmer territory was an area of marshland and forest before the first colonizers arrived by sea in the 16th century. During the rule of the Nguyen Lords great expanses of marshland were reclaimed and a network of small canals were built.

By the end of the 18th century two huge canals, the Thai Hoa which linked Rach Gia and Long Xuyen and the Vinh Te, linking Chau Doc and Ha Tien, were operational.

The Delta region is still peopled by a large percentage of Khmer *krom*, people of Khmer origin, Chinese and Chams as well as Vietnamese, among them are followers of diverse religious beliefs including Buddhism, Catholicism, the sects of Cao Dai, Hoa Hao and Brahman.

The delta's nine provinces: Long An, Dong Thap, An Giang, Kien Giang, Tien Giang, Ben Tre, Cuu Long, Hau Giang and Minh Hai are served by well over 100 ferries and an adequate road network. On the whole the roads are in good shape – by Vietnamese standards – and the comprehensive waterway network carries a busy and greatly varied flow of traffic.

The best time to travel in the delta is between January and March when the temperature ranges between 22 and 34°C. From May onwards the rainfall and humidity increases. During the wettest months, between July and October, some provinces are badly flooded and travel is considerably restricted.

In contrast to North Vietnam, the people here appear well clothed and fed. The region has greatly recovered from the ravages of the chemical defoliants and bombs dropped on it during the war. The markets in the region are abundantly supplied with fish and a variety and quantity of produce yielded by the delta's rich alluvial soil – rice, soyabeans, maize, sesame, peanuts, pineapples, pumpkins, potatoes, tangerines, melons, cabbages, durians and tobacco.

The province of **Long An**, which stretches from the Cambodian border in the west right across the country to the east coast, is more of historical that scenic significance. It was here, at Nhat Tao on the Vam Co Dong River, that the French battleship *L'Esperance* was completely burnt by the Vietnamese in 1861. This decisive battle cost the life of everyone on board and forced the French out of the South.

The North is slightly hilly although most of the province occupies a level plain a few metres above sea level. The Vam Co Dong, Vam Co Tay and Saigon rivers flow through the province, bringing rich alluvial silt to the extensive rice fields. Plantations of pineapple, cassava, coconuts, sugar cane and bananas are a common sight, so too are fresh water fish farms.

The Delta's Western Provinces: Dong Thap Province, can be reached by the ferry from **My Thuan** or via Highway 49. Bordering Cambodia in the north, it is one of the three provinces lying in the marshy area known as Dong Thap Muoi or the Plain of Reeds. The province takes its name from the 10 storey **Thap Muoi Tower**, built in the town of **en Phong**. The tower, since disappeared was used as a lookout by the resistance forces during the war against the French.

The province was formerly inhabited by the ancient Phu Nam Kingdom and later the Chan Lap (Tchen La) civilization, a people who in the 1700s exchanged the area of **Sa Dec** with Vietnam for military aid that restored order to the area. The Chen Lap were subsequently wiped out and assimilated by the Vietnamese and today the area is peopled mainly by people of Chinese, Khmer, Cham and Thai extraction.

Among the archaeological vestiges uncovered in the area of Dong Thap Muoi and the ancient alluvial area of Duc Hoa, the site of **Binh Ta**, 15 km from Ben Luc township is the richest in historical remains. Among the objects unearthed were gold artifacts, precious stones, fine ceramic pieces of the Oc Eo civilization, iron objects, attesting to the earlier presence of the **Phu Nam** (Funan) **Kingdom**. Among the golden artefacts was a plate engraved with ancient sanskrit, in the Southern Indian style, recording the order given to withdraw troops by the king of Phu Nam in the year 550 A.D. Excavations at the **Go Xoai Temple** revealed the location of the troop withdrawal ceremony at the center of Dac Muc, the capital of the Phu Nam kingdom. This excavation marked the first time that Vietnamese archaeologists uncovered evidence linking the Phu Nam kingdom and the Oc Eo civilization. A large number of

prehistoric remains were found within a 6¼ mile (10 km) radius of the temple.

Among the other archaeological discoveries in the province are the remains of a town buried 1,000 years ago which have been excavated at the archaeological site of **Go Thap**.

In addition, Dong Thap Province is famous for its scenery, particularly its extensive reedbeds, lakes and ponds where lotus grows in profusion. Its cajeput forests are home to many species of rare birds and animals.

To the south **An Giang Province** borders the Cambodian Province of Takeo. This border remains a somewhat politically sensitive area. Here the Mekong enters the province and splits into two branches, forming the Tien and Hau rivers, which every year deposit millions of cubic metres of alluvium in the adjacent areas. This prosperous region, rich in natural resources and fertile land produces many varieties of fruit trees and crops of soya bean, tobacco, groundnut, tobacco and mulberry.

Phu Tan Village in the north of the

From Chau Doc, Cambodia looms in the distance.

province is the birth place of Huynh Phu So, founder of the Hoa Hao sect. Its male followers are easily identified by their long beards and long hair tied in a bun.

Long Xuyen, the provincial capital located in the east of the province has a population of about 100,000 and its Catholic Church which can seat 1,000 is one of the largest in the delta. From here a road heads west to Ba Chuc, passing many fishing villages built beside the canals. Very flimsy bamboo "monkey bridges" stretch across the canals. These were built for the lighter and more agile Vietnamese and are to be avoided, or negotiated with extreme care, unless you want to end up in the canal, an all too easy feat which causes the locals no end of amusement.

Some 19 miles (30km) from Long Xuyen township, in the hilly area of Ba Thi are the **Ruins of Oc Eo** which was a major trading port during the first centuries A.D. Oc Eo lay submerged for centuries until it was rediscovered in the 1940s. Traces of architectural structures and other finds made by archaeologists here, indicate that it was a city closely linked with the ancient kingdom of Phu Nam (Funan), which dates back to the first centuries A.D. and reached its peak in about the 5th century.

Most of what we know about this ancient civilization has been gleaned from archaeological excavations at Oc Eo which revealed evidence of contact with the Roman Empire, Persia, China, Thailand, Malaysia and Indonesia, and the written accounts of Chinese travellers and emissaries. Oc Eo's elaborate canal system was used for transportation and irrigation.

You may need special permission to visit the area; if in doubt consult the local Vietnam Tourism office.

The province is renowned for its unglazed black pottery, pieces of which were excavated at Oc Eo. This is produced using diato-mocaolinite, a type of clay formed from the dried remains of living creatures. After firing, this pottery is so light that it can float on the surface of the water.

Birds of a feather flock to the Delta.

The early morning market on the canal in **An Chau** is a lively and very visual affair. Not far from here are the long irrigation canals of the district of **Tri Ton** where a great percentage of the population is now Khmer, after thousands of refugees fleeing Pol Pot's forces poured into the area during 1977-78.

The town of **Chau Doc**, not far from the Cambodian border is situated on the right bank of the Hau Giang River. The **Dinh Than Chau Phu** (Chau Phu temple) in the township was built in 1926. Here, the locals worship Thai Ngoc Hau, the man responsible for the nearby **Chau Doc Canal** which delimits the frontier between Cambodia and Vietnam. He held a high official rank under first the Nguyen Lords and later the Nguyen Dynasty.

Mass is held twice a day in the town's small Catholic church built in 1920. You may like to take the ferry across the Hau River from the Chau Giang terminal in the town to visit the **Chau Giang Mosque** which serves Chau Giang district's Muslim Cham community. From here you can pick up a lift to Tan Chau district which is famous throughout the south for its silk industry and prosperity. The market here offers many imported goods from Thailand which are brought into the country via Cambodia.

Three miles (5 km) from Chau Doc stands **Mount Nui Sam**, so named because from a distance the hill resembles a *sam*, king crab. This beautiful site holds many important monuments and relics, among them, the **Tomb of Thoai Ngoc Han** which holds the remains plus those of his two wives and the **Thoai Ngoc Hau Temple** where he is worshipped.

Also sharing the Nui Sam hillside are the Indian style **Tay An Pagoda** which dates from 1847, famous for its many finely carved religious figures, the **Temple of the Goddess Saint** (Den Thanh Mau), where a granite statue left by the Cambodians is worshipped which was and Den Thanh Mau was founded in the 1820s.

Every year on the 22nd day of the fourth lunar month a large procession of

In a Mac Cuu temple at Ha Tien.

religious followers begins a week long series of festivities and ceremonies to celebrate their pilgrimage.

Halfway between Tay An Pagoda and Thoai Ngoc Hau's tomb you'll find the Hoa Phuong Restaurant where you can enjoy delicious local specialities, including turtle and snake.

About half way up Mount Nui Sam's western flank, set apart from the main body of religious buildings, is a pagoda, **Chua Phuc Dien Tu** which backs onto a cave containing a shrine dedicated to the Quan Am.

Kien Giang Province, in the southwest of the delta, shares a common border in the northwest with Cambodia and in the west is washed by waters from the Gulf of Thailand. Forests, plains, offshore islands and a 200 km coastline contribute to Kien Giang's rich scenic diversity. It features the most beautiful of all the towns in the delta, **Ha Tien**. Located less than 4 miles (6 km) from the border with Cambodia, this charming town of Chinese origin was founded towards 1674 by Mac Cuu,

a Chinese immigrant from Canton who arrived here after the fall of the Ming Dynasty. He refused to serve the Manchu rulers and instead explored the South seas with his men. After procuring the agreement of the Cambodian kings and the Vietnamese Nguyen Lords, he and his men installed themselves at Ha Tien, transforming it in no time into a prosperous principality equipped with a maritime port.

In 1714 Ha Tien was given to Lord Nguyen Phuc Chu from Hue, who recompensed Mac Cuu with the title, Generalissimo of Ha Tien. The principality prospered from the revenue accumulated from a gambling house and a tin mine. The governor used the tin to make coins for commercial exchanges. His son, Mac Thien Tu continued his father's work in improving the sectors of administration, social and economic development. He organized an army equal to the task of repelling the Cambodian and Siamese invasions and also founded an Academy of Arts, the Chieu Anh Cac (Pavilion of Quintessential Welcome).

One for the album at the Tay An Pagoda.

The provincial capital, **Rach Gia**, is an active fishing port with a population of around 120,000, bordered by marshland, much of which has been drained for rice growing.

The town has quite a number of interesting temples and pagodas. The large Khmer **Phat Lon Pagoda** was established about two centuries ago. The **Ong Bac De Pagoda** on Nguyen Du Street in the town center was built by the local Chinese community about a century ago. The central altar is occupied by a statue of Ong Bac De, the reincarnation of the Jade Emperor of Heaven. To his left is Ong Gon, the guardian spirit of happiness and virtue and on his right is Quan Cong. **Nguyen Trung Truc Temple** at 18 Nguyen Cong Tru Street, is dedicated to Nguyen Trung Truc, who lead the resistance campaign against the French during the 1860s. He led the attack on the French ship *L'Esperance*. Although the French repeatedly tried to capture him, it wasn't until 1868 that they succeeded, after taking his mother and a number of civilians hostage and threatening to kill them unless he gave himself up. He did so and was executed by the French in the Rach Gia marketplace on October 27, 1868.

The small **Pho Minh Pagoda** on the corner of Co Bac and Nguyen Van Cu streets, was built in 1967. A garden full of trees pruned in the shape of animals surrounds the **Tam Bao Pagoda** near the corner of Tran Phu and Thich Thien An streets.

The town also has a small Cao Dai Temple near the bus station on Nguyen Trung Truc Street and a Protestant Church further along the street in the direction of the river.

Rach Gia is well known for its seafood and has a good selection of restaurants serving both Chinese and Vietnamese food and specialities such as eel, turtle, snake, frogs legs, deer and cuttlefish.

Ferries leave for Chau Doc (5.30 p.m.), Long Xuyen (12.30 p.m.) and Tan Chau (4.30 p.m.) from the Muoi Voi ferry terminal on Bach Dang Street.

The road from Rach Gia to Ha Tien is

On the beach at Binh An.

284

a bit rough but passes many duck farms and provides an interesting look at life on the canal. The Khmer **Soc Soai Temple** in **Hon Dat District** stands in a beautiful setting of lush tropical vegetation. Completed in 1970, it houses over seventy monks. The temple's interior with its old fashioned furnishings has a well worn charm and no shortage of atmosphere.

Many Khmer people live in this area and a little detour off the main road leads to the Khmer village of **Binh An**.

The **Chua Hang Grotto** and **Duong Beach**, one of the best beaches in the area, lie about 20 miles (32 km) from Ha Tien. The grotto is entered from behind the altar of the pagoda which is set back into the base of the hill. The grotto's thick stalactites are hollow and give off a bell-like resonance if tapped. Inside the grotto is a plaster statue of the Goddess of Mercy, Quan Am.

The beach, **Bai Duong** next to the grotto takes its name from the duong trees growing beside it. Its white, clear water and picturesque surroundings make it an ideal spot to break the journey and enjoy a swim.

Roughly 7 km further on is the **Hang Tien Grotto** or Coin Grotto, which takes it name from the zinc coins found buried within it by Nguyen Anh, the future Emperor Gia Long, and his troops, who sheltered in it recesses from the pursuit of the Tay Son rebels.

About 17 km from Ha Tien, 3 km from the main road is the **Mo So Grotto**. During the wet season it is only accessible by boat, but for the rest of the year you can reach it on foot. Be sure to take a torch with you and a local to accompany you if you intend to explore the labyrinth of tunnels beyond the three main caverns.

A floating toll bridge completes the last watery stretch of the journey to Ha Tien. Nestling in a cove formed by the **Gian Thang River**, Ha Tien has a population of 80,000. The region belonged to Cambodia until 1708 when, unable to deal alone with the repeated attacks from the Thai's, its Khmer-appointed governor Mac Cuu, requested help and protection from the Vietnam-

ese. Thereafter Mac Cuu acted as governor under the protection of the Nguyen Lords. His son, Mac Thien Tu succeeded him. In 1798, this region and the southern tip of the delta came directly under Nguyen rule. Ha Tien's unspoilt natural beauty attracts many visitors, among the most picturesque spots are the **East Lake** (Dong Ho) and mounts **Ngu Ho** and **To Chau**, which dominate the mouth of the **Giang Thanh River**.

The town has several temples dedicated to the Mac family and an even greater number of tombs which rest on the eastern flank of **Mount Binh San**. These are built of bricks cemented together with vegetable resin from the o duoc shrub and contain the remains of both Mac Cuu and his relatives. His own tomb, built in 1809, is the largest and decorated with finely carved figures of the Blue Dragon and the White Tiger.

The **Bao Pagoda** at 328 Phuong Thanh was founded by Mac Cuu in 1730. A statue of Quan Am standing on a lotus stands in front of the pagoda. Nearby is the **Phu Dung Pagoda** which was

The Grotto That Swallows the Clouds.

founded by Mac Cuu's second wife about the middle of the 18th century. Her tomb is built on the hillside behind the pagoda's main hall. The pagoda contains some rather interesting statues, in the center of the main hall is one of a the new born Sakymouni Buddha in the embrace of nine serpents and on the main dais in a glass case is a bronze Chinese Buddha. The small temple dedicated to the Taoist Jade Emperor of Heaven beyond the main hall contains papier mache statues of a number of Taoist divinities, the gods of the Northern and Southern Stars, the God of Happiness and the God of Longevity.

Ha Tien does a lively trade in beautiful items hand-crafted from sea turtle shells. The unfortunate creatures are reared in pools along the coastline. Looking out to sea from the headlands you will see the Father and Son Rocks whose grottoes are a favorite haunt of sea swallows. It is also famous for its seafood and black pepper and its beautiful white sand beaches such as Bai No with its coconut palm-shaded shore, Mui Nai, 4 km west of the city and Bai Bang with its dark sands lined with bang trees.

One of the main attractions located 2 miles (3½ km) from town on Mac Tu Hoang Street is **Thach Dong Thon Van**, the Grotto that Swallows the Clouds. The grotto shelters a Buddhist sanctuary and funerary tablets and altars to Quan Am and Ngoc Hoang, the Jade Emperor of Heaven, are contained in several of its chambers. Nearby is a mass grave where 130 people, victims of a massacre by Pol Pot's troops in March 1978, are buried. The stele to the left of the sanctuary's entrance, known as Bia Cam Thu – the stele of hatred – commemorates the victims.

Hon Giang Island lies about 9 miles (15 km) off the coast of Ha Tien and can be reached by boat, its lovely secluded beach is well worth the trip.

Phu Quoc Island: Perhaps better known for the former French penitentiary of Poulo Condor, this beautiful forested archipelago comprising 16 islands, lies about 19 miles (30 km) as the crow flies west of Ha Tien and forms part of Kien

Below and right, tropical fruits at the central market in My Tho.

Giang Province. The 30 miles (48 km) long island has a population of about 18,000 and covers an area of 495 square miles (1,320 square km).

The future Emperor Gia Long was sheltered here from the Tay Son rebels by the French missionary Pigneau de Behaine, who had himself used the island as a base between the 1760s and 1780s.

Today Phu Quoc is renowned for its bountiful fishing grounds and its prime-quality *nuoc mam* production.

Flights leave from Saigon every Friday to the island's main center, Duong Dong. The unspoilt beaches, snorkelling and fishing are exceptional.

The Eastern Provinces: Tien Giang Province represents one of the country's main rice growing areas. Land reclamation began in this extremely fertile region during the 17th century. This ancient Khmer territory was colonized by the South Vietnamese towards the end of the 17th century, then taken over by the French in April 1861.

Major rivers such as the Tien, Go Cong, Ca Han and Bao Dinh, flow through the province. These, combined with the extensive canal network, provide excellent waterway access to Ho Chi Minh City and Phnom Penh. The sites of Rach Gam and Xaoi Mut by the Tien River are where the peasant hero, Nguyen Hue won his first victory in an historic river battle which claimed the lives of 40,000 Siamese troops in 1785.

My Tho, the provincial capital with its population of 90,000, lies on the left bank of the My Tho River, the northernmost branch of the Mekong. It is easily reached from Saigon by a one and a half hour bus journey or a six hour ferry trip. The city was founded in the 1680s by political refugees from Taiwan.

This region is famous for its orchids, coconut palms and fruit – mangoes, longans, bananas and oranges.

The old Saigon to My Tho railway, the earliest built in Indochina, no longer operates, but the province has a more than adequate road network.

The central market is located on Trung Trac and Nguyen Hue streets and is

closed to traffic. Stalls selling all manner of goods fill the streets.

The Catholic church here was built at the end of last century. Masses are held twice daily for My Tho's 7,000 strong Catholic congregation.

The Vinh Trang (a real tourist trap) and Quan Thanh Pagodas are definitely not worth visiting unless you're into the tacky and kitsch ultimate in bad taste, in which case you won't be disappointed. You would be better advised to give them a miss and spend your time taking a boat on the Mekong to one of the nearby islands, a thoroughly interesting and enjoyable excursion.

Phung Island lies a few km from My Tho and can be reached by either ferry or by hired boat.

The island was the home of the Coconut Prophet, Ong Dao Dua and his followers, a charismatic character who founded a religion known as Tinh Do Cu Si which was a synthesis of Buddhism and Christianity. Both Buddhist and Christian symbols represented a unique sect – Jesus and Buddha, the Virgin Mary – a unique and very interesting triumvirate.

Born Nguyen Thanh Nam, in 1909, he studied physics and chemistry in France between 1928 and 1935 before returning to Vietnam where he married and had a daughter. In 1945 he left his family to live the life of a monk and for three years is said to have sat on a stone slab beneath a flag pole meditating, eating only coconuts – thus the name. His philosophy advocated peaceful means of reunifying his country and this did not go down at all well with the successive South Vietnamese governments in whose prisons he was a frequent guest. He died some years ago, a prisoner of the communists who arrested him for anti-government activities. After his arrest his band of followers dispersed.

The island boasts the remnants of a bizarre open air sanctuary where the Coconut Prophet addressed his following. Today its faded dragon-entwined columns and multi-tiered tower with a great metal globe atop, stand rather for-

Floating market on the Hau River.

lorn and neglected. **Tan Long Island** is a five minute boat ride from the dock at the bottom of Le Loi Boulevard. Its shores are lined with lush coconut palms and many wooden fishing boats. The island is famous for its longan orchards.

Seven miles (12 km) from the town is a snake farm whose occupants yield a variety of medical substances used in traditional medicines. Their flesh is believed to be an effective remedy against a number of ailments ranging from mental disorders to rheumatism and paralysis. Snake gall combined with other drugs is used to treat coughs and migraine. An excellent tonic alcohol is obtained by steeping three special varieties of snake in alcohol.

Ben Tre Province lies between the My Tho and Co Chien Rivers. A ferry runs between Ben Tre and My Tho further south. The provincial capital, Ben Tre, is located on the Mi Long tributary. More coconut palms are grown here than in any other province in the country. These contend for space with the province's extensive rice fields.

A boat trip along the Bai Lai - Ham Luong waterway provides an opportunity to become better acquainted with the scenes of everyday life on the river. Ba Tri district's bustling market place is a good place to buy locally produced silk. The **Nguyen Dinh Chieu Temple** here is dedicated to a 19th century poet who lived in Ba Tri.

Many species of birds can be seen in the Cu Lao Dat Bird Sanctuary in An Hiep village which covers 30 hectares of forest.

Cuu Long Province (Nine Dragons) further south takes it name from the stretch of the Mekong River that flows through southern Vietnam and the vast delta area. Its landscape, crisscrossed by canals, lies just 6½ feet (2 metres) above sea level.

A number of interesting temples and pagodas can be visited in the provincial capital of **Vinh Long**. Boats leave from in front of the Cuu Long Hotel for the An Binh and Binh Hoa Phuoc islands in the Tien River. The one hour trip is a treat for fruit lovers as it takes in villages

On the waterfront at Can Tho.

whose gardens and orchards produce a great variety of seasonal fruit such as mangoes, mandarins, rumbutans and plums.

Can Tho, the capital of **Hau Giang Province**, is the most modern and only university city in the delta. This important bustling commercial center and river port with its population of 150,00 lies on the banks of the **Hau River**, the Mekong's southernmost tributary. Can Tho University, founded in 1966, conducts valuable agricultural research that has contributed substantially to improving production and pest control.

A visit to the animated Can Tho Market which spreads out along Hai Ba Trung Street and in its main building at the intersection of Hai Ba Trung and Nam Ky Khoi Nghia streets reveals the rich variety and abundance of fruit, seafood and vegetables produced in the region.

Several restaurants along the waterfront serve specialities of the region – frog, turtle, snake and fish.

The city has a friendly feel about it but there is not a great deal of sightseeing to be done in the city itself, although the **Vang Pagoda** on Hoa Binh Avenue in the center of town is worth visiting.

Boat trips on the Hau River provide an opportunity to see life on the waterways. A lively floating market takes place at the junction of seven canals, where all manner of boats and sampans gather, their occupants busily engaged in buying or selling a wide variety of fruit, fish and vegetables.

About 22 miles (35 km) southeast of Can Tho is the town of **Soc Trang**. Many Khmer people live in the area and just outside the town is a Khmer temple, richly decorated with elephants, griffins, tigers and statues of dancing girls. A Ghe Ngo, Rowing Boat Festival, is held here on the 14th day of the tenth lunar month. A 52 man crew displays its skills in a 200 year old Kampuchean war canoe, 82 feet (25 metres) long. Canoes from other villages race against them to the noisy accompaniment of a gong.

Minh Hai Province: The southernmost province of Vietnam, Minh Hai, is hardly a tourist destination. Cau Mau, the largest town, lies 111 miles (179 km) south of Cantho on the Gan Hao River in the heart of an immense submerged plain covered in mangrove forest the U Minh forest – the largest of its kind in the world outside the Amazon. The forest was seriously damaged by defoliants dropped by the Americans during the war. The dense swampy undergrowth is home to many varieties of venomous snakes, leeches and mosquitoes. The locals catch the snakes for farms which supply the pharmaceutical industry and also for food. Another unusual animal eaten by the locals is the *te te*. The meat of this creature, which resembles something between a snake and a lizard, is reputedly delicious. Large tortoises are found in the drier areas. Cajeput forests thrive in the brackish water and the cajeput is collected to provide a variety of special oils. Honey and royal jelly is collected from wild bees' hives.

Cau Mau Point marks the extreme southernmost tip of Vietnam and the end of our journey.

Active business day in Can Tho market. **Right**, eyeing boats at Ben Tre.

"NAMSTALGIA" – LEGACY OF THE VIETNAM WAR

Tim Page, who wrote this piece, was a war photographer in Vietnam. He has returned to photograph the country several times in recent years.

Who was Dave, where is he now and will he ever come back to see his old charger resting, rusting in the center of downtown Dong Ha? His name is still preserved on the front glacis plate on an M-48 tank just below the driver's hatch; one of a motley collection of American fighting vehicles given over to the old

Korean, Taiwan and, as always, the Japanese. The ploughshares come back as Toyotas, ghetto blasters and beer cans. Business is booming although the folks are having to dig deeper in the old battle fields and firebases to find the spent shell casings. Now they are resorting to returning chunks of shrapnel as the country is being cleared of every vestige of its struggle for unification. One has to be something of an industrial waste detective to spot the traces, the remains of the intense campaigns and opera-

regime's force (the ARVN) during the Vietnamization campaign in the early 1970s.

Five years ago, it would have been possible to find a tank, APC or some other artefact of war in a hundred different places. They have mostly gone to the recyclers' heap with the rest of the scrap that a war produces, the proverbial guns to ploughshares syndrome. In Vietnam's case, the vicasa – literally steel rolling mills – outside Long Binh in the South and Hoa Binh up North smelt the resting debris down to reinforcing rod, plate and girder or ingots for export. The clientele for the stuff often includes the foes that the North once fought against for liberation:

tions that once waged up and down the stunning beauty of the land.

An amateur sleuth has to really leave the beaten track to find anything of strategic interest, much less something to pick up as a souvenir for even the most usable surplus has almost disappeared from the markets. The GI waterbottles, aluminium mess cans, marmites and cutlery are now prized durable possessions, while any engine or piece of machinery is carefully stripped and the parts cleaned up and resold at specific stalls in all the *Cho* (markets). Should you want some odd bearing for your GM six-by-six, the Danang market could fill your need. Jeep spares are better down in the Mekong Delta, the deeper the better. The traffic is enormous as Indochina still runs on a collection of ex-army vehicles, mainly American in the South, Russian and Chinese the further north you go.

Few veterans had the luxury at the time of their tours in-country to take in the sheer beauty of the country, let alone vignettes of it. Too often their perceptions only extended to their perimeters and on into the local ville with its tacky row of steam and cream truck washes and sordid bars with their complement of equally sorry bargirls. The trench lines, entanglements and concertina are all gone, it is just possible – with the aid of an old

as human mine detectors extracting shell casings. Originally all those enjoying the reeducation process were put to work excavating the trash dumps for the soda and beer cans which were recycled into the first coinage of the new nation. There were ten washer-like Hoa coins to the *dong*, Today they are sold for thousands of times their original value to visiting tourist collectors. Should you have a large wad of old *pee* (the piastres of the day), you could have a viable sideline in downtown Saigon. Memorabilia is making a comeback as more vets start to take up the mental challenge and come back to see the font of all their fantasies, their chrysalis to manhood, the birthplace of all

wartime map – to pick out where the landscape was modified to accommodate the occupying units. The hooches, huts and buildings were the first to go, liberated by the people to improve their own housing in an epoch when there was nothing new on the market, a time of desperation and depravation, the *dong* at rock bottom, the country ostracized from the world scheme. The vicasa mills were slow coming on line and folk busily spooled in barbed wire and acted

dreams and all nightmares.

Going back to Vietnam has to be the biggest exorcism available for those who served long enough to have had the Nam bug planted. It is an easy place to fall in love with. Even under conditions of duress, its fertility, fecundity, peaks and panoramas, glimpsed then from the open door of a chopper, the back of a jeep down a possible mine-implanted road, or when plodding through paddies or forests, left their mark. Those once familiar frames come flooding back, a sense of order returns to the mind when the familiar is recognized. It initially strange to drive down a road where decades ago an ambush

Preceding pages: Ageing US transport planes at Tan Son Nhut. **Far left**, Dave's old charger. **Left**, stopped in its tracks. **Above, helicopter graveyard.**

was sprung, until it dawns on you that this is the place where *hoa binh* (peace) is a cherished thing. No one is really interested in the war any more. Economics has overtaken history. If you want to visit a familiar locale, the authorities are only too happy to organize it; you are, after all, the customer.

Virtually the only places still off limits are the military-active parts of the airfields where internal flights land at Danang and Tan Son Nhut, and an occasional compound still used by the army.

Red Beach in Danang, the site of the first US Marine landing on March 8, 1965 is now the depot for the trucks plying the tortuous Annaminite cordillera range to the Mekong

the remains of 22,000 men and women killed in the battles of the DMZ, the 17th parallel. One faction of the American military had the inspired concept of building a fence to keep the Northerners out, so in 1967 the MacNamara line came into being. This sterile zone below the DMZ was a conglomeration of fences, minefields, electronic listening devices, the whole gamut of sophisticated military technology supposedly strung and laid from the mouth of the Ben Hai at Cua Viet to the Lao border. In reality, it ran but a short stretch at a cost of untold millions, the invading troops simply walked around the end of it. Since the war some 17,000,000 pieces of live ordnance have been dug up at

in Laos over notorious Route 9 from Dong Ha through Cam Lo, Con Thien, past the Rockpile to Khe Sanh, Lang Vei and then on to Tchepone the other side of the border. As you pass the Rockpile, displaced Bru ethnics sort through assorted artillery and cluster bomb casings in the shade of a woven bamboo hut, their menfolk chiselling up flattened drums for scrap parcels. All along the pitted highway, small piles of unidentifiable distorted material are accumulated until a monthly truck doles out hot *dong*.

How many medals were won in that strip of land? The Liet Si (liberation cemetery) at Con Thien, the largest in Vietnam, contains

the cost of 2,000 or so limbless and dead. The stretch of land from Dong Ha up to the Ben Hai is only just relinquishing its sterility. On the first ridge you hit south at Gio Linh where five years ago only lateral and manioc flourished around a newly built Liet Si, an emergent eucalyptus plantation grows around a stripped ARVN M-42 tank now integrated into a farmer's back porch.

A similar lonely barrel-dropping vehicle resides in the new rubber plantation at the museum/tunnel complex at Cu Chi 15 miles (25 km) from downtown Ho Chi Minh where the Viet Cong had a tunnel system right beneath the 25th Division base camp. The network extended to the outskirts of the city and north to the rubber plantation in the battle zone which was formerly christened the Iron Triangle. Back in 1980 countless blown apart APCs were still serving duty as chicken coops or integrated into the back of a kitchen. Now a dirty Huey, gutted tank and pierced track lines up in a dusty courtyard at the post junction on Route 4, at Hoc Mon. Further along at Tran Bang, an incongruous M-48 lurks behind a gas station next to a restaurant veranda, neatly fenced around.

Behind you on the main road to Cambodia and Tay Ninh a constant cacophony of belching over-loaded six-by-sixes, semi-tractors and ammunition trucks trundle by. Lacking

responsible for creating the potholes in the first place.

Probably the ultimate idiom of the Vietnam War was the chopper, the whole of the southern conflict vibrated to the sound of their rotor thud. There are rumors that there are some still flying, there must be, but the only ones on view are a gutted dozen out on the flight line at Ton San Nhut. Probably the only place where chopper carcasses still hang apocalyptically in the trees up in the A Shau and A Loui valleys back on the Lao border in Quang Nam province. Here, there were days when up to 40 choppers were lost in these primal forested mountains.

The high valley was base camp to divi-

radiator repair facilities, the cooling is dealt with by a 55-gallon (250-litres) fuel drum atop the cab, directly feeding the block water through hydraulic hosing. (It is becoming possible to creep slowly north from Ho'ville on this system, the ride to Danang costing 20,000 *dong*, approximately $4) The roads took punishment beyond belief. The disintegrating infrastructure was piecemealed back together by Rumanian-built road rollers which were hauled to the potholes on the deck of a transporter that had carried tanks

Left and above, the machinery of war now serves as play tools at the B-52 Park in Hanoi.

sions of North Vietnamese troops, a major junction on the Ho Chi Minh (Truong Son) Trail. They defined it with radar controlled, anti-aircraft batteries so the scrap piles are Russian mixed with the boat-shaped casings from the cluster bomb units. The 200 bombs they dispersed are still blowing limbs off both new settlers and wandering Pac O tribal folk. A keen eye can pick out a strange object in front of a stilted longhouse, a long chunk including the hub of a chopper rotor assembly. To find more would require a day's hike back up through impenetrable jungle to mountaintop crash sites that even the MIA missions are only now getting around to checking out.

Three million Americans were cycled through Vietnam during that 10,000-day epoch, a culture was affected, temporarily warped and inevitably modified, changed. The essence of all that is Vietnamese was layered over with a crass cola plastic veneer, representing the worst of all that is American. The more subtle French influence has left behind the best *baguette* outside of France. The French were also more open to intermarriage with the enchanting long-tressed Viet women, their offspring stunningly handsome metisses. The average GI had his one tour, 365 days, to survive then home to the big PX, the new Firebird GT

The real shock, the numbing truth is how much damage modern warfare can inflict. It is hard even as a European who witnessed post-World War II Europe to countenance what the firepower could do to a mainly rural agricultural society. South of Vinh to Dong Ha, the most intense interdiction campaign – Rolling Thunder – attempted to arrest the flow of supplies and men down the Ho Chi Minh Trail. The road and railway running almost parallel to the coast, were easy targets, especially for the battleship *New Jersey*, with its 16-inch (40-cm) guns just off the coast, or the cruisers and destroyers which freely ranged the length of the gulf. The landscape was radically altered, the road

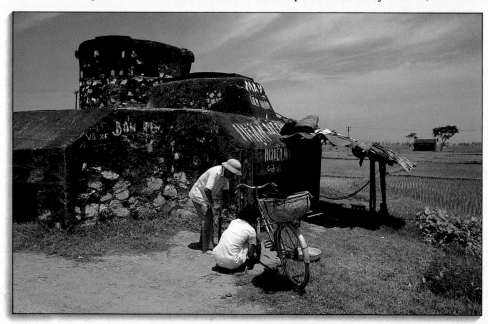

ordered from a catalogue deep in the heart of the war zone. Few took local brides though thousands of 'children of the dust' – the Amerasians, the progeny of those lustful moments away from the horror – still remain, leading a nowhere life in a society that initially condemned them as non-persons. Many have been reunited with their erstwhile fathers, some have been adopted to Europe as well as the US, fewer are integrated totally into the local life. In the areas where there was a major US presence, you will still exchange eye contact with teenagers, their features accented with a sharp Caucasian-edge, a blue eye.

today still a roller coaster dodging bomb craters, the paddies, from the near misses, take on Mondrian patterns. Industry such as it was, was forced into the caves, transport rolled at night as did the planting and harvesting. Night-time was for working, fighting, day time for recovering. A grudging respect for their sheer resilience seeps through you, admiration for their history. The once-razed towns between Nam Dinh and the border are now creeping back to a ferro concrete nouveau reality. Vinh, a city of 30,000, still has no running water.

The cost of delivering this damage did not come cheaply to the USAF, Navy and Marine Corps. Attacking the Ham Rong (Dragon's Jaw) rail and road bridge north of Thanh Hoa cost 73 planes before it was finally taken out in 1972 by a laser-guided missile. Thousands of planes were downed, even 27 B-52s, in the last strikes at Christmas 1972 against Hanoi and Hai Phong when the SAM missiles went up like telephone poles. Hundreds of pilots were doomed to spend their war days in one of Hanoi's infamous POW camps. The Plantation, the Zoo, the Hilton; the latter now the facility for Vietnam Films, the cells acting as cutting rooms. The war museum in Hanoi has a superb collection of 1960s and 1970s flying paraphernalia. In Thanh Hoa the authorities have

'Ranch Hands' with the motto "We Prevent Forests" sprayed 11 million gallons (50 million litres) of the defoliant Dioxin, known as Agent Orange. This chemical, designed to kill trees by stripping the foliage, poisoned everything its vapours touched before seeping into the soil and watertable.

Re-forestation is a gradual and painful process with much stunted or retarded growth. The folk, military and civilian doused in it ended up with more toxic-related diseases than anywhere. Their offspring accounting for a spectrum of mutation and deformity beyond Bosch, the genetic malfunction occurring in the male. The women affected comprise the greater percentage of

thoughtfully put their exhibition of AA guns in the same courtyard as the city's only other attraction, a 17th century Ly Dynasty house. North and South, the B-52s worked silently from over 35,000 feet (10,700 metres), raining horrific damage which finally only strengthened the North's resolve to overcome.

The blight upon the land was convoluted by another element. A unit flying C-123 flying boxcar tankers, calling themselves

Left, bunkers are a common sight in Vietnam. **Above**, Amerasian kids – living legacies of the Vietnam War.

the miscarriages and stillbirths in the south. An orphanage of the victims in Ho Chi Minh City just behind the Zoo, is the most heart-rending stop of any vets visit, albeit a somewhat orchestrated one.

I imagine that not only Americans and the Free world allies who served in whatever capacity before, during and after the war suffer Namstalgia.

The thrall that Vietnam casts around and over you in moments is both ludicrous, insane and horrific, moments of life and death. Everyone remembers in Vietnam someone dear, someone dead, someone missing – that is Namstalgia.

GETTING THERE

BY AIR

Virtually all visitors to Vietnam arrive and depart by air. An increasing number of scheduled flights link Hanoi's Noi Bai International Airport, 30 km from the capital and Ho Chi Minh City's Tan Son Nhat Airport, 7 km from the city with overseas destinations. Hanoi is served by direct flights from Bangkok (Thai International, Air Vietnam), Vientiane (Lao Aviation, Air Vietnam), Phnom Penh (Air Vietnam, Kampuchea Airlines), Moscow via Tashkent, Karachi and Calcutta (Aeroflot), Prague (Czechoslovakian Airlines) and East Berlin via Karachi (Interflug).

The cost of a taxi from the airport into Hanoi is fixed at US$33 , alternatively you can take an Air Vietnam bus for 5,000 dong (about US $1).

Ho Chi Minh City is served by flights from Bangkok (Thai International, Air Vietnam), Kuala Lumpur (MAS), Denpasar, Jakarta and Batam Island (Garuda),Singapore (Lufthansa and a charter service run by Cassidy for Air Vietnam) Paris (Air France, Philippine Airlines), Phnom Penh (Air Kampuchea, Air Vietnam), Manila (Philippine Airlines, Air Vietnam), Moscow (Aeroflot) and Prague (Czechoslovakian Airlines)

A taxi from Tan Son Nhat Airport into the city should cost no more than US$5.

If you are considering flying from Singapore, bear it in mind that the nearest Vietnamese diplomatic representation is in Kuala Lumpur and that a return ticket for the Garuda flight from Batam Island is much cheaper to purchase in Indonesia than in Singapore.

BY SEA

Although no real passenger service exists, some cargo vessels accept a limited number of passengers and in this way visitors may enter Vietnam at the ports of Saigon, Danang or Haiphong from a number of countries including Hong Kong, Japan, Thailand, Singapore, the Soviet Union, France and Poland. Inquire with local travel and shipping agents for schedules and fares. A ferry service operates between Cambodia and Chau Doc, the provincial capital of An Giang Province in the Mekong Delta.

BY ROAD

It is possible to enter Vietnam by road from Cambodia (and vice versa) by bus and non-official vehicles which run every day between Phnom Penh and Ho Chi Minh City. If price is no object, the Cambodian Foreign Ministry will be only too happy to provide a car and driver for a wildly exhorbitant price per head, far in excess of the cost to fly between the two cities.

The overland routes between Laos, China and Vietnam remain closed to foreigners.

TRAVEL ESSENTIALS

VISAS & PASSPORTS

All visitors to Vietnam, including overseas Vietnamese, must possess a valid passport, an entry visa, and very often, an unlimited reserve of patience.

Acquiring a visa is not quite the straightforward process one would hope for. The time it takes between applying and actually acquiring one is subject to considerable variation and the price to considerable fluctuation. The Vietnamese Tourist Authorities have the system well sewn up as far as visas and getting around the country go. Going with them all the way on one of their all inclusive package tours certainly oils the wheels of bureaucracy and produces a visa relatively quickly.

Visas fall into a number of categories: tourist, business, journalist, official, multiple entry business and family visit, and there are several ways of going about acquiring one. They are usually made out on a separate sheet of paper rather than stamped directly into the passport. The reputedly fastest and easiest way is to apply directly, by telex or telegram, to an official tourist organization in either Bangkok, Ho Chi Minh City, or Hanoi, with the details of your full name, date and place of birth, nationality, address, profession, passport number, duration of stay, port of arrival and departure and the Vietnamese Embassy or Consulate you will be dealing with. Specify clearly in your application the area you intend to cover in your travels or your visa will only allow you to travel within the region of your arrival point in Vietnam. For example if you intend to enter at Ho Chi Minh City, travel up to the North and depart from Hanoi, state your intentions clearly in the visa application. The tourist organization will apply for approval from the local Foreign Ministry Office and then forward the approval to the relevant Vietnamese Embassy or Consulate. If once you have entered the country you wish to exit from somewhere other than where you have specified on your visa, ensure that you get the Foreign Ministry office in either Ho Chi Minh City or Hanoi to add this amendment to your visa. Bangkok would seem to be the best place to acquire a visa in terms of speed and efficiency. Alternatively you can apply for a visa through a Vietnamese Embassy or diplomatic representation. You are required to complete 3 copies of the visa application form accompanied by three 4x6cm photographs. One copy you submit to the Embassy or diplomatic representation, the other two you retain and hand to the official tourist representative on your arrival in Vietnam. The delay in obtaining a visa is basically the time it takes for the Embassy to obtain approval from Vietnam Tourism and the Ministry of Foreign Affairs. Once approval has been received your visa can be issued immediately and is valid for the duration asked for (as a rule the maximum is 30 days).

Overseas Vietnamese wishing to visit Vietnam as tourists or visit relatives are required to add the date and number of their exit visa (if in possession of one), or the date, reason and means of exit, plus the full names and addresses of their relatives in Vietnam and their relationship to them.

For those who wish to visit Vietnam on business the procedure is slightly different. If you are in contact with any local business organization or individual you need a letter, telex, fax or telegram of invitation from them before a Vietnamese Diplomatic Representation will issue you with a visa. Your local sponsor is expected to have made arrangements for you and officially these trips are expected to be planned. If you have no local business contact there are organizations you can contact stating the purpose of your visit and they can provide you with the required paperwork and make arrangements for you. Vietcochamber (Vietnamese Chamber of Commerce) provides an imformation service and can put you in touch with a local state run company. They publish a trade directory and foreign trade magazine which list the state companies.

If your application has been accepted but your visa does not arrive before you depart, you can obtain a transit visa on arrival and resolve the matter from there. Theoretically visas for visitors on business or for official purposes should be ready for collection from the Vietnamese representation within seven days of Vietnam Tourism receiving the application. In reality there is no such guarantee, it usually takes twice as long and the earlier you embark upon the process the better. Tourist visas take even longer.

Some individuals have traveled to Vietnam without having first acquired a visa, if you are willing to risk it you may acquire a visa at the airport at a price in the region of anything between US $85 and $150 or more, you may be fined first then granted a visa, or you may find yourself on the next flight back. There are no apparent set rules or regulations and to enter the country this way is a gamble that may or may not pay off. Some airlines, however, require that you have your Vietnamese visa before they will carry you.

Discrepancies over the time it takes to be issued with a visa and its price are unfortunately to be expected, although the *Ho Chi Minh City 1990 Guidebook for Foreign*

Tourists and Businessmen, published by the Saigon Tourist Association, quotes the fixed price for obtaining an entry visa at US$14 and states that on the tourist authorities receiving the paperwork and requests for a visa, formalities should take at most 3 days. This at best is wishful thinking on their part.

Although individual travel is not greatly encouraged by the authorities who stand to lose out financially, it is possible, but you're likely to encounter difficulties both in acquiring a visa and getting around once inside the country. Visas may also be extended within the country through the official tourist authorities. The regulations governing this are continually changing, but you have more chance of doing so in Ho Chi Minh City or Hanoi than in one of the provinces. Vietnam Tourism may inform you that you will only be granted one if you book a tour through them and the Immigration police may tell you they require a letter from Vietnam Tourism before they can issue you with one, so if you don't book a tour you may feel that you will get nowhere, but don't believe all you hear.

You will be given a copy of your landing card on your arrival. This, along with your visa, must be kept with you at all times and handed back on your departure.

FOREIGN REGISTRATION & INTERNAL TRAVEL PERMITS

By law, all visitors must register with the police within 48 hours of arrival in Vietnam and periodically thereafter. If you are on an organized tour all this is normally taken care of for you. If you are traveling independently it is vital that you do this, yet for some inexplicable reason you are not likely to be informed of the fact or of the procedure. Individual travelers can get Vietnam Tourism to handle this registration for them. For business people, registration arrangements can be made through a hotel or sponsoring organization. You can however, also register personally, but for the time and hassle this entails its preferable to pay someone or have a local contact do this for you. While your visa, which is issued by the Foreign Ministry will get you into Vietnam, this registration, issued by the Immigration police, who are branch of the Interior Ministry,

allows you to stay. Hotels are required by law to register all their guests with the local police which is why you are required to hand over your passport in hotels, so there is no way your presence goes unnoticed by the police.

You must also obtain an internal travel permit before leaving the city or town where you have registered with the police. These permits are issued by the Immigration Police in Ho Chi Minh City and through TORESCO in Hanoi. Usually this is unnecessary if you're just making a day trip, but if you're moving on to spend the night elsewhere it is and once you arrive you may also need to register again with the police. You cannot be blamed for being unaware of these regulations — many people have had the unpleasant experience of learning about them the hard way. One of the only constant things in Vietnam is change. The Interior Ministry is continually changing its policies on the issue of travel permits to individual travelers, so it's difficult to know if application requests will be granted and what the prevailing policy will be from one week to the next. One can only hope that once Vietnam's authorities become more familiar with the common concept of tourism, travel will become less subject to restrictions and visitors will no longer find themselves having to pay the price for violating regulations that they were unaware of in the first place.

Hanoi Police Office for the Registration of Foreign Visitors,
63 Tran Hung Dao,
Hanoi.

Ho Chi Minh City Police Staion,
161 Nguyen Du,
Quan 1.
Tel: 99398, 97107
Opens 8 - 11am and 1 - 4pm.

Vung Tau Immigration Police,
14 Le Loi Street.

CUSTOMS

All visitors to Vietnam are required to fill in a very detailed customs declaration in duplicate upon arrival. Customs officials are thorough and will probably inspect your luggage to verify you have made a correct declaration. Any amount of foreign currency can be brought into the country but officially must be declared. The same applies for cameras, transistor radios and recorders, videocassettes, unexposed film, jewelry, personal effects, and medicine in reasonable quantity. Gifts officially must not exceed the value of more than US$50, this however does not apply to overseas Vietnamese, *Viet Kieu*, who may bring in gifts valued at up to US$300 per person or at a limit of US $600 per family. 200 cigarettes, 50 cigars, 250 gms of tobacco and 2 liters of alcohol can be brought in duty free. Items strictly prohibited include arms, explosives, narcotics, inflammable products, Vietnamese dong, animals and any articles considered incompatable with, or forbidden by, the regime in Vietnam.

You will be given a copy of your declaration which you must keep with you during your stay and the items you decalre as temporary imports will be expected to accompany you on your way out. You are also required to record all your currency exchanges and financial transactions, including hotel bills. On your departure it is not unlikely that you will be asked to produce the items you declared plus valid receipts for exchange transactions and purchases made with foreign currency or Vietnamese dong changed while in the country. In any event it pays to keep all your receipts. You will be required to fill in a further declaration form on your departure, but examination on leaving the country is often only a formality as officially Vietnam welcomes you and your money.

Official authorization from the General Commission of Customs is required for clearance to export or take any antiquities out of the country. Visitors are prohibited to take out any Vietnamese currency, ancient artifacts, antiques, or national objects.

On both arrival and departure your luggage will be exposed to an X-Ray examination by antiquated equipment, so keep all cameras, film, software and any other sensitive equipment well clear of it. Ignore any customs official who tries to tell you otherwise, their equipment is lethal.

MONEY MATTERS

Vietnam's unit of currency, the dong, currently circulates in banknotes of 5,000, 2,000, 1,000, 500, 200, 100, 50, 30, 20 and 10, 5, 2, and 1 denominations.

The performance of the Vietnamese dong is a hard act to follow. In August 1988, with an inflation rate of between 80 percent to 100 percent and an active free market, the official rate was 368 dong to one US dollar, by December 1988, the dong had depreciated to 3,000 against the dollar. The free market rate at the beginning of 1988 put the dong at 900 to the dollar, by May it had reached 3,000 and by the beginning of October 4,300. The current rate now stands at about 5,000 dong to US$1. The rate of inflation is currently about 45 percent and the great discrepancy between the the official and free market rate no longer exists, although the latter is usually worth an extra 400 dong per dollar. If you wish to avail yourself of the free market rate (your *cyclo* driver will invariably be able to help you out) offered by certain shops, money lenders or directly on the street, particularly in Ho Chi Minh City and Hanoi, it is essential that you do not declare all your foreign exchange to customs when entering the country.

The US dollar note is the most favored and easily exchangeable foreign currency. Other currencies are not accepted in hotels or tourist shops. Travelers checks in US dollars and foreign currency can be changed at state banks, the few foreign banks now open in Vietnam, and hotels, but travelers checks are not readily accepted elsewhere. The Visa card has recently begun to have a very limited acceptance in Vietnam, but don't count on it, as this could change at any moment and places with the facility to deal with Visa cards are virtually non-existent.

The law and Vietnam's desire for US dollars collectively require that you pay many of your expenses directly in US dollars. This applies in hotels, for national and international flights, purchases made in state-run tourist shops and hotel boutiques, and for all Vietnam Tourism services.

Money transfers may be cabled into Vietnam through the Overseas Vietnamese Export Company, COSEVINA, (102 Nguyen Hue Boulevard, Ho Chi Minh City, Tel: 92391, 96648, telex: 18255 COSEVIN), but this takes at least three weeks and the money can only be collected in dong. This service is meant primarily for overseas Vietnamese to send money to their relatives back home.

HEALTH

No vaccinations are officially required, but immunisation against cholera, hepatitis, Japanese encephalitis, typhoid, tetanus, polio, and a course of an anti-malarial such as Mefloquine or Halfan is advised.

Avoid drinking the local water and ice unless using water purifying products. Bottled mineral water is readily available.

Vietnam suffers from a considerable lack of medical preparations and equipment so take your own comprehensive personal pharmacy. Include something for possible stomach and intestinal disorders, insect repellent, painkillers, eyedrops, a broad spectrum antibiotic, an antifungal preparation such as pevaryl, antiseptic, eyedrops, and an antihistimine for insect bites. Any medication you don't use on your trip would be very gratefully received in Vietnam.

Should you need medical aid during your trip, your hotel reception or Vietnam Tourism would be able to point you in the direction of the nearest hospital or medical service.

WHAT TO WEAR

For the South and Ho Chi Minh City, light casual clothing is suitable all year round. Warmer clothes are needed if you are visiting Hue, Danang and especially Dalat during the Winter months from December to April and really warm clothing, including a coat, is required when visiting Hanoi, Halong Bay, and the mountainous regions of the North at this time.

During the rainy season (May to September) forget about footwear that wouldn't survive a soaking. An umbrella would be an invaluable accessory.

Swimwear, sunglasses and sunfilter preparations are a must for the coastal areas.

WHAT TO BRING

Slide films are not available in Vietnam and only a limited selection of print films are available at rather inflated prices so bring enough to cover your trip. If you have to buy film in Vietnam, check the expiry date.
—Extra passport size photographs
—Water purifying tablets
—A universal travel plug adapter would be useful, also a torch as no visit to Vietnam is complete without the inevitable and untimely power cuts, particularly after dark.
—A portable shortwave receiver.
—You would probably live to regret not including some form of mosquito deterrent in your survival kit.

Tea and coffee would be a good thing to take along as most accommodation provides flasks of boiling water in the rooms.

Dunhill and 555 cigarettes are the brands most favored by the locals and can be used as a form of currency. The import of foreign cigarettes became illegal in August 1990.

GETTING ACQUAINTED

HOW VIETNAM IS GOVERNED

Vietnam is a socialist republic ruled by the Vietnamese Communist Party since the fall of Saigon in 1975, and the country's subsequent imposed reunification in 1976. In principal the state is run by a State Council, currently headed by President Vo Chi Cong, as the official Chief of State. However in real terms the country's present leading man is Nguyen Van Linh, the Secretary General of the party.

The government is nominated by the National Assembly, proposed by the party and theoretically elected by the people.

The republic is divided into 40 administrative areas comprising three city provinces: Hanoi, Ho Chi Minh City and Hai Phong; 36 provinces and one special zone, Vung Tau, all of which come directly under the central administration in Hanoi.

In the Vietnamese Communist Party, the Politburo wields all power in decision making, directing party line and policies. The bottom level of the party hierachy is occupied by the Chapter which elects delegates to attend congresses at district levels from where delegates are appointed on up to the National Congress. Congresses at all levels elect members to party executive

THE PROBLEMS OF A

HEAVY TRAFFIC.

You'll come across massive Thai jumbos at work and play in their natural habitat. In Thailand, elephants are part of everyday rural life.

FALLING MASONRY.

A visit to the ruined cities of Sukhothai or Ayutthaya will remind you of the country's long and event-filled history.

EYESTRAIN.

A problem everyone seems to enjoy. The beauty of our exotic land is only matched by the beauty and gentle nature of the Thai people.

GETTING LOST.

From the palm-fringed beaches of Phuket to the highlands of Chiang Mai there are numerous places to get away from it all.

OLIDAY IN THAILAND.

GETTING TRAPPED.

n bunkers mostly. The fairways, superb club
nouses and helpful caddies make a golf trap for
players of all standards.

HIGH DRAMA.

A performance of the 'Khon' drama, with gods
and demons acting out a never-ending battle
between good and evil, should not be missed.

EXCESS BAGGAGE.

Thai food is so delicious you'll want to eat more
and more of it. Of course, on Thai there's
no charge for extra kilos in this area.

MISSING YOUR FLIGHT.

In Thailand, this isn't a problem. Talk to us or your
local travel agent about Royal
Orchid Holidays in Thailand.

Thai
We reach for the sky.

*This region was the cradle of the **Insight Guides** and is their special domain. It all started on the enchanted island of Bali with the idea to create a very different guidebook — one that combines visual and intellectual insight. What is the magic of Bali, island of the gods? How do you avoid giving offence in Thailand? Does the nightlife of Bangkok live up to its reputation? Where do you find the best dining experiences in Singapore?*

***Insight Guides** provide the answers.*

Bali
Bangkok
Burma
Indonesia
Malaysia
Philippines
Singapore
South East Asia Wildlife
Thailand
Vietnam

A P A
INSIGHT
GUIDES

committees. At the national level, the Party Congress of Delegates appoints members to the Central Committee, from where members are appointed to the Politburo which usually comprises of 14 members, thus supreme power is monopolized by a small body of very senior individuals.

The Vietnamese Communist Party organization can be divided into three main bodies: the National Congress of Delegates; the Central Executive Committee; and the Control Committee. Theoretically the National Congress of Delegates holds all power, yet is only an association of 1,129 individuals which meets once every 4 or 5 years to hear reports and vote on resolutions already drafted by the Politburo. Essentially it transfers all power to the 173-member Central Committee which meets every 3 to 6 months, but functions merely as an accompaniment to the all powerful Politiburo and its secretariat. The Control Committee is not independent of the Politburo, but plays the role of enforcing party discipline.

Party members do not automatically have the right to run for office, but must first be screened by appropriate executive committee levels before their names can appear on a list of candidates. They are then screened again when congresses evaluate those who meet the criteria set by the Central Committee. Although encouraged to exercise initiative, party members are not at liberty to disagree with party line, policies or decisions hailing from above. Re-education camps and other disciplinary measures ensure that party members toe the line, as expulsion from the only ruling party means losing the many privileges that go with the position. The party encourages criticism and self-criticism within its ranks through its media, but few voluntarily subject themselves to this form of public confession.

THE ECONOMY

Vietnam is essentially an agricultural country, with rice cultivation accounting for 45 percent of the GNP and employing 72 percent of the population. Other major crops include tea, coffee, maize, bananas, manioc, cotton, tobacco, coconut and rubber.

Industry represents 32 percent of the country's GNP and occupies 11 percent of the active population. Electricity, steel, ce-ment, cotton fabrics, fish sauce, sea fish, wood, paper and the growing oil exploration and production industry represent Vietnam's major areas of industrial production. Ho Chi Minh City now boasts a small oil refinery and has become Vietnam's economic capital, accounting for 30 percent of the national industrial production.

Plagued by high unemployment and a shortage of housing and consumer goods, the country's standard of living ranks amongst the lowest in the world. Despite a protracted effort to revive the rural economy, disasterous economic polices coupled with the drain of more than 50 percent of the country's budget on supporting its occupation forces in Cambodia and Laos, have had devastating effects on Vietnam's economy. In an effort to revive the ailing economy the country has recently opened its doors to encourage foreign investment and tourism, while further reform policies have been geared to re-establish a market economy and encourage production in the private sector, agriculture and light industry.

TIME ZONE

Vietnam, like Laos, Cambodia and Thailand, lies in the zone seven hours ahead of Greenwich Mean Time.

The sun sets relatively early, around 5.30pm in Winter and 8pm in Summer.

CULTURE & CUSTOMS

The concept of tourism is very new to Vietnam. Even before reaching the country, you may encounter attitudes in official representives that try your patience to the limit. However, firmness, perseverence and diplomacy will achieve a great deal more than losing your cool. Patience is a necessity in this long-suffering country. If misunderstandings do arise and things do not seem to be going the way you anticipated, or you don't feel you're getting what you paid for, raising your voice, shouting and loudly criticizing the offending party will only result in loss of face all round and make matters worse. If you have a complaint to make, do so in a manner that will not be taken as threatening or insulting. On the whole the Vietnamese are very friendly, polite, hospitable and helpful. Like anywhere else in the world, these attributes take a back seat during rush hour traffic and in the battle for space on the overcrowded public transport, situations that tend to bring out the worst in everyone.

Very direct questions about one's age, family status and income are quite natural topics of conversation and not considered rude or personal. Vietnamese who have not had much exposure to foreign visitors are often very shy but curious and those who speak English or French enjoy an opportunity to converse with foreigners and make friends. Be sensitive to anyone who may appear ill at ease or not wish to be seen talking to a foreigner, locals have been arrested for less and the past is hard to shake off. A gentle handshake is usual when you meet, but public demonstration of affection is not quite the done thing.

The working day starts very early in Vietnam and business meetings can take place from as early as 7am.

Gifts are much appreciated and its a good idea to bring a supply of pens, lighters, shampoo, foreign cigarettes, spirits and perfume to give to the friends you will make in Vietnam.

People in the North are generally more reserved and have had less exposure to Europeans than those in the South.

Tips are much appreciated, but bear in mind that whatever you do sets a precedence for those who follow and the average wage is very low. A small donation is much appreciated when you visit a temple or pagoda —there is always a little contribution box for this.

It is a matter of courtesy to ask before you take someone's photograph and to ask permission to take photographs in religious buildings, although permission is usually granted. Formal dress is expected when you visit religious buildings.

In Ho Chi Minh City particularly, you will be approached by beggars, if you give anything, do so discreetly otherwise you will be plagued by a very persistent and ever increasing following. It is very difficult to ignore these people, whether their plight is genuine or not, but in the long run it does not help to foster an attitude whereby foreigners are seen as a soft touch and preyed upon as a source of easy income.

ELECTRICITY

The voltage in the cities and towns is generally 220v, 50 cycles sometimes 110v in the rural areas. Electric sockets are standard European or American. Voltage in some of the hotels is very irregular, although practically all have their own generators. Some of the wiring you will come across may shock you. If you intend using any sensitive electronic equipment it is best to use a surge suppressor to deal with the frequent current surges and cuts.

BUSINESS HOURS

Offices and public services generally open early from around 7.30am and close for lunch at around 12pm or 12.30pm, opening again around 1pm until 4.30pm Monday to Saturday. Banks are open from 8am to 3pm Monday to Friday and closed on Saturday afternoons and Sundays. Private shops are open from 8.30pm until late in the evening.

OFFICIAL HOLIDAYS & COMMEMORATIVE DAYS

The most important celebration of the year in Vietnam is Tet, or Lunar New Year, which falls either in late January or early February on the day of the full moon between the Winter solstice and the Spring Equinox. Festivities last three days (officially), preceded, particularly in Ho Chi Minh City and Hanoi by a week-long flower market.

OFFICAL PUBLIC HOLIDAYS

1 January, New Year's Day.
3 February, the Foundation of the Communist Party of Vietnam.
30 April, the Liberation of Saigon.
1 May, International Labour Day.
19 May, Ho Chi Minh's Birthday.
2 September, State Proclamation of Independence, 1945, now National Day of the Socialist Republic of Vietnam.

TRADITIONAL & RELIGIOUS FESTIVALS

Many other traditional and religious festivals take place throughout Vietnam, particularly in the North in and around Hanoi during Tet. All dates, unless otherwise stated, fall in the first lunar month.

Dong Ky Festival, a firecracker competition festival, held on the 15th in Dong Ky village, Tien Son District. One of the largest and most spectacular festivals.

Mai Dong Festival, which takes place from the 4th to 6th at the Mai Dong Temple in Hai Ba Trung District, Hanoi, is held in honor of Le Cham, the Trung Sisters' brave female general who fought against the Chinese in the first century.

Dong Da Festival, held on the 5th, in Hanoi's Dong Da District, commemorates King Trung Quang's victory at Dong Da and those who died in this battle against the Tsing in 1789.

An Duong Vuong Festival, occurs between the 6th and 16th, in the temple of the same name in Co Loa village near Hanoi. Held in memory of King Thuc An Duong Vuong, one of the founders of ancient Vietnam who built the Co Loa Citadel.

Le Phung Hieu Festival, on the 7th, at the temple of the same name in Hoang Hoa district, Thanh Hoa Province.

Lim Festival, held on the 13th in the Lim village pagoda, Ha Bac Province. Features singing and a wide range of cultural and artistic activities.

Ha Loi Festival, held on the 15th at Ha Loi Temple in the Me Linh suburb of Hanoi. Commemorates the Trung Sisters.

Den Va Temple Festival, dedicated to Tan Vien, God of the Mountain, held in the Bat Bat suburb of Hanoi on the 15th.

Ram Thang Gieng,, the most important Buddhist festival, takes place on the 15th.

Van Village Festival, celebrated in Hanoi's Viet Yen District from the 17th to the 20th.

Khu Lac and Di Nau Festival, occurs on the 7th and 26th in Tam Nong District, Vinh Phu Province.

Lac Long Quan Festival, from the 1st to 6th days of the third lunar month, at Binh Minh village, Ha Son Binh Province. Dedicated to Lac Long Quan, the quasi-legendary ancestor of the Vietnamese people. Features traditional music, elders dressed in traditional silk robes, fireworks displays and a stunning display of young ladies carrying altars laden with fruit and flowers through Binh Minh's narrow streets.

Huong Tich Festival, held throughout the Spring in the spectacular Huong Son mountains West of Hanoi in Ha Son Binh Province, can be visited at the same time as the the Lac Long Quan Festival.

The Buffalo Immolation Festival, held during Spring in the Tay Nguyen Highlands.

Thay Pagoda Festival, held on the 7th day of the 3rd lunar month in Quoc Hai, Ha Son Binh Province, is dedicated to To Dao Hanh, a revered Buddhist monk and teacher. An excellent opportunity to see the traditional water puppet theater in an historical and idyllic setting. Also features rowing contests and mountain climbing.

8th March, Womens Day.

12th March, the Den Festival takes place at the site of the ancient capital of Hoa Lu in Ha Nam Ninh Province. It commemorates King Dinh Bo Linh and General Le who fought against the Sung invaders.

16th March, De Tham Festival in Hanoi's Yen The district.

8th April, the Dau Pagoda festival in Thuan Thanh.

Easter, celebrated more in the South.

12th April, the anniversary of Vietnam's first King, Hung Vuong.

15th May, Buddha's birth, enlightenment and death, celebrated in pagodas, temples and private homes throughout the country.

1st June, Children's day

July/August, on the first day of the 7th lunar month offerings of food and gifts are made in homes and temples for the wandering souls of the dead.

September/October, the Mid-Autumn Festival on the day of the full moon in the 8th lunar month. Celebrated with sticky rice mooncakes filled with lotus seeds, salted duck egg yolks, peanuts and melon seeds. Brightly colored lanterns depicting all manner of things—dragons, boats, butterflies —are carried by children in evening processions.

The Kiep Bac Temple Festival, held in Hai Hung Province on the 20th day of the 8th lunar month commemorates the national hero Tran Hung Dao who wiped out the invading Mongol forces in the 13th century.

November 20th, Teachers Day.

25th December, Christmas.

COMMUNICATIONS

NEWSPAPERS

Between 100 and 135 publications are currently published in Hanoi and about 35 in the provinces. Among the foreign language reviews published by the Vietnamese Information Agency (VNA) periodically available in English and French are *Vietnam Weekly, Vietnam Foreign Trade, Women of Vietnam, Vietnamese Studies, Vietnam Courier, Vietnamese Trade Unions,* and *Vietnam Youth.* These are not all that easy to get hold of. Only the national newspapers are readily available and these without exception reiterate the views of the party.

Some foreign magazines, such as *Time,* are on sale in a limited number of outlets.

RADIO & TELEVISION

The Voice of Vietnam, the official radio station, broadcasts twice a day. Two stations transmit worldwide from Hanoi and Ho Chi Minh City in 11 different languages—English, French, Spanish, Russian, Mandarin/ Cantonese, Indonesian, Japanese, Khmer, Lao, Thai, and likewise international stations can be received on a shortwave receiver, but the reception is quite variable. Provincial radio stations broadcast cultural programmes and national news.

Television made its debut in Vietnam in September 1970. UNESCO aid further developed the service, particularly in Hanoi and Ho Chi Minh City. The central television network transmits a vast majority of Soviet and local emissions via satellite throughout the country—not a viable source of entertainment.

POSTAL SERVICES

Post Offices open every day from 7am to 8pm. Every city, town and village has a post office of some sort, however, the service in the South is more reliable than that in the North. Generally mail reaches its destination in 10 to 15 days. Pre-stamped aerogrammes may also be purchased when in stock. Overseas postage rates are among the highest in the world. Major Hotels also provide postal services.

Telegram and telex facilities are available 24 hours in the larger towns. Telegrams are charged at a minimum rate of 7 words.

CENTRAL POST OFFICES

Ho Chi Minh City
125 Hai Ba Trung, Quan 1.
Tel: 92997
Open 7 days a week from 6.30am to 7.30pm.

Hanoi
75 Dinh Tien Hoang.
Tel: 54413
Open every day from 6.30am to 8.30pm, 24 hour telex and telegram services, also telephone service from 7.30am to 12pm and 1am to 11pm in an adjoining building.

Haiphong
3 Nguyen Tri Phuong,
Haiphong.

Danang
Bach Dang,
Danang.
Hours: 9am to 1pm and 5pm to 9pm.

Phu Khanh Province
2 Tran Phu,
Nha Trang.

Hue
8 Hoang Hoa Tham,
Hue.
Hours: 6am to 9pm.

Vinh
Nguyen Thi Minh Khai Street,
Vinh.

Vung Tau
4 Ha Long Stree.
Tel: 2377, 2689

International telephone services are available at Central Post Offices and Hotels. For international calls it is best to use the satellite service via Moscow. Australian Telecom haS recently installed another satellite link which has made communications via satellite more reliable. Hotels add a 10 percent tax for international calls, which are always charged in US dollars for a minimum of three minutes.

Telex services are available at Post Offices and in most large hotels with the minimum charge for three minutes.

Both telephone and telex services leave something to be desired however, and are often subject to delay. It is often more difficult to contact Hanoi from Ho Chi Minh City than to get an international link.

Fax facilities are now becoming more available, mainly in the larger hotels and in companies conducting regular international business. The main Post Offices in Ho Chi Minh City, Hanoi and Danang offer fax services.

SECURITY & CRIME

Vietnam's difficult past and consequent economic deprivation have left their mark on its people. Extremely low wages combined with high living costs, contribute further to the people's struggle to survive. Poverty is often all too evident and sadly there are problems associated with such deprivation. In Ho Chi Minh City, begging, particularly by young children and mothers carrying babies and experienced pickpockets are all too common. It pays to travel light and prudently. Deft fingers are well experienced in lightening the pockets and bags of the wary and unwary alike, particularly in crowded streets and marketplaces. In the case of theft, if you report the matter immediately to the local police it is guite possible that they'll find the culprit and be able to recover some, if not all, of your goods. It doesn't pay to go out wearing an excessive amount of gold and rings and it is better to carry limited amounts of money on you.

Hotel security is good and safe deposit facilities are available.

Undetonated mines, mortars, bombs, rockets, and artillery shells have maimed or killed thousands of Vietnamese since 1975. Towns and cities, cultivated areas, well travelled tracks and paths are safe, but if you get off the beaten track it is still possible to wander into an area where undetonated ordnance has lain undisturbed since the war. If you do come across any such souvenir of the war don't touch it —it simply isn't worth the risk. Unexploded ordancemay also be lying inside bomb craters, so resist any desire to climb inside one.

GETTING AROUND

Getting around in Vietnam is not always easy. The war and years of neglect have left the road network in a very bad state, especially in the North. Vietnam's main trunk road, National Highway 1, cuts across the country from Ca Mau in the extreme South, to Dong Dang at the Chinese border in the North. Apart from the major routes, roads are generally dirt tracks which become quagmires during the rainy season.

Infrastructure aside, the greatest obstacle to traveling in the country is the bureaucracy, particularly for individual travelers.

How does one get around in Vietnam? For those who opt for organized tours with Vietnam Tourism or any of the other official tourist agencies, theres no great difficulty. However, for the individual traveler who wishes to use the local transport services the options are solely for the patient and the adventurous. If it's not comfort you're after, old pre-war trucks offer a taxi service of sorts and some collective bus services exist between certain large towns and bus stations. These, although very cheap, can prove very difficult for the visitor to negotiate. Vietnam's very extensive bus network reaches practically every accessible corner of the country and many cities and larger towns have several bus stations which operate local, intercity, express or non-express services.The express tag is rather casually applied to such services, but the real express services are a good deal faster than local buses which stop for everyone anywhere en route. The official line, which is of course subject to change and varies considerably with the telling, holds that foreigners are forbidden to travel between towns and provinces without prior authorisation. More than likely you'll be told that you may only travel on a tour organized by officially recognized authorities and that no other option lies open to you. The expense of such travel packages is considerably more than public transport. In reality, it is difficult to to travel outside any of the main cities individually. Officially you are required to obtain authorization from the nearest Police Office for foreign registration. If you are granted permission you are then officially able to travel to the areas specified in the authorization, by any means of transport, including public bus, train, rented bicycle, or even riding pillion on a motorscooter if you get to know a local who proposes to show you around. Should you wish to bypass the bureaucracy altogether, you wouldn't be the first, but should a curious official catch up with you and find you without the necessary papers your excursion will most certainly be curtailed and you may have to account and or pay for your actions.

A considerably more comfortable and expensive option is to hire a car or minibus with a driver, either by the hour or for the day through your hotel or one of the tourist organizations who can apply for the police permit for you. This way you have a much better chance of getting anywhere. For example, Vietnam's Youth Travel rent vehicles on either a daily basis or for several days, depending on your requirements. Rates are charged in US dollars, usually per km for short distances and on an all inclusive basis for longer excursions. Prices vary depending on the type of vehicle and whether you opt for air-conditioning or not. Self-drive rental cars have yet to hit the scene in Vietnam.

Another possibility is to travel by train, providing you're not in a hurry to get anywhere and wish to travel between Ho Chi Minh City and Hanoi. The trains are old and cover the 1,730km along the coast at a speed of 25km per hour. You have a choice between the slow train, minus couchettes or restaurant service which takes 68 hours, the "rapid" which does have couchettes and covers the

distance in 58 hours, or the new twice-weekly fast service which takes 48 hours and offers 4 berth sleepers for the price of 320,000 dong (about US$64) payable at the station in either dong or US dollars. This is an interesting way to see the country. One other line exists between Hanoi and Haiphong served by two trains daily which make the journey in around 4 hours.

Your most practical and rapid means of covering any great distance is by plane on the domestic routes served by the national airline, Hang Khong Vietnam. Bookings must be made as soon as you arrive in the country to ensure a seat as flights become fully booked very fast. Flights are very much subject to change and delay, with no apparent warning or assured alternative notice given. At least two daily flights link Ho Chi Minh City and Hanoi at a cost of US$150 one way. Another service linking Da Nang to Hanoi and Ho Chi Minh City operates three times a week and takes about 45 minutes. Some irregular services exist between Ho Chi Minh City and Nha Trang, Phu Quoc Con Dao and Dalat, Ho Chi Minh City and Hanoi via Hue, and other destinations within the country. It is best to enquire at a Vietnam Airlines office or the airport for detailed information. On board service is minimal and the aircraft are old Tupolev TU134's or Ilyushin IL18's. Tickets are payable in US dollars, although occasionally travelers checks are accepted. Internal flights are usually fully booked so don't leave booking and confirmation to the last minute if you really need to get anywhere. The national airline company has no computerized system, so do not rely too much on any reservations you may have been able to make outside the country, once you arrive confirm these without delay. Should you be traveling on the domestic airline to Bangkok or any other destination where you expect to catch a pre-booked and confirmed connecting flight, you may be in for an unpleasant surprise. Telex services and communications not being all that they could be, it is quite possible that unless you arranged a firm booking before leaving for Vietnam, your on-going flight confirmation request never reached its destination and will need to sorted out once you get there.

Scheduled Hang Khong Vietnam flights from Ho Chi Minh City serve Buon Me Thuot, Dalat, Danang, Hanoi, Hue, Nha

Trang, Phu Quoc Island, Pleiku, Qui Nhon and Rach Gia.

From Hanoi regular flights serve Buon Me Thuot, Dalat, Danang, Dien Bien Phu, Ho Chi Minh City, Hue, Nha Trang, Qui Nhon, Pleiku and Na San near Mai Son in Son La Province in the North.

Hanoi and Ho Chi Minh City's tram and comprehensive bus services are not really geared for the visitor and will probably appear totally incomprehensible. Beyond the major cities, collective urban transport is almost nonexistant. For short distances, apart from walking, the easiest and cheapest form of transport is the trishaw (*cyclo*), but always agree on and fix the price in advance. Some of the drivers speak reasonable English and if you strike a good one you will be well set up with a local guide, interpretor and mine of information for the duration of your stay.

Bicycles, by far Vietnam's most common means of transport, can be hired, but this very much depends on who you meet, as cycle hire is not yet readily available.

Another means of travel, a little less scenic, is a two day coastal voyage by passenger ship between Haiphong and Ho Chi Minh City which currently runs every 10 days. The *Thong Nhat* is operated by the state operated VINASHIP. Good accommodation in a single or double berth cabin may be had for 76,000 dong (about US$15) one way.

Vietnam Tourism (Du Lich Viet Nam) and Saigon Tourist are state run and responsible for everything from visas to accommodation and transportation. They can supply you with maps and any information you need on getting around and you may have to avail yourself of their services to acquire your visa extensions and internal travel permits. Every province has a tourism authority or Vietnam Tourism representative office. Alternatively enquiries at your hotel reception may provide you with some very helpful information.

The main border crossings from Vietnam to Cambodia are at Ha Tien in Kien Giang Province, Moc Bai in Tay Ninh Province and Chau Doc in An Giang Province. Daily buses ply the route between Phnom Penh and Ho Chi Minh City via Moc Bai, but the authorities on both sides do not take kindly to foreigners using this alternative to the substantially more expensive chauffeur driven alternative. Saigon Tourist arranges

tours from Ho Chi Minh City into Cambodia.

Passenger and goods ferries to the Mekong Delta depart from a dock at the river end of Ham Nghi Boulevard in Ho Chi Minh City . You can buy your tickets on board.

DOMESTIC TRAVEL

TRAIN & BUS STATION

Hanoi Railway Station
Nam Bo Street,
Hanoi.

Hanoi Bus Station
Kim Lien Street,
Hanoi.

Saigon Railway Station
I Nguyen Thong Street,
District 3. (10km from the city center)
Ho Chi Minh City
Ticket Office opens from 7.15 - 11am and 1-3pm daily.

Ho Chi Minh City Bus Stations
Northbound buses for Hanoi leave from Van Deng Bus Station, and from the bus station near Lam Son Place for Hue and Danang.

Southbound buses leave from Mien Tay Bus Station, situated about 10 km West of the city in An Lac. Buses from here serve:

An Phu, Bac Lieu, Ben Tre, Camau, Can Tho, Chau Doc, Ha Tien, Long An, Long Phu, Long Xuyen, My Thuan, My Tho, Phung Hiep, Rach Gia, Sa Dec, Tay Ninh, Tra Vinh, Vinh Chau, Vinh Long and a host of other smaller towns in the South.

Express and mimibus services leave daily from the bus station at 39 Nguyen Hue Boulevard, tel: 90541, for Vung Tau, Dalat and Nha Trang.

Daily buses to Phnom Penh leave from the garage at 155 Nguyen Hue Boulevard. Tel: 93754.

Nha Trang Bus Station,
Corner of Hung Vuong and Nguyen Tinh Minh Kai.

Express buses leave from the Youth Tourism Express Bus Office, Tel:22010 at 6 Hoang Hoa Tham Street for Buon Me Thuot, Dalat, Danang and Ho Chi Minh City, and from the Express Bus Station, Tel: 22397, 22884, at 46 Le Thanh Ton Street. Buses from here serve Buon Me Thuot, Dalat, Danang, Hue, Ho Chi Minh City, Quang Binh, Quang Ngai, Qui Nhon and Vinh.

Nha Trang Railway Station
19 Thai Nguyen.
Ticket Office opens between 7am and 2pm. Northbound trains to Hanoi depart daily at 9.45am and 10pm.

Nha Trang Express Bus Station
46 Le Thanh Ton Street.
Open daily between 6am and 4.30pm.

Hue Bus Stations
An Cuu Bus Station for southbound buses, An Hoa to northward destinations and Dong Ba for short haul destinations. Contact the bus station at Hung Vuong Street.
Tel: 3817, for further information.

Hue Railway Station
Le Loi Street.
Ticket office opens between 6.30am and 5pm.

Dalat Bus Station
Beside the old Caltex petrol station.
From here a daily express service runs to and from Nha Trang and Ho Chi Minh Express services also run to Danang, Quang Ngai and Qui Nhon two or three times a week.

Non-express buses depart for various destinations throughout the country, including Hanoi, Ho Chi Minh City, Phan Rang, Cat Tien, Danang, Quang Ngai, but these only leave when they're full.

Danang Railway Station
Haiphong Street—about 1.5km from the city center.

Bus tickets for express and some non-express services from Danang Intercity Bus Station can be purchased from the ticket office at 200 Dien Bien Phu Street which opens from 7 to 11am and 1 to 5pm.

Express services run to Buon Me Thuot, Dalat, Haiphong, Hongai Hanoi, Ho Chi Minh City, Gia Lai, Lang Son, Nam Dinh and Nha Trang and non-express services to Kontum, Vinh and Sathay.

Other non-express services depart from Danang Bus Station to Dong Ha, Hoi An, Hue, Quang Hgai, Qui Nhon, Tra My and various other destinations.

Vung Tau Bus Station
52 Nam Khoi Nghia Street.
From here non-express services depart for Ho Chi Minh City, Bien Hoa, My Tho, Tay Ninh.

Express and minibuses also leave from in front of the Ha Long and Hoa Binh hotels for Ho Chi Minh City.

WHERE TO STAY

The Western concept of tourism is something completely foreign to Vietnam and the country has a very long way to go before it can offer the standard of services and accommodation found in other more developed tourist destinations. Vietnam's hotel infrastructure, particularly in the North and Center, has a long way to go before it reaches international standard. Rooms are often under-equipped, or equipped with fixtures and appliances that don't work and power cuts are frequent. Room rates are quite high, more in line with demand, which often exceeds availability, than the standard of accommodation. Some very good hotels have been built recently in Ho Chi Minh City, Vung Tau, Nha Trang and Danang and other existing hotels are being refurbished. The hotels built during the French and American eras in Ho Chi Minh City, Hanoi and Danang, retain a certain faded charm and well worn comfort.

On the plus side, hotel staff are friendly and helpful, the food is good and services and facilities are improving.

Hotel rates are charged in US dollars, although some of the smaller hotels outside the main centers may accept payment in dong. While the rates given below serve as an indication they are not to be taken as gospel.

HO CHI MINH CITY (SAIGON)

The Continental
132-134 Dong Khoi Street.
Tel: 99201, 99255
Telex:811344 HOCON VT
Fax: 84890936
Recently reopened after a 2 year face lift, the French colonial facade was spared and has been lavishly restored/ The interior has been entirely rebuilt according to the original design.
72 air-conditioned rooms, 3 restaurants, cafe, telex & fax facilities, car service, hair salon, beauty parlor, 30 seat conference room, massage and sauna, terrace souvenir shop.

Saigon Floating Hotel
1A Me Linh Square (P.O. Box 752).
Tel: (84 8) 90783, 90624
Telex: 812614 HOTL
Fax: 84 890784/3
Opened in December 1989 after being towed from its previous location on Australia's Great Barrier Reef. With 201 rooms, Vietnam's only 5 star hotel boasts a business center, IDD, telex and credit card facilities, photocopying, secretarial, and courier services, personal computers and overseas reservations facilities, in-house video, nightclub, sauna, swimming pool and tennis court.

Ben Thanh Hotel (The Rex)
141 Nguyen Hue Boulevard.
Tel: 92185/6/7
Telex: 8201 HOT BT-HCM
Fax: 84891469
87 air-con rooms: single $US30 to $66, double $30 to 77 plus 10 percent surcharge. 2 Restaurants, roof top bar, swimming pool, tailor, hairdresser, sauna, massage, acupuncture souvenir shops, conference hall, cinema, dance hall, money changing, photocopying, telex, IDD, fax and postal facilities. The former US Army officers quarters.

Cuu Long Hotel (The Majestic)
1 Dong Khoi Street.
Tel: 95515, 95517
Telex: 8275, 8276 HOTCL-HCM
Fax:84891470
91 air-conditioned rooms, singles from $30 to $40, doubles from $40 to $70, suites $60 to $90, plus 10 percent.
Restaurant, cafe-bar, conference room, telex, IDD and postal services, dance hall, souvenir shop and laundry.
A charming hotel of the colonial era, although a little run down, the city's only hotel beside the Saigon River. There is an excellent view of Saigon from the restaurant on the 5th floor.

Doc Lap Hotel (The Caravelle)
19-23 Lam Son Square.
Tel: 93704/5/6
Telex: 811259 HOTDL-HCM
Fax: 84 899902
113 air-conditioned rooms, single $25 to $38, double $33 to $50
Restaurant, penthouse bar, disco, conference hall, exchange and telex and IDD facilities, laundry. Air France travel agency on the ground floor. The terrace patio on the 10th floor has an excellent view over the city.
Situated in the center of town opposite the Continental.

Tan Binh Hotel (First Hotel)
201 Hoang Van Thu, Tan Binh District.
Tel: 41167, 41175, 44207
Telex: 8558 HOT TB
52 rooms, 42 with air-conditioning, from $25 to $45 with air-conditioning and $10 to $12 without, plus 10 percent.
Restaurants, coffee shop, boutique, swimming pool, tennis, disco, massage and sauna. A modern and comfortable hotel, near the airport about 5km from the city center.

Huu Nghi Hotel (Palace)
56-64 Nguyen Hue Boulevard.
Tel: 97284, 94722
Telex: 8202, 8204, 8208 HOTHN-HCM
Fax:84 899872
112 air-conditioned rooms, singles $23 to $43, doubles $28 to $52
Restaurant, bars, disco, video, swimming pool, souvenir shop and money changing facilities, laundry. Wonderful views from the 14th floor restaurant and terrace above.

Bong Sen Hotel (Miramar)
115-119 Dong Khoi.
Tel: 99127, 90545, 91516
85 air-conditioned rooms, singles $28 to $42, doubles $33 to $52 plus 10 percent.
Restaurant, bar, disco, souvenir shop.

Thang Long Hotel (Oscar)
68a Nguyen Hue Boulevard.
Tel: 93416
70 rooms from $14 to $31 inclusive of tax.
Restaurant and boutique.

The Kim Do Hotel
133 Nguyen Hue Boulevard.
Tel: 93811
Near the Rex, an excellent hotel for about $8 to $15.

The Dong Khoi Hotel
8 Dong Khoi Street.
Tel: 92178

The 69 Hai Ba Trung Hotel
69 Hai Ba Trung Street.
Tel: 91513

Huong Duong Hotel (Central Palace)
150 Nguyen Thi Minh Khai.
Tel: 92404, 92805
80 air-conditioned rooms, singles $18 to $25, doubles $22 to $35
Restaurant, bar, tennis court, souvenir shop.

Huong Sen Hotel
66-70 Dong Khoi.
Tel: 91415, 90916
50 air-conditioned rooms, singles $20, doubles $28.
Bar and boutique.

Thien Hong Hotel (Arc-en-Ciel)
52-56 Tan Da Street, Quan 5.
Tel: 52550, 56924
90 rooms from $22 to $55.
2 restaurants, bar, dancing, handicraft shop.
The only large hotel in Cho Lon.

Que Huong Hotel
49 Nguyen Dinh Chieu, Quan 3.
Tel: 98822
Rooms from $20 to $40 plus 10 percent tax.
Restaurant, cafe, boutique, dancing, sauna, massage.
2km from the city center.

Hai Au Hotel
132 Dong Khoi, Q1.
Tel: 94456

Le Lai Hotel
76 Le Lai Street.

Tel: 95147/8/9, 91246
Telex: 8500 HOTLL HCM
Fax: 84890282
IDD, fax, telex and postal servies, exchange, 2 restaurants, bar, dancing, souvenir shop.

Vin Loi Hotel
129-133 Ham Nghi, Quan 1.
Tel: 23184
Restaurant.

Tan Son Nhat Hotel (near the airport)
200 Hoang Van Thu Boulevard.
Tel: 41079/39
25 rooms from $31 - $33

Nha Kach Viet Kieu
311 Nguyen Troi Street.
Tel: 40897.

Phu Tho Hotel
871 Ba Thang Hai Street, Quan 11.
Tel: 41167, 44027
Swimming pool, bar. Situated near the airport, reserved for transit passengers.

Phuong Huong Hotel (The Phoenix) (Central Cholon)
411 Tran Hung Dao Boulevard.
Tel: 51888

Bat Dat Hotel
238-244 Tran Hung Dao.
Tel: 51662

Quoc Thai Hotel
41 Nguyen Duy Duong Street.
Tel: 51657

Hanh Long Hotel
1025-1029 Tran Hung Dao Boulevard.
Tel: 50251

VUNG TAU

Hoa Binh Hotel
11 Nguyen Trai,
Chau Thanh Ward.
Tel: 2265, 2411
Telex: 307
145 rooms, 82 air-conditioned rooms, from $27, suites $42, plus 10 percent tax.
Superb restaurant specializing in sea food, conference room, bar, dancing, Vietnamese massage salon, steam bath, tennis.

Tam Thung Hotel
On Quang Trung Street.
Double rooms from $12 to $14.
Verandah restaurant, small Japanese garden, dancing.

Thien Thai Hotel
Next to the Hoa Binh on Nguyen Trai Street.

Thai Binh Duong Hotel
6 Le Loi,
Chau Thanh Ward.
Tel: 2279

Thang Loi Hotel
1 Duy Tan,
Chau Thanh Ward.
Tel: 2135
Souvenir and art shop, sauna, dancing, laundry, hairdresser, postal service.

The International Hotel (Khach San Quoc)
242 Bacu Street.
Tel: 2571
25 rooms from $6 to $20.

Lam Son Hotel
94 Thanh Thai.
Tel: 2588

Tho Nguyet Hotel
48 Quang Trung.
Tel: 2590

Truong Son Hotel
2 Phan Dinh Phung.
Tel: 2486

Hanh Phuoc Hotel
Opposite Hoah Binh Hotel at 11 Nguyen Trai Street.

Thang Muoi Hotel
5 Thuy Van Street,
Chau Thanh Ward.
Tel: 2665, 2674

Vietnamese Youth Tourist Centre
46A Thuy Van.
Bungalows of one or more rooms from $10 along the the east coast beachfront.

Song Hau Hotel
5 Duy Tan.
Tel: 2589

Song Huong Hotel
1 Truong Vinh Ky.
Tel: 2419

Song Hong Hotel
1 Hoang Dieu Street.
Tel: 2137

Thanh Liem Bungalows
46A Thuy Van Street.
22 thatched wooden bungalows which sleep two.

Rung Duong Bungalows
Thuy Van Street - near the prawn hatchery.
Camping is permitted if you have a tent.

The Vietnamese Youth Tourism camping ground at 46A Thuy Van Street hires out rooms and tents.
Three km North of central Vung Tau at Bai Dau Beach, old villas converted into guest houses provide alternative accommodation.

THE DELTA

CAN THO

Quoc Te Hotel (the International)
12 Hai Ba Trung, Can Tho City.
Tel: 20973, 35795, 35793
41 large, air-conditioned, modern and comfortable rooms, $15 to $20 for a single and $19 to $25 for doubles.
3 restaurants, souvenir shop, beauty parlour, dancing, laundry, video room. Located on the Ninh Kieu Pier beside the Hau River.

Hau Giang Hotel
34 Nam Ky Khoi Nghia, Thanh Po,
Can Tho City.
Tel: 35537, 25181, 20180, 20152
Doubles $17 to $22 and singles $13 to $20.
A very friendly hotel, excellent food, souvenir shop, dancing, laundry, video room.

Hao Hoa Hotel
6 Lu Gia Street.
Tel: 35407

Hoang Cung Hotel
55 Phan Dinh Phung Street.
Tel: 35401

Huy Hoang Hotel
35 Ngo Duc Ke Street.
Tel: 35403

Thuy Thien Hotel
6 Tran Phu Street.
Tel: 35412

Phuoc Thanh Hotel
5 Phan Dang Luu Street.
Tel: 35406

DON THAP

Sa Dec Hotel
108/5A Hung Vuong, Thi Xa, Sa Dec.
Tel: 2498
40 air-conditioned rooms. The service, staff
and food are excellent.

MY THO

Rach Gam Hotel
33 Trung Trac Street.

Ap Bach Hotel
Tel: 3593

Lac Hong Hotel
Thang 4 Street.
Tel: 3918

Khach San 43
43 Ngo Quyen Street.
Tel: 3126

Tien Giang Province Guest House,
on the corner of Hung Vuong Boulevard and
Rach Gam Street.

RACH GIA

1/5 (First of May) Hotel
38 Nguyen Hung Son, Thi Xa.
Tel: 414
18 air-conditioned rooms—when the
electrics are working. The plumbing is also
very temperamental. Very basic and over-
priced accommodation at $26 for doubles
and $20 fo singles.
15 other rooms are even more basic, but so is
the price, $15 for doubles and $12 for singles.
The food however is good.

To Chau Hotel
4F Le Loi Street (next to the cinema),
Thi Xa.
31 rooms, the first class rooms have air-
conditioning.

Binh Minh Hotel
48 Pham Hong Thai Stree.
Tel: 016

Thanh Binh Hotel
11 Ly Truong Street.
Tel: 053

Nha Kach Uy Ban
31 Nguyen Hung Son Stree.
Tel: 237

BIEN HOA

Dong Nai Hotel
57 Highway 15.
Tel: 2267

Vinh An Hotel
107 Highway 1.
Tel: 2377

LONG XUYEN

Thai Binh Hotel
12 Nguyen Hue, Thi Xa.
Tel: 52184
32 rooms, with fans, doubles 4,000 dong and
singles 3,000 dong. Good restaurant and
dance hall.

Long Xuyen Hotel
17 Nguyen Van Cung Street, Thi Xa.
Tel: 52927, 52308
Special rooms have adjoining sitting rooms.
Showers and electrics are a bit off and on but
the restaurant is excellent. Air-conditioned
rooms begin at $10-$12.

Cuu Long Hotel
35 Long van Cu, Thi Xa.
Tel: 52365, 52865

Song Hau Hotel
10 Hai Ba Trung Street.
Tel: 52979

An Giang Hotel
42 Phan Chu trinh Street.
Tel: 52297

Binh Dan Hotel
12 Nguyen Anh Ninh Street.

Phat Thanh Hotel
2 Nguyen Anh Ninh Street.

CHAU DOC

Chau Doc Hotel
17 Doc Phu Thu, Thi Xa.
Tel: 6484
30 rooms, 1,500 dong per night for a double room.

Thai Binh Hotel
37 Bao Ho Thoai Street.

VINH LONG

Cuu Long Hotel
Duong 1 Thanh 5.
Tel: 2494
20 air-conditioned rooms, restaurants, bar, laundry, souvenir shop and video.

BEN TRE

Dong Khoi Hotel
16 Hai Ba Trung.
Tel: 2240

MINH HAI

Minh Hai Hotel
Tel: 261

HA TIEN

Has four hotels, all of about the same standard:

Ha Tien Hotel
On the corner of Ben Tran Hau and Phuong Thanh streets.

Phuong Thanh Hotel
Tu Chau Hotel.
Tel: 80

Dong Ho Hotel
On the corner of Ben Tran Hau and To Chau streets.

HUE

Huong Giang Hotel (Perfume River)
51 Le Loi Street.
Tel: 2122, 2288
42 air-conditioned rooms with fridge and interphone, from $22 to $60 plus 10 percent service.
Terrace restaurant, souvenir shop, post office, telex, Vietnamese massage, tennis, ping pong, billiards dancing - Saturday evenings, small private jetty, boat trips.
Hue's best hotel, very comfortable, situated beside the Perfume River.

Thuan Hoa Hotel
7B Nguyen Tri Phuong.
Tel: 2553, 2576
66 rooms—44 air-conditioned, with fridge and interphone. From $22 to $28.
Restaurant, terrace cafe, small boutique.

Nha Khach Hue
2 Le Loi Street.
Tel: 2153
Fairly basic accommodation around $10 per room. Close to the railway station.

Nha Khach Hue Tourism
18B Le Loi.
Tel: 3720
10 double rooms run by the Hue Tourist Office.

Nua Thu Hotel
26 Nguyen Thu Phuong.
Tel: 3929
Excellent restaurant.

San Thuong Tu Hotel
1 Dinh Tien Hoang Street.

Hang Be Hotel
173 Huynh Thuc Khang Street.
Tel: 3752
Ground floor restaurant.

Thuong Tu Hotel
5 Dinh Tien Hoang

Tan My Hotel
Tan My Harbor.
Souvenir shop, laundry.

Three small villas on Ly Thuong Kiet Street provide some of the most pleasant accommodation in Hue:
Nha Kach
11 Ly Thuong Kiet Street.
$16 - $20
16 Ly Thuong Kiet Street.
Tel: 3679
and at number 18
Tel: 3889
$16 - $20.

A grand villa at 5 Le Loi Street, built beside the river, was formerly the residence of the Governor of Central Vietnam.

SAM SON

Sam Son Hotel
Sam Son

DONG HA

Nha Kach Dong Ha
Tran Phu Street.
Tel: 361
24 rooms at $12

Dong Truong Son Hotel
Tel: 239

DONG HOI

Dong Hoi Hotel
Tel: 22

Nhat Le Hotel

DANANG

Phuong Dong (the Oriental)
93 Phan Chu Trinh.
Tel: 21266, 22854
36 air-conditioned rooms from $23 to $31 plus 10 percent service.
Restaurant, bar, telex aan IDD services, souvenir and craft shop, laundry.

Thai Binh Duong Hotel (the Pacific)
80 Phan Chu Trinh.

Tel: 22931, 22137
60 air-conditioned rooms from $20 to $25 plus 10 percent service.
Restaurant, bar, laundry.

Hai Chau Hotel
215 Tran Phu St.
Tel: 22722

Huu Nghi Hotel
10 Ly Thuong Kiet.
Tel: 21101
Souvenir shop, dancing, laundry.

Danang Hotel
1 Dong Da St.
Has seen better days, but rooms are priced accordingly at $12.
Restaurant.

Dong Da Hotel
7 Dong Da Street.
Tel: 22563

Hai Van Hotel
2 Nguyen Thi Minh Khai Street.
Tel: 21300

Song An Hotel
24 Bach Dang Street.
Tel: 22540

Thanh Binh Hotel
Situated at the end of Ong Ich Khiem Street on Thanh Binh Beach.

Tu Do Hotel
65 Hung Vong.

Non Nuoc Hotel
10 Ly Thuong Kiet,
Hua Nghi.
Tel: 21470, 22137
Air-conditioned rooms from $20 to $30.
14 km from Danang at the foot of the Marble Mountains, situated on a lovely beach. Advance booking necessary due to its popularity with the Soviets. Restaurant and bar on the beach.

VINH

Chuyen Gia Giao Te Hotel
Thanh Ho Street.
Tel: 4175

A very large hotel used mostly by Eastern bloc visitors and Vietnamese. 90 rooms, 25 with air-conditioning. Restaurant, laundry, video room, table tennis.

Nghe Tinh Guest House
Dinh Cong Truong Street.
Tel: 3175
$10 - $20.

Vinh Railway Hotel
Tel: 24.

Ben Thuy Hotel
Nguyen Du Street.
Tel: 4892

Cua Lao Hotel
Nghe Tinh.
Tel: 13 Cua Lo
Located on the beach 14 km northeast of Vinh.
48 rooms, half of which are air-conditioned. Restaurant and laundry service.

International Hotels 1 & 2
Dinh Cong Trang Street.

Quang Trung Hotels 1 & 2
Quang Trung Street.

QUY NHON

Quy Nhon Hotel
12 Nguyen Hue.
Tel: 2401

NHA TRANG

Hai Yen Hotel
40 Tran Phu.
Tel: 22974
104 air-conditioned rooms, from $20 to $33
Restaurant, bar, disco, souvenir shop, laundry, barber shop.
Opposite the beach. US$11 per night, breakfast included.

Thong Nhat Hotel
18 Duong Thong Nhat,
Thanh Pho.
Tel: 22966.
Opposite the beach
70 rooms at $17.
Restaurant, souvenir and art shop, laundry.

Thang Loi Hotel
4 Rue Pasteur,
Thanh Pho.
Tel: 22226, 22241
70 rooms from $20 to $24
Restaurant, souvenir shop, money changing facilities, laundry.

PHAN THIET

Vinh Thuy Hotel
Duong Nguyen Tat Thanh, Thi Xa.
Tel: 2622, 2655
38 rooms, the most expensive 5,500 dong. Very good restaurant and swimming beach.

Phan Thiet Tourist Hotel
40 Tran Hung Dao, Thi Xa.
Tel: 2901, 2573/4
This far from clean establishment has 14 dirty rooms, first class 1870 dong, others 1210 dong. Services include restaurant, laundry, barber, souvenir shop and video.

BIEN HOA

Ninh Chu Hotel
Tel: 2042
Situated on the beach

Han Nghi Hotel
Le Hong Phong,
Phan Rang.
Tel: 2049

Thong Nhat Hotel
Duong Thong Nhat.
Tel: 74 Thong Nhat

DALAT

Palace Hotel
2 Tran Phu.
Tel: 2203
42 rooms from $18 to $45.
Restaurant, banquet room, billiard room, video between 5 and 7pm.
A charming hotel of the colonial era, complete with fireplaces in the bedrooms, a large breakfast room and a superb view over the lake.

Dalat Hotel (Khach San Da Lat)
7 Tran Phu.
Tel: 2363

67 rooms priced a little less than the Palace although it's not quite in the same league. Services include a restaurant, bar, laundry, souvenir shop and dancing every night except Monday.

Minh Tam Hotel
20A Khe San.
Tel: 2447
A little far from the town center (3km), but comfortable and relatively modern.

Hotel Anh Dao
52-54 Hoa Binh Square.
Tel: 2384
Well situated, near the market and modestly priced.

Duy Tan Hotel
83 Duy Tan.
Tel: 2216
40 rooms. Restaurant, bar, laundry and tennis court.
24 rooms from $8 to $15.

Ngoc Lan Hotel
54 Nguyen Tri Phuong.
Tel: 2136
Overlooks the bus station.

Thuy Tien Hotel
73 Thang 2 Street.
Tel: 2444

Lang Biang Hotel
Place du Marche.

Bao Loc Hotel
11A - 12 Tran Phu,
Bao Loc.
Tel: 10 (ext. 105)

Phu Hoa Hotel
16 Tang Bat Ho Street.

Lam Vien Hotel
20 Hung Vuong.

Phuoc Duc Guest House
4 Khu Hoa Street.
Tel: 2482

Lam Son Hotel
5 Hai Thuong.
Tel: 2362, 2124

An old French villa one km west of the town center.

Lan Huong Guest House
190 Phan Dinh Phung Street.

The Mimosa Hotel
170 Phan Dinh Phuong.
Tel: 0320

Huong Son Hotel
29 April 30th Street.
Tel: 2124

Le Lai Compound
7 Le Lai, Dalat.
Tel: 2218

Alternative accommodation can be had in one of Dalat's many villas which are rented out through Lam Dong Province Tourism. You can also stay in the former Governor General's residence or Bao Dai's Summer Palace. The Lang Bian Youth Hostel at 6b Nguyen Thi Minh Khai St., near the central market is run by the Lam Dong Province Ho Chi Minh Communist Youth Committee. For information on camping, trekking and hill tribe visits in the region get in touch with Lam Dong Youth Tourism whose office is on the second floor of the youth hostel - tel: 2136, 2318.

THE CENTRAL HIGHLANDS

BUON ME THOUT

Thang Loi Hotel
1 Phan Chu Trinh.
Tel: 2322

Hong Kong Hotel
30 Hai Ba Trung.

Hoang Gia Hotel
2 Le Hong Phong

THE NORTH

HANOI

Finding accommodation in Hanoi can be quite difficult as the new hotels in the center of the city are most sought after, so it is best to book in advance. Hotels are more plentiful and of a more recent vintage in the suburbs.

Thong Nhat Hotel (Metropole)
15 Ngo Quyen.
Tel: 52785, 52755, 52787
192 rooms, with or without air-conditioning, rooms from $24 to $50.
Restaurant, bar, souvenir shop, conference room, hairdresser, laundry.
Situated in the heart of Hanoi beside the Lake of the Restored Sword. A 60's style dance is held here every Saturday night from 8 to 10. Just around the corner is the Bao Chi Club—reserved for Western journalists. Recently renovated.

Hoa Binh Hotel
27 Ly Thuong Kiet.
Tel: 53315
59 air-conditioned rooms from $28 to $40.
Restaurant, bar, souvenir shop. Central.

Dan Chu Hotel
29 Trang Tien.
Tel: 54937, 53323, 54344
28 air-conditioned rooms from $28 to $45.
Restaurant, bar, laundry. Central.

Hoan Kiem Hotel
25 Tran Hung Dao.
Tel: 54204
15 air-conditioned rooms from $36 to $46.
Restaurant, bar. Central.

Thang Loi Hotel
Duong Yen Phu.
Tel: 58211, 58215
160 air-conditioned rooms from $41 to $64.
2 restaurants, 3 bars, large conference room, fishing, tennis, physiotherapy massage, swimming pool, mini-zoo, post office, hair salon, supermarket, dancing—Wednesdays Thursdays and Saturdays, telex, money changing facilities which accept travelers checks.
The largest hotel in the North, situated on the edge of the Ho Tay (West Lake) in the north of the city.

Thang Long Hotel
Giang Vo area.
Tel: 57796, 52270
61 air-conditioned rooms from $22 to $28, suites $38.
2 restaurants, bar, billiard room, souvenir shop, post office, table tennis, telex, dentist.

Bo Ho Hotel
1 Ba Trieu.
Tel: 52075

HAIPHONG

Huu Nghi Hotel
62 Dien Bien Phu.
Tel: 47486, 47206
30 rooms, 14 of which are air-conditioned, prices start from $20
Restaurant, souvenir shop, laundry.

Bach Dang Hotel
42 Dien Bien Phu.
Tel: 47244, 47657
30 air-conditioned rooms. Restaurant, laundry, souvenir shop, dancing Thursdays and Saturdays.

Hong Bang Hotel
64 Dien Bien Phu.

Ben Binh Hotel
Dien Bien Phu.

Duyen Hai Hotel
5 Nguyen Tri Phuong.
Tel: 47657
5 air-conditioned rooms, 2 restaurants, bar, souvenir shop and laundry service.

Cat B1 Hotel
29 Tran Phu.

HALONG BAY

Ha Long Hotel
Bai Chay Street.
Tel: 238
100 rooms from $10 to $34 with air-conditioning.
Restaurant, laundry service. Charming colonial hotel with beautiful view over the bay.

Son Long Hotel
Bai Chay Street.
Tel: 254

Hoang Long Hotel
Bai Chay Street.
Tel: 264

Bach Long Hotel
Bai Chay Street.
Tel: 281
Laundry, souvenir shop, dancing, video room.

Villa Hotel
Bai Chay Street.
Tel: 08

THAI BINH

Huu Nghi Hotel
Ly Bon.
Tel: 270

TRIEN HAI

Dong Chau Hotel
Dong Minh Beach.

DO SON

Do Son Hotel
Tel: Do Son no 10
Souvenir shop, laundry, hairdressers, sauna.

HOA BINH

Hoa Binh Tourist Hotel
Tel: 01 Hoa Binh

MY DUC

Huong Son Hotel
Huong Son.
Tel: 46 My Duc

NAM DINH

Vi Hoang Hotel
115 Nguyen Du.
Tel: 439362

THANH HOA

Tourist Hotel
21 A Quang Trung.
Tel: 298

HA DONG

Song Nhue Hotel
Ha Dong Tel: 46 My Duc

VIN YEN

Vinh Yen Hotel
Ngo Quyen Square.

VINH PHU

Lam Thao Hotel
Cao Mai Phuong Chau.

Tan Dao Hotel

VIET TRI

Song Lo Hotel
Tan Dan Square.
Tel: 318 Viet Tri

FOOD DIGEST

Vietnamese cuisine offers the visitor a wide variety of fine dishes, delicately flavoured with fresh herbs spices and *nuoc mam* (fish sauce), usually accompanied by *nuoc cham*, a condiment sauce of nuoc mam, lime juice, a little grated carrot, chilli, garlic and sugar. Steamed rice (*com*) and soup are eaten at every meal. Different regional specialities lend even more variety to this widely varied menu. Due to the highly inflated price of meat, seafood and river fish play an important part in the Vietnamese menu, particularly in the South. Pork, chicken, beef, duck and pigeon feature widely on the menu, plus a wide variety of vegetables and tropical fruit. A leftover from the colonial era, French bread is available throughout the country. Sandwiches made with these baguettes, the local pate and salad vegetables make an excellent snack.

Most localities have their particular noodle soups which vary in the noodles and meat used and the use of spices and herbs. The most celebrated dish in the North is *pho*, a delicious soup of rice noodles, beef stock, ginger, to which beef, bean sprouts, fresh coriander, basil and mint are added at the very last. In the South an excellent soup, *ho tieu* is enjoyed, this is often made with prawns or crab meat and pork. Another very popular soup is *bun bo*. rich and spicy it is eaten with mint, bean sprouts and a twist of lime. The people from Hue make their own special version of this. One of the favorite soups is *canh chua*, made with fish, pineapple, star fruit, okra, and fresh herbs. The famous national dish, *cha gio* is made from crab and pork, mushrooms, prawns, rice vermicelli and beansprouts, rolled in a thin rice pancake then deep fried. These delicious crisp rolls are eaten wrapped in a lettuce leaf with fresh herbs and dipped in an accompanying sauce. *Go cuon*, another national favorite, is made without pork and eaten raw. Look out for *chao tom*, a dish of fried minced crab and pork on sugarcane, served with vermicilli, vegetables and coriander leaves. Another celebrated dish is *cha ca*, fish marinated with *nuoc mam* and saffron then barbecue grilled and served with rice vermicelli, herbs, grilled peanuts and a special sauce. One of Hanoi's oldest streets is named after this delicious speciality. For the more adventurous some speciality restaurants serve turtle, snake, eel, bat and wild game. The fresh seafood, particularly lobsters, flower crabs and oysters are excellent. Numerous restaurants specialise in French and Chinese food. An endless variety of Vietnamese dishes await you, ask the locals for recommendations and they will be very happy to initiate you into the discovery of Vietnam's delicous and unique cuisine.

WHERE TO EAT

Hanoi and Ho Chi Minh City's large hotel restaurants offer both Vietnamese specialities and Western dishes, particularly French, but be sure to check on the hours and book in advance if you're not a guest. Wherever you are in country, don't hesitate to frequent the small local eating places serving a variety of Vietnamese dishes at any hour; you will be in for some delicious surprises.

HO CHI MINH CITY

Ben Thanh Hotel Restaurant
Probably the best in the country, serves Vietnamese specialities and Western dishes.

Vinh Loi Hotel Restaurant
Serves Vietnamese specialities that you would probably never find outside the country—tortoise, snake, eel, bat, frogs—not for the faint-hearted.

Cuu Long Hotel Restaurant
Serves Vietnamese and Western food.

Lam Son Hotel Restaurant
Specializes in goat and mutton dishes and Indian-style rice.

Maxims
Dong Khoi.
Tel: 96676
Floor show, dancing.

Dong Phat
79 - 81 Nguyen Cong Tru.
Offers Vietnamese, Chinese and Western dishes.

La Bibliotheque and the Floating Hotel are for the less adventurous who prefer Western food. For those who aren't too bothered about the decor, the Ben Thanh Market food stalls offer an oppotunity to try many of the local dishes amongst curious onlookers. The stall holders are delighted to serve you. The only drawback here is that as soon as you finish your leftovers are fallen upon by some very hungry people who appear out of nowhere.

Cholon is the place to go for Chinese food.

HANOI

Ho Tay Floating Restaurant
Than Nien Street, next to the nautical club. Specialities include pigeon and *banh tom* (prawn pancakes).

The "202"
202 Rue de Hue.
Regional specialities, pork, chicken, birds, crabs, eel, sea turtle. Serves Vietnamese, Chinese and Western dishes. Has an excellent cellar of fine wines from both Europe and Asia.

The Cha Ca
14 Rue Cha Ca.
Grilled fish served with peanut-flavored vermicelli is a speciality.

The 17
17 Ly Quoc Su.
Regional specialities.

Kim Ma
Van Phuc area.
Offers a menu of fish dishes

Nha Trinh
28 Luong Van.
Serves a variety of excellent soups.

Hanoi's Ta Hien District is famous for its Chinese and Vietnamese cuisine.

HUE

Huong Giang Hotel Restaurant
Menu includes sea food, Vietnamese and Western dishes and specialities of Hue.

Thuanh Hoa
Reputed for its cuisine and certainly not its interior.

Song Huong Floating Restaurant
Tel: 3738
Situated on the Perfume River between the Huong Giang Hotel and the old Clemenceau Bridge.

SPECIAL INFORMATION

DOING BUSINESS

A growing number of foreign banks and Trading companies provide various services for businesspeople and visitors alike. Many of the trading companies are involved in tourist services such as tours to neighbouring Cambodia and Laos, transport, visa services and form, import export services, hotel bookings, guides, rail, boat and even helicopter tours, foreign exchange and banking services and shipping.

HO CHI MINH CITY

Import Export Corporation of Ho Chi Minh City _ "IMEXCO"
1 Nam Ky Khoi Nghia, Quan 1.
Tel: 95232, 95931
Telex: 8223, 8224 IMEX HCM

OSC Tourism Transactions and Guide Office
101 Nguyen van Cu Street.
Tel: 54717, 51520, 51271

Riverway Transport Corporation
94 Nam Ky Khoi Nghia, Quan 1.
Tel: 24342, 24535

Ocean Transport Company
23 Nguyen Hue, Quan 1.
Tel: 90197

Vietnam Overseas Shipping Agent
57 Nguyen Hue, Quan 1.
Tel: 97694, 90194

Ocean Shipping Company
142 Nguyen Tat Thanh, Quan 4.
Tel: 93124

Transimex - Ministry of Foreign Economic Relations
406 Nguyen That Thanh, Quan 4.
Tel: 22415, 25663

VUNG TAU

OSC (Oil Services Company)
Head Office, 02 Le Loi Street.
Tel: 97562
Telex: OSC SGN 307

HANOI

Hanoi Foreign Trade Company
56 Ly Thai To.

AIRLINES

HO CHI MINH CITY (SAIGON)

Aeroflot
4 Trang Thi.
Tel: 56184

Air France
1 Quang Trung.
Tel: 53484
Hours: 8am to 11.30am and 2pm to 4.30pm,
closed Saturday afternoons and Sundays.
Also at 127 Tran Quoc Thao.
Tel: 90985, 93770

Air Vietnam (Hang Khong Vietnam)
Representitive for Thai Airways and Lao
Aviation.

International Flights
25 Trang Thi.
Tel: 53842
Hours: 7.30am to 11.30am and 1.30pm to
3pm, except Saturday afternoon.
Tickets payable in US dollars, travelers
checks also accepted.

Domestic flights
16 Le Thai Tho.
Tel: 55283
Hours: 8am to 11am and 1pm to 3.30pm.

Interflug
Ba Trieu Street.
Tel: 56061, 56134

GO CHI MINH CITY

Aeroflot
4B Le Loi.
Tel: 93489

Air France
112 Dong Khoi.
Tel: 90981, 90982 and at the airport 41278
Hours: 8am to 12pm and 2pm to 4.40pm,
closed Sundays.

Air Vietnam International flights
116 Nguyen Hue.
Tel: 92118

Domestic flights
27B Nguyen Dinh Chieu.
Tel: 99980, 99910
Hours: 7.30am to 11am and 1.30pm to 4pm,
closed Sundays.

Philippines Airlines
116 Nguyen Hue.
Tel: 25538

Thai International
116 Nguyen Hue.

Danang Booking Office
35 Tran Phu, Danang.
Tel: 21130

TRAVEL PACKAGES, TOUR OPERATORS & TOUR GUIDES

Vietnam's tourist industry is being developed along the organised tour line. It is administered by the National Office of Tourism, which carries with it a ministerial rank. Vietnam Tourism is the official representative, responsible for promoting the industry both within the country and abroad. Its network of representitve offices throughout the country provides information and services such as transport hire, hotel reservations and at least 17 different organized tours. These range from between 3 to 21 days, with an option of trips into neighboring Laos or Cambodia, at a price fixed more for the foreign wallet than the actual standard of the service. A little patience is needed to overcome the complications that can arise in the absence of sufficient guides and chaffeurs competent in foreign languages.

Vietnam for the most part is open to tourism, yet some areas in the country remain closed to tourists and even to the Vietnamese themselves. "No go" areas include the North's high plateau region, Cao Bang and Lang Son in the North on the Chinese border and Cam Ranh Bay in the Center. However it is not impossible to visit these areas "unofficially", although its not advisable to tempt fate too far. Any area can suddenly become sensitive these days due to the growing discontent with the present system and if your request to visit an area is completely stonewalled, this may well be the reason.

Organized tours are available through a growing number of overseas agencies and both official and unofficial agencies within the country. You may feel that you are not getting what you paid for or have been misled, but try to deal with any misunderstandings that may arise with as much tact and patience as you can muster, it will get you further in the long run. Many operators advertise their services, both within Vietnam and elsewhere, particularly Bangkok. It pays to shop around as prices vary considerably.

Visas may be acquired more easily, at a price, through a specialist agent or tour operator, who can arrange an all inclusive package of visa, flight and hotel accommodation. Taking an all inclusive package outside Vietnam is usually considerably more expensive than if you make your arrangements yourself once you have arrived.

AUSTRALIA

Intercontinental Travel Pty. Ltd
307 Victoria Street, Abbotsford,
Victoria 30567.
Tel: (03)42877849 4298377
Telex: U Five AA 38432

Intercontinental Travel
1st Floor, 113 Swanton Street,
Melbourne 3000.
Tel: (03) 633745
Telex: AA 3065 ME 1228

Orbit Tours Pty Ltd
C 29 Mlc Centre, Castlereagh St.,
Sydney, Box 3484 GPO,
Sydney, NSW 2001.
Tel: 2333288
Telex: AA 27081

ACT International Ltd
16 Railway Street, Lidcombe,
NSW., 2141 Sydney.
Tel: 61 (02) 6432099
Fax: 61 (02) 7491609

Keyline Trading Co.
2/2 Albion Street,
Annadale NSW, 2038.
Tel: (02) 5502021
Fax: (02) 5502021

Tara International Travel Pty. Ltd
Level 3, 427 George Street,
Sydney NSW 2000.
Fax: 612 2645811
Telex: AA 171350 ARATVL

AUSTRIA

View Travel
Sankt Voitgasse 9, A-1130 Vienna.
Tel: (222) 8218532
Telex: 13667 Mrd A.

BRITAIN

TBN World Travel Ltd
Celveley Mill, Tarporley,
Cheshire, CW6 9JU,
England.
Tel: (0829) 260591

Regent Holidays Ltd
13 Small Street, Bristol BS1IDE.
Tel: (0272) 211711
Telex: 444606

Voyages Jules Verne
10 Glentworth Street, London NW1.
Tel: 01-486 8752
Telex: 27104

TBN North West Travel
92 North Gate Street,
Chester CH1 2HT.
Tel: (0244) 374915

Bales Tours Ltd
Bales House, Barrington Road,
Dorking, Surrey RH4 3EJ.
Tel: (0306) 885991

BULGARIA

Balkantourist Agency
1 dai 10 Vitosha, Sofia.
Tel: 855039
Telex: 22567/8, 22584

CANADA

Hoi Van Hoa Que Viet
1700, Berri,
Suite 29 Montreal,
PQ Canada H2L 434.
Tel: 8424551
Telex: 03560848

New Asia Tours
Tour Nouvelle Asia Inc.,
210 Quest Rue Chabanel,
Que, Canada Hzn IG2.
Tel: (514) 4180
Telex: 4959321
Fax: (514) 3847045

Keyline Trading Co.
5068 Manorst, Vancouver, B.C., 3Y3.
Tel: (604) 4301937

Saigon Tours - Club Voyages Berri
1650 Berri, Montreal, Quebec H2L 4E6.
Tel: (514) 982 6168/6169
Fax: (514) 9820820

CZECHOSLOVAKIA

OKM Agency
12105 Praha 2,
Zitna Ulice 12.
Tel: 299941
Telex: 122299, 122886 OKM.

FRANCE

Nouvelles Frontieres

Jet Tours
22 Quai de la Megisserie,
75001, Paris.
Offer a hunting and fishing tour of Vietnam.

Hit Voyages
21 Rue des Bernadins,
Paris 75005.
Tel: 43529904, 43541717
Telex: Hit Vge 201 475 F

Loisirs et Vacances de la Jeunesse
4 & 6 Rue de Chateau-Landon,
75005 Paris.
Telex: LVJ 230G9748F

International Tourisme
26 Bd. St. Marcel,
75005 Paris.
Tel: 45870770
Telex: 201647 F

Locotour
Le jardin Tropical 3,
Rue des Cgenes Poupres,
95000 Cergy.
Telex: CESVLOC 607784 F.
Pacific Holidays
34 Avenue du General Leclerc,
75014 Paris.
Tel: 45415258

Akiou et Planete
2 Rue de la Paix,
75002 Paris.
Telex: 230970 F

GERMANY

Indo Culture Tours
Indoculture Reisedienst GmbH,
Bismarckplatz 1 D-7000 Stuttgart 1.
Tel: 0711/61 7057-58
Telex: 0723368 iclt d.

Jugendtourist
1026 Berlin Alexanderplatz 5.
Tel: 2150
Telex: 114657 RSBJT DD

Reiseburo
Berlin
Tel: 2150
Telex: 114648, 114652 RSBO DD

Saratours
Sallstr. 21 D 3000,
Hanover 1.
Tel: 0511 282353
Telex: 4 170329 Asi va 17. 6997263.

HONG KONG

Vietnam Tours and Trading Co.
Room 302 Leader Commercial Building,
54 Hillwood Road,
T.S.T. KLN.
Tel: 3682493, 3676663
Telex: 74237 TME. HX
Fax: (852) 5766635

Vietnam Tours
Friendship Travel,
Houston Center,
63 Mody Road, Kowloon.
Tel: 3666862
Telex: 31712 WHLTCHX

Skylion Ltd
Suite D,
11F Trust Tower,
68 Johnston Road, Wanchai.
Tel: 5 8650363
Telex: 66971 WSKYHX
Fax: (852) 5 8651306

Chu and Associates Co Ltd
Unit E, 5/F,
8 Thomson Road.
Tel: 5278828, 5278841
Telex: 61113 CHULE HK.

HUNGARY

IBUSZ Agency
1364 Felszabadulas,
Ter 5 Budapest.
Tel: 259915
Telex: 224676 A IBUS HT

ITALY

Going Tours
Via Aresenale, 27/G.
Torino.
Tel: (011) 517475
Telex: 213558 LO121 Torino.

Jonas Ways
Via Aracooli,
300187 Rome.
Tel: (06)6792953

Club VIACCI
Piazza Leonardo da Vinci,
32 20133 Milan.

Aventure Nel Mondo
Via Cino da pistoria,
7-00 152 Rome.
Tel: 5891400, 5898097
Telex: 620855 V Mondo.

JAPAN

Disc Tours
3rd Floor, Grandeur Yotsuya Building,
2-1 Samoncho,
Shinjuku-ku, Tokyo 16.
Tel: (03) 3532246
Telex: DISC JJ2325172
Fax: (03) 2536160

Rainbow Tours
7th floor, Crystal Building,
1-2 Kanda, Awaji-Cho,
Chiyoda-ku, Tokyo 101.
Tel: (03)2535855
Telex: 2222611 IDITYOJ
Fax: (03) 2536819

S.M.I. Travel Co. Ltd
1-2-7 Hamamatsu-cho,
Minato-Kku, Tokyo.
Tel: 4381014
Telex: 2425253 SMICHI.J.
Fax: 03 4591385

NEW ZEALAND

Keyline Trading Co.
31 Pleasant Street,
Onehunga, Auckland.

PHILIPPINES

IMPEX International PHILS
Suite 201 Centrum Bldg,
104 Perea St.,
Legasapi Village Makati MM.
Tel: 81648656667
Telex: 66687 MBC PN.

Vietnam Tours
Ground floor, Corinthian Plaza Building,
Paseo de Roxas, Makati, MM.
Tel: 810-4391 to 94
Telex: 45013 IMEXPM
Fax: (632)801-1010

POLAND

Orbis Agency
16 Bracka Street,
00-028 Warsaw.
Tel: 260271
Telex: 817781 ABZTW PL.

Polish Tourism Cooperative
23 UL Podwale,
00952 warsaw.
Tel: 312135
Telex: 312386 CROM PL.

SOVIET UNION

Intiurist Agency
16 Marx Prospekt,
Moscow.
Tel: 2922756
Telex: 4118438 INTU SU.

SPAIN

General Tours
Monteleen, 30-10 Madrid.
Tel: 4486963/12
Telex: 42804 Viju e.

SWITZERLAND

Nayak
Steinengrabes 42 Ch 4001 Basel.
Tel: 061224343
Telex: 640/47 Naya Ch.

Fer Nost Reisen
Welchogasse 4, 8050 Zurich
Tel: 013124040

M B Reisen Travel Agency
Limattal STR 200,
CH 8049 Zurich Hongg.
Telex: 823913 mbzh SBG Zurich-Hongg

THAILAND

Diethelm Travel (Representitive of the Australian Agency Orbitours)
544 Ploenchit Road, check address
Bangkok 10500.
Tel: 2559150/60/70
Telex: 81183, 21763, 22700/1 DIETRAV TH
Fax: (662) 25602248/9

Global Union Express Company
21/4 Thai Wah Tower,
3rd Floor, South Sathorn Road,
Bangkok 10120.
Tel: 2409004/9
Telex: 21132 GUE

Air People Tour and Travel Co. Ltd.
30/7 Saladang,
1 Silom Road,
Bangkok 10500.
Tel: 2352668/9, 2333864

Exotissimo Travel
21/17 Sukhumvit Soi 4,
Bangkok 10110.
Tel: 2535240/1
Telex: 20479 ASIAN TH

Fergusson and Associates
426/1 Soi 10, Paholyothin Road,
Bangkok 10400.
Tel: 2713905, 2713818
Telex: 81070 Fergusn

Orientours
8/27- Soi 16 (Soi Sam-mit) Sukhumvit Road,
Bangkok 11.

Tel: 3926091
Telex: Oriens TH 20586 Ortours TH

Air People tour and Travel
307 Sa La Daeng Road, Bangkok 10500.
Tel: 2352668, 23333864
Telex: 21132 Gueth
Fax: (662) 2409003

TAIWAN

Stone International Development Co., Ltd.
Unit 1/4F Pao Chiao Road,
Msien Tien, Taipei.
Tel: (02) 9186556
Fax: (02) 9186373
Telex: 35576 SIGMA

USA

Indochina Consulting Group Ltd.
844 Elda Lane, Westbury,
New York 11590.
Tel: 5163336662, 5168723885

Internet Asia
1341 Ocean Ave., Suite 232,
Santa Monica, California 90401.
Tel: (213) 8227908

US-Indochina Reconciliation Project
5808 Green Street,
Philadelphia. PA 19144.
Tel: (215)8484100
Telex: 254830 USIN UR.

TRAVCOA
857 North Michigamn Avenue,
Chicago, Illinois 60611.
Tel: (312)9512900

Viet Tours Holidays
8907 Westminster Avenue,
Garden Grove CA 92644-2609.
Tel: (714)8952588

Linblad Travelinc
1 Sylvan Road,
NPO Box 912,
Westport CT 06881.
Tel: (203)2268531
Telex: 4759015 (Lind UI)

Marazul Tours
New York.
Tel: 2125829570

Mekong Travel
151 First Avenue, Suite 172,
New York, NY 10003.
Tel:(212)5292891
Telex ITT 4933786 MKNG UI PAX
(212)5292891

Pacific Hemisphere International
8942 Garden Grove Boulevard,
Suite 220, Garden Grove,
California 92644.

TOURIST INFORMATION CENTERS

Apart from Vietnam Tourism, some other
state organizations offer much cheaper and
more flexible organized tours. For example,
Trung Tam Du Lich Thanh Nien Vietnam
(Vietnam's Youth Tourism Centre), 31 Cao
Thang, Quan 3, Ho Chi Minh City, tel:
90553, 94602, provides a very accommo-
dating service and will tailor a guided tour to
suit your requirements.

HO CHI MINH & THE SOUTH

VIETNAM TOURISM
69 - 71 Nguyen Hue.
Tel: 90772/3/4/5/6
Telex: 295. Dulivina SGN.

SAIGON TOURIST
205 Dong Khoi
Tel: 93944
Telex: 8275 Saigon;
39 Le Thanh Ton
Tel: 95000, 95515/17
Telex: 275 SG.

SAIGON TOURIST ASSOCIATION
112 Cach Mang Thang Tam.
Tel: 38653
Telex: 811514 EPO-VT
Fax: 84824744

CANTHO
Hau Giang Tourist Office in service of
Shipping,
27 Chau van Liem.
Tel: 20147, 35275

RACH GIA
Tourist Office,
12 Ly Tu Trong.
Tel: 2081

LAM DONG - DALAT
12 Tran Phu, Dalat.
Tel: 2021, 2034

PHU KHANH HOA AND NHA TRANG
1 Tran Hung Dao,
Nha Trang.
Tel: 22753, 22754, 22721

THUAN HAI - PHAN THIET
82 Trung Trac,
Phan Thiet.
Tel: 2474, 2475

VUNG TAU
Tourist Agency in Service of Vung Tau Oil
and Gas Enterprise,
2 Le Loi.
Tel: 90195
Telex: 370 VT

HUE & THE CENTER

Hue - Thua Thien Tourist Agency
51 Le Loi, Hue.
Tel: 2288, 2355

Binh Tri Thien Province Tourist Office
51 Le Loi, Hue.
Tel: 2288, 2369

QUAN NAM - DANANG
48 Bach Dang,
Danang.
Tel: 21423, 22213

BINH DINH - QUY NHON
4 Nguyen Hue,
Quy Nhon.
Tel: 2524, 2206
NGHE TINH
Truong Thi Square, Vinh.
Tel: 692 Vinh.

HANOI & THE NORTH

Hanoi Tourism
18 Ly Thuong Kiet,
Hanoi.
Tel: 54209, 57886

HAIPHONG
15 Le Dai Hanh.
Tel: 47486

HOA BINH
24 Tran Hung Dao,
Ha Dong.
Tel: 37

HALONG
Bai Chay Street.
Tel: Halong 08

HA NAM DINH
115 Nguyen Du.
Tel: 439, 362

THANH HOA
21a Quang Trung.
Tel: 298

THAI BINH Tourist Agency
Ly Bon Tel: 270

BANKS

Bank of Vietnam for Foreign Trade
47 Ly Thai To,
Hanoi.
Tel: 52831
Hours: 8am to 11am and 1.30pm to 3.30pm,
closed Saturday afternoons and Sundays.

Hong Kong and Shanghai Banking Corporation
29 Den Chuong Dong,
Ho Chi Minh City.
Hours: Monday to Friday 8am to 11.30am
and 2pm to 4pm and Saturday 8am till noon.

Banque du Commerce Exterieur
29 Ton Duc Thang,
Ho Chi Minh City.
Tel: 97245, 97247
Foreign Trade Bank
29 Ton Duc Thang,
Ho Chi Minh City.
Tel: 97238(245)

Banque Nationale de Paris (BNP)
Ho Chi Minh City.

MUSEUMS

HANOI

History Museum
1 Pham Ngu Lao.

Army Museum
Dien Bien Phu Boulevard.

Beaux Arts Museum
66 Nguyen Thai Hoc.
Closed Mondays.

Museum of the Revolution
25 Ton Dan.

Museum of Independence
48 Hang Ngang.

HUE

Hue Museum
3 Le Truc.

Ho Chi Minh Museum
7 Le Loi.

NHA TRANG

Marine Biology Museum

Ho Chi Minh Museum
16 Tran Phu.
Hours 7.30 to 10.30am, 1.30 to 4.00pm and
6.30 to 8.30pm.

VINH

The Museum of Nge Tinh
In the Citadel of Nge Tinh.

The Museum of the Nge Tinh "Soviets"

DANANG

Museum of Cham Sculpture

HO CHI MINH CITY

The History Museum
2 Duong Nguyen Binh Kheim.

The War Crimes Museum
28 Vo Van Tan.
The Revolutionary Museum
114 Nam Ky Khoi Nghia.

MEDICAL SERVICES

Bach Mai Hospital
Nam Bo Street,
Hanoi.
Tel: 53731

Viet Duc Hospital
Trang Thi Street,
Hanoi.
Tel: 53531

Hospital of Traditional Medicine
Nguyen Binh Khiem Street,
Hanoi.
Tel: 52850

Pharmacy
52 Trang Tien,
Hanoi.

A French and Swedish doctor may be contacted at their respective embassies in Hanoi.

Hue Hospital
16 Le Loi.
Tel: 2325, 2326

Pharmacy of Traditional Vietnamese medicine
34 Nguyen Hue,
Ho Chi Minh City.
Open every day 7.30am to 6pm.

SHOPPING

WHAT TO BUY

Traditional Vietnamese handicrafts offer a wide variety of wares to choose from. These include lacquerware, mother-of-pearl inlay, ceramics, pottery, precious wood, tortoise shell, embroidery, silk paintings, bamboo and wickerware, baskets, wool carpets, sculpture, wood, marble and bone carvings, jewelry, jade, engraving, silk and brocade. You may like to add a *non la*, the famous Vietnamese conical hat and an *ao dai*, the traditional costume worn by the Vietnamese fairer sex, to your wardrobe.

Heavy taxation has discouraged the sale of antiquities, which has become almost clandestine and very limited in the North and strictly surveilled in the South. Only after enquiring of the proprietor will you discover all that may be available as the best pieces are never displayed. Antique shops in the center of Ho Chi Minh City and the old town of Hanoi sell Vietnamese wood or Laotian bronze Buddhas, old porceline, objects in silver and ivory, small jade statuettes and objects used by the various cults. Prices are in US dollars and subject to bargaining. However, bear in mind that it is forbidden to export certain objects and in principle clearance must be obtained before you take antiquities out of the country.

Russian vodka, caviar and even French champagne may be found at very reasonable prices.

Clothing is comparatively cheap and local tailors can very quickly produce well made garments to the design of your choice.

HO CHI MINH CITY

Cultrimex (state run)
94 Dong Khoi.
Tel: 92574, 92896
Handicrafts, paintings, lacquer work, reproductions of antiquities.
Closed Sundays.

Artexport (state run)
159 Dong Khoi.
Objets d'art and antiquities.

Hoang Oanh
45 Dong Khoi.
Antiquities and objets d'art.

"47"
47 Dong Khoi.
Antiquities and objets d'art.

Sodasy
115 Le Than Ton.
Tel: 97752
Produces Natural shell and ivory articles.

Cuu Long
177 Dong Kho.
Ao dai and fabrics.

Lac Long
143 Le Than Ton.
Leather and skin goods.

Fahasa Bookshop
185 Dong Knoi.
Books in English, French, Vietnamese and Russian.

The city's major markets are Ben Thanh Market, in the center of the city and Bin Tay Market, in the Chinese quarter of Cholon. You will find the main commercial area along the streets of Le Loi, Nguyen Hue, Le Than Ton and Dong Khoi. Dong Khoi Street is full of shops selling good quality souvenirs, check out particularly the shops at numbers 62 and 63.
Also here are a few art galleries selling paintings, ranging from traditional to surrealism, by local artists.

Souvenirs of Vietnam
30A Ly Thuong Kiet.
Vietnamese handicrafts

Cultrimex Gallery
22B Ha Ba Trung.
Silk paintings, paintings, antique reproductions.

Xunhasaba
32 Hai Ba Trung.
Ministry of Culture sponsored society for the sale and export of books, periodicals, reproductions of objets d'art and handicrafts. Foreign language publications are also available.

Souvenir Shop
89 Dinh Thien Hoa.

Rong Dat
105 Hang Gia.
Embroidery

Han Art
43 Trang Tien.

Hanoi Gallery
61 Trang Tien.

International Bookshop
61 Trang Tien Street.
Tel: 57043

Book Sach
57 Trang Tien.
Foreign language publications.

Vietnamese Bookshop
On the corner of 19 Ngo Quyen and 40 Trang Tien.
Foreign language publications.

Hanoi Foreign Trade Company
56 Tran Tien.

Souvenir Shop
89 Dinh Thien Hoang.

Hanoi has two principal markets, Dong Xuan Market in the heart of old Hanoi and Hom Market on the corner of 81 Pho Hue and Tran Xuan Soan. You will find Hanoi's main commercial area on Trang Tien Street and the southern area around Hoan Kiem Lake. For antique hunters, if you start at Hang Dao Street and walk through the old town of Hanoi to Le Duan Street and above Lenin Park you will discover numerous small antique shops selling some lovely pieces, particularly in Kim Lien Street, and at numbers 66 to 74 Rue de la soie and 8 Cha Ca Street.

DANANG

Art Articles Shop
48 Bach Dang.
Tel: 21423

LANGUAGE

Vietnamese, the national language, is spoken by practically all the population. Variations in dialect, accent and pronunciation exist between the North, South and Center and among the ethnic minorities who have their own dialects.

The Vietnamese language has its origins in the Austro-Asiatic languages and has been influenced by the Sino-Tibetan Thai language. Through the centuries of Chinese occupation the Vietnamese adopted the Han characters. In the 13th century they developed their own written language—Nom. In the 18th century, on the initiative of a French Jesuit priest, Alexandre de Rhodes, missionaries translated the language into its Romanized form, Quoc Ngu, which was first used by the Catholic church and the colonial regime's administration. Gradually its use spread, replacing the old written form by the 19th century. Variations of spelling, particularly noticeable in place names, is common and there appears to be no hard and fast standardization of spelling. The languages of Vietnam's ethnic minority groups are drawn from the many Southeast Asian linguistic groups of Austro-asiatic,

Austronesian or Malayo-polynesian, Tibetan-Burman, Kadai and Mia-Yao.

VIETNAMESE PRONUNCIATION

Vietnamese is no easy language to pronounce. The syllable is the language's base unit. Most syllables have their own particular meaning and each syllable can be pronounced in six different tones to confer a totally different meaning. In the romanized written form these tones are expressed by five diacritical accents and one atonic, where the syllable has no accent. For example the syllable "ma", depending on the tone, can mean ghost, mother, a term of relationship, rice shoot, tomb, or horse. Obviously that leaves much room for confusion for any novice and anyone on the receiving end of a beginner's efforts.

French is still spoken by any of the older generation in Vietnam, so with that option the prospect of communicating with the locals is not quite as daunting.

English is now very much in demand as a second language and particularly in the South you will find the younger generation speak English.

GREETINGS

The basic hello - *chao*, is always followed by another word that varies depending on the age and sex of whom you address.

for an old lady	*Chao ba*
for a young lady	*Chao co*
for an older lady	*Chao chi*
for an old man	*Chao ong*
for a young man	*Chao anh*
for an older man	*Chao bac*
for a young person	*Chao em*
goodbye	*Tam biet*
See you again	*Hen gap lai*
I am sorry	*Xin loi*
please	*Xin moi*
thank you	*cam on*
yes	*da*
no	*khong*
My name is ...	*Toi ten la ...*
What's your name?	*Ten ong la gi?* (pronounced zee)
How are you?	*Bac co khoe khong?*
Fine thankyou	*Cam on binh thuong*
I	*toi*

a little	*it*
how much?	*bao nhieu?*
today	*hom nay*
tomorrow	*ngay mai*

ASKING FOR DIRECTIONS

O dau? - where?, comes at the end of the sentence directly after the noun. For example if you want to ask for the Post Office - *Buu dien, Buu dien o dau?*

hotel	*khach san*
bank	*ngan hang*
hospital	*benh vien*
bookshop	*hieu sach*
taxi station	*ben xe tac xi*
bus station	*ben xe*
train station	*ga xe lua*
airport	*san bay*
swimming pool	*ho boi*
cathedral	*nha tho*
restaurant	*nha hang an*
Where is the toilet?	*Nha ve sinh o dau?*
Turn left/right	*Re ben trai/phai*
Continue straight ahead	*Hay di thang*
This way	*Loi nay*
street	*pho/duong*
district	*quan*

MISCELLANEOUS

stamp	*tem thu*
car	*xe hoi / o to*
film	*phim*
rice	*com*
bread	*banh mi*
fish	*ca*
boiled water	*nuoc soi*
tea	*che*
coffee	*ca phe*
beer	*bia*

I am thirsty/very thirsty	*Toi khat/lam*
I am hungry	*Toi doi*
I am sick	*Toi binh*
I have stomachache	*Toi bi da day*
I have diahorrea	*Toi bi di rua*
I have a fever	*Toi bi sot*
I have toothache	*Toi bi rang*

Monday	*Thu hai*
Tuesday	*Thu ba*
Wednesday	*Thu tu*
Thursday	*Thu nam*
Friday	*Thu sau*
Saturday	*Thu bay*
Sunday	*Thu nhat*

one	*mot*
two	*hai*
three	*ba*
four	*bon*
five	*nam*
six	*sau*
seven	*bay*
eight	*tam*
nine	*chin*
ten	*muoi*
eleven	*muoi mot*
fifteen	*muoi lam*
twenty	*hai muoi*
twenty-one	*hai muoi mot*
twenty-five	*hai muoi lam*
thirty	*ba muoi*
fifty	*nam muoi*
ninety	*chin muoi*
one hundred	*mot tram*
two hundred	*hai tram*
nine hundred	*chin tram*
one thousand	*mot nghin*
ten thousand	*muoi nghin*
100,000	*tram nghin*
one million	*mot trieu*

FURTHER READING

NON-FICTION

The Birth of Vietnam - Keith Weller Taylor. University of California Press, Berkeley 1983.

In the Midst of War - An American's Mission to Southeast Asia. - Major General Edward Geary Landsdale. Harper & Row, New York, 1972.

We the Vietnamese - edited by Francois Sully. Praeger Publishers, 1971.

Tradition on Trial 1920-1945 - David G. Marr. University of California Press,

Berkely, 1981.

Vietnamese Anti-colonialism 1885-1925 - David G. Marr. University of California Berkely, L.A. & London, 1971.

Fire In the Lake - Francis Fitzgerald. Vintage Books, New York, 1972.

Why Vietnam?- Archimedes L. Patti. University of California Press, Berkeley, L.A. & London, 1980.

Vietnam: A History - Stanley Karnow. Viking Press, New York, 1983.

Henry Mouhot's Diary: Travels in the Central Parts of Siam Cambodia and Laos During the Years 1858-61 - edited by Christopher Pym.

A Dragon Apparent - Travels in IndoChina - Norman Lewis Charles Scribner's Sons, New York, 1951.

River Journeys - William Shawcross. Describes the author's Mekong River trip made in 1983.

Xunhasaba in Hanoi publishes a comprehensive series—Vietnamese Studies which deals with all manner of subjects encompassing history, archaeology, ethnography and politics.

FICTION

Blue Dragon, White Tiger - Tran Van Dinh
Saigon - Anthony Grey
The Quiet American - Graham Greene

USEFUL ADDRESSES

HO CHI MINH CITY

Service of Foreign Affairs
6 Thai Van Lung,
Tel: 24127

Office of Foreign Registration
161 -163 Nguyen Du.

Customs
125 Ham Nghi.
Tel: 90095, 90096

The Vietnamese Information Agency (V.N.A.)
120 Xo Viet Nghe Tinh.

Import - Export
IMEXCO,
8 Nguyen Hue.
Tel: 97424

Office for the Control of Cultural Item's Import and Export
178 Nam Ky Khoi Nghia.

Institute of Franco-Vietnamese Cultural Exchange
31 Don Dat Street,
Ho Chi Minh City.
Tel: 24577

Saigon Port
Ho Chi Minh City.
Tel: 91825

Tan Son Nhat Airport
Tel: 43250, 42339

International Booking Office
116 Nguyen Hue.
Tel: 92118, 23848.

International Airlines represented at Tan Son Nhat Airport:

Air France	Tel: 41278
Aeroflot	Tel: 43774
Thai International	Tel: 46235

HANOI

Office for Foreign Registration (Immigration Police)
63 Tran Hung Dao.
Open Monday to Saturday between 8 and 11am and 1 to 5pm.

Department of Foreign Affairs for Quang Nam Danang Province
136 Ong Ich Khiem,
Danang.
Tel: 21092

DIPLOMATIC MISSIONS & CONSULATES

CONSULS IN HO CHI MINH CITY

BULGARIA
6 Phung Khac Khoan.
Tel: 95075

CZECHOSLOVAKIA
170 Nguyen Van Thu.
Tel: 91475

CUBA
126 Nguyen Dinh Chieu.
Tel: 97345

FRANCE
127 Xo Viet Nghe Tinh.
Tel: 97231

KAMPUCHEA
41 Phung Khac Khoan Street.
Tel: 92751

POLAND
2 -2A Tran Cao Van Street.
Tel: 95737

SOVIET UNION
36 - 38 Phung Khac Khoan Street.
Tel: 92937

EMBASSIES IN HANOI

AUSTRALIA
66 Ly Thuong Kiet.
Tel: 52763

BELGIUM
B3 Khu Van Phuc,
Room 201-2.
Tel: 52263

CHINA
46 Hoang Dieu.
Tel: 53737, 53726

CZECHOSLOVAKIA
13 Chu Van An.
Tel: 54231, 54132

FINLAND
D1 Khu Van Phuc.
Tel: 56745, 57096

FRANCE
57 Tran Hung Dao.
Tel: 54367, 54268

GERMANY
25 Phan Boi Chau.
Tel: 53663, 55402

ITALY
9 Le Phung Hieu.
Tel: 53388, 56246, 56256

JAPAN
E3 Khu Trung Tu.
Tel: 57902, 57924

KAMPUCHEA
71 Tran Hung Dao.
Tel: 53788

LAOS
22 Tran Dinh Trong.
Tel: 54576

PHILIPPINES
E1 Ku Trung Tu.
Tel: 57948, 57873

SOVIET UNION
58 Tran Phu.
Tel: 54631, 54632

SWITZERLAND
27 Quang Trung.
Tel: 54751

THAILAND
E1 Khu Trung Tu.
Tel: 56043, 56053

UNITED KINGDOM
16 Ly Thuong Kiet.
Tel: 52510, 52349

VIETNAMESE OVERSEAS MISSIONS & TRADE REPRESENTATIVES

ALBANIA
Embassy of the SR Vietnam,
Tirana.

ALGERIA
Embassy of the SR Vietnam,
30 Chenoua Hydra.

AUSTRALIA
Embassy of the SR Vietnam,
6 Timbarra Section,
O'Malley, A.C.T. 2606.
Tel: 866059
Telex: 62756

BULGARIA
Embassy of the SR Vietnam,
12 Oborichte Street,
Sofia.
Cable: Viethuong

CUBA
Oficina Commercial de la RSVN,
Calle 16 No. 5 y 7,
Miramar,
Havana.
Cable: Vietthuong

CZECHOSLOVAKIA
Embassy of the SR Vietnam,
V. Tisine 2 (Bulenec),
Praha 6.

FRANCE
Ambassade de la SRVN,
62 rue Boileau,
75016 Paris.
Tel: 45245063, 45276255

Ambassade de la SRVN,
Section Commercial,
44 Avenue de Madrid,
92200 Neuilly sur Seine,
Paris.
Tel: 6248577
Telex: 612922
Cable: COVIETNAMEX

GERMANY
Botschaft der Sozialistischen,
Republik Vietnam,
Konstantin Strasse 37,
5300 Bonn, BRD.

HONG KONG
The Representation of the National
Export Import Corporations of the SRVN,
17th floor Golden Star Building,
20 -24 Lockhart Rd.

Tel: 5-283361-3
Telex 63771 VNCOR
Cable: VINACOR

HUNGARY
Embassy of the SR Vietnam,
24 Benczur Utca I/1,
Budapest VI.
Cable: VIETKULKER

INDIA
Embassy of the SR Vietnam,
E 48 Panch Shila Park,
New Delhi 110017.
Cable: THUONGVU

ITALY
Embassy of the SR Vietnam,
Piazza Barberini 12,
00187 Rome.
Tel: 4755286, 4754098

JAPAN
Embassy of the SR Vietnam,
50-11 Motoyoyogi-cho Shibuya-ku,
Tokyo 151.
Tel: 466-3315
Telex: 32440 Vietnam
Cable: VIETTRADE

LAOS
Embassy of the SR Vietnam,
Route de That Luang,
Vientiane.
Tel: 5578, 2707

MALAYSIA
4 Persiaran Stonor,
Kuala Lumpur 5040.
Tel: (03) 2484036

POLAND
Embassy of the SR Vietnam,
U1. Swiedtorkrzyska 36 M-32,
Warsaw.
Cable: VIETHUSU

RUMANIA
Embassy of the SR Vietnam,
28 Hrito Street,
Bucarest.
Cable: VIETHURU

SINGAPORE
The Representation of the National
Import Export Corporations of the SRVN,
10 Leedon Park.
Tel: 4683747
Telex 26936
Cable: VINATRADE

SWEDEN
Embassy of the SR Vietnam,
Parkvagen 42,
S-13141 NACKA.
Tel: (08) 7182841
Telex: 15716 COMVIET S
Cable: VIETNAMHANDEL

THAILAND
Embassy of the SR Vietnam,
83/1 Wireless Road,
Bangkok.
Tel: 252-6950, 251-7201

UNITED KINGDOM
The Embassy of the SR Vietnam,
12-14 Victoria Road,
London W8.
Tel: 9371912
Telex: 887361

USSR
Embassy of the SR Vietnam,
58 Gorki Street,
Moscow.
Telex: 414411, 414321
Cable: BETTOP

ART/PHOTO CREDITS

INDEX

E

F

G

H

N

O - P

V

W

X - Y

A
C
D
E
F
G
H
I
J
a
b
c
d
f
g
h
i
j
k
l